INCORPORATING WOMEN

A History of Women and Business in the United States

Angel Kwolek-Folland

For Nathan

INCORPORATING WOMEN: A HISTORY OF WOMEN AND BUSINESS IN THE UNITED STATES

Copyright © Angel Kwolek-Folland, 1998, 2002.

First published in 1998 by Twayne Publishers.

First paperback edition, PALGRAVE™
175 Fifth Avenue, New York, N.Y. 10010 and
Companies and representatives throughout the world.

PALGRAVE™ is the new global publishing imprint of St. Martin's Press LLC Scholarly and Reference Division and Palgrave Publishers Ltd. (formerly Macmillan Press Ltd.).

ISBN 0-312-23349-3 paperback

Library of Congress Cataloging-in-Publication Data

Kwolek-Folland, Angel.
    Incorporating women : a history of women and business in the
United States / Angel Kwolek-Folland.
        p.   cm.
    Includes bibliographical references and index.
    ISBN 0-312-23349-3 pbk.
        1 . Businesswomen—United States—History.   2. Women-owned business
enterprises—United States—History.   I. Title.
HD6095.K85   1998
331.4'0973—dc21   98-7619
                                                                          CIP

First paperback edition: March 2002
10   9   8   7   6   5   4   3   2   1

Printed in the United States of America.

Contents

Foreword

Does business have the same meaning for women as it does for men? This provocative question frames Angel Kwolek-Folland's history of women in business. Beginning with the "business of colonization," Kwolek-Folland shows how women participated in the American economy as entrepreneurs, managers, and organizers in a variety of ways over the past four hundred years. Though they faced severe legal restrictions on their ability to own and use property and mobilize capital, they also played key roles in the family-based economy of America before the twentieth century. As partners with their husbands on family farms and in urban establishments, they shared duties and contributed human labor and capital. In times of difficulty or following the death of a spouse, they took over the family firm. In frontier areas, they bent the legal system to find opportunities denied them in more settled areas. Sometimes they engaged in business publicly, other times they were forced to operate behind the scenes. Their strategies varied depending on their location, their class, and their ethnicity.

What remained constant for businesswomen, however, was the link between their participation in the economy and their role in the family. Women were generally allowed greatest freedom when acting as mothers, wives, or widows. As a result, they have historically brought values beyond those of profit and individual success to their enterprises. For nineteenth century women, business might involve running a religious order or educational institution, two areas of public life in which women were allowed to assume prominent roles. In other cases, business might mean translating traditional "female" activities, such as sewing, cooking, cleaning, or butter making, into profitable enterprises as dressmakers, restaurateurs, laundresses, seamstresses, or storekeepers. Immigrant and minority women found opportunities in supplying to their ethnic group services and products largely ignored by business enterprises.

Whatever the case, women could never assume that business was simply a means of individual upward mobility. There were children to think about, family patrimonies to protect, social prejudices and suspicions to overcome. Women could only ignore these matters at great risk, in extraordinary circumstances, when operating beyond the pale of respectable society. One of the most profitable areas of female enterprise, for example, was the sex business. Women operated brothels or moved in the demimonde of the theater, where the growing importance of "celebrity" status allowed them to circumvent the normal restrictions on capital mobilization.

We are used to thinking of the history of women in business as one of slow, sometimes tortuous liberation from gender restrictions. Yet in this book we also see other patterns. Though the nineteenth and twentieth centuries have witnessed the growing liberation of women from sexist laws and customs, economic "modernization" was a step backward for many women. After the Civil War, as large-scale national corporations replaced small, entrepreneurial firms, some opportunities for women narrowed. Upper management and professions closed ranks against women. Entrepreneurship required connections to banks and other financial institutions, not friends and relatives, shutting out women who had manipulated the old family-based economy. The professionalization of medicine eliminated women from once lucrative careers as midwives. Much of the history of women in the twentieth century has been a long, slow climb back into business by breaking down the walls of the corporate and professional worlds that excluded them.

In the late twentieth century, with the rapid growth of women in modern business, we are once again wondering whether management, entrepreneurship, and business organization are really gender neutral or whether corporations should accept the differences between men and women. Kwolek-Folland points out the dangers of simple assumptions. Business has long had a gender dimension, rooted deeply in the historical sex division of work. Women have always found ways of balancing family responsibilities with the constraints of the market and opportunities for profit. What has changed is the once close connections between career and personal life, business enterprise and family.

Too many of today's discussions assume that the problem is the presence of women in an otherwise sexless organization composed of employees with no family or personal life. In fact, as Kwolek-Folland shows, the entry of women into corporate America has from the beginning forced male managers to reconsider their assumptions about how to motivate, reward, and direct white-collar workers. If we do not yet know how men, women, and corporations will handle these conflicting currents, Angel Kwolek Folland's outstanding new history of women in business shows us that the issues of today are not unprecedented. In their own way for their own aims, women too have found that the business of America can be business.

Kenneth Lipartito

Acknowledgments

Once in awhile one is lucky enough to be in the right place at the right time. When Ken Lipartitio approached me about writing a book on the history of women's business experience I happened to be in the market for a project—preferably one that would bridge my previous work on women in the banking and insurance industries and my growing interest in women's role in economic development. The idea of having the chance to read extensively everything I could find on women and business and putting together a coherent narrative of that history sounded challenging and fun. It has been both, although at times more one than the other. *Incorporating Women* is the result. In addition to original research, it builds on a foundation of solid scholarship by many others and the informed criticism and helpful suggestions of numerous colleagues and friends.

This book owes a great deal to the scholarship of many diverse individuals, who have recreated over the years various aspects of women's business experience. The bibliographic essay at the end of this volume lists these sources, but a few deserve specific mention here. It is hard to imagine the history of women during the colonial period, for example, without the work of those pioneer historians of women's business experience, Elisabeth Dexter and Julia Cherry Spruill. At the other end of the time frame, a new cadre of young scholars even as I write are infusing both the history of women and the history of business with new goals, new ideas, and new information. At the risk of overlooking someone, I have found especially exciting the work of Wendy Holliday, Karen Ward Mahar, Katina Manko, and Debra Michals.

Some wonderful colleagues and friends have contributed their time, energy, and encouragement as they read and commented on portions of the manuscript. David Sicilia, Sara Alpern, and my editor, Ken Lipartito, read and thoroughly critiqued the entire manuscript. I am extremely grateful for their help (not to mention the occasional bad puns). Ann Boylan, Richard Butsch, Chuck Cheape, Jonathan Chu, John Ingham, Roger Horowitz, Betsy Kuznesof, Naomi Lamoreaux, Peter Mancall, Sharon Popper, Josh Rosenbloom, Ann Schofield, Phil Scranton, Stanley Shapiro, Carl Strikwerda, and Mary Yeager each brought their critical skills to various portions and helped make the book, and the process, a delightful interchange. I do, of course, take full responsibility for any errors of fact or omission.

Archivist Lynn Catanese of the Hagley Museum and Library, Wilmington, Delaware, provided unfailing interest and suggestions. She was finishing her own comprehensive book on sources related to women in the Hagley's collections and introduced me to some of the fascinating women inventors documented in the archives. I wish there had been more room here to include them all.

Several institutions, including the Hall Center for the Humanities and the Women's Studies Program at the University of Kansas; the Hagley Museum and Library; and the Art History and History Seminar at the University of Delaware, provided funding for research or forums for presentation of portions of the book. I want specifically to acknowledge the enormously stimulating conference in May 1996 sponsored by the Hagley, which brought together about 30 scholars of business history for intense discussions about the role of gender, race, and ethnicity in the history of business.

The staff at Twayne/Macmillan and Impressions Book Services smoothed the complex process of bringing a book into print. I would especially like to thank Mark Zadrozny and Jill Lectka for their attention to the book.

There are also a few people who, while not directly involved in the creation or production of this book, still made it possible. For all of the good times, special thanks to Lois Spatz for her stories, Wendy Gamber for her sense of humor, Roger Horowitz and Phil Scranton for the big dreams and unorthodox schemes, Jackie McGlade for the fly-fishing lessons, and Juliet Walker for her supportive encouragement, even from the other side of the globe. I managed to write this book while serving as the graduate director of the University of Kansas's history department, thanks to the help of the delightful, smart, and funny Ellen Garber. As the graduate secretary, Ellen's patience with me, dedication to the students, and knowledge of "corporate culture" helped open up spaces for the research and writing. I could not have worn simultaneously both a scholar's and an administrator's hat without her. Finally this book is for Nathan, who remains good-natured about being a Wildcat among the Jayhawks.

I hope you will find this book as enjoyable to read as I did to write and that it will send you to at least some of the original scholarship on which it is based.

Chapter One

Incorporating Others: The Social Categories of Business History

This is not about money. I would like to feel I could have an impact on people's lives in a broader venue.
        —*Oprah Winfrey, Founder, Chair, and CEO*
                Harpo Entertainment Group

My grandmother was my real mentor. . . . Grandma was a truly liberated woman and matriarch who said that a woman should never ask her husband for anything and should earn things herself through making her own money.
        —*Josie Alemeda Cruz Natori, Founder and CEO*
                The Natori Company

Women have always been in business in America. From the Ojibwa women who mediated the seventeenth-century fur trade to the early-twentieth-century management theorist Lillian Gilbreth and from the nineteenth-century African-American seamstress and entrepreneur Elizabeth Keckley to Kim Polese, one of the "architects" of the Internet, women have initiated and managed firms and contributed their expertise and resources to business development. However, the history of women in American business has long been overlooked and obscured. It is a largely forgotten, but fascinating, story.

This book surveys the history of women and business in the United

1

States from the colonial period to the present. Five chapters address the main themes of women's and business history, synthesizing the two fields. This analysis involves more than merely adding women to business history by pointing out that "women were there, too." Rather, the presence of women's organized economic activity challenges the assumptions of business history, forcing us to rethink the nature of economic activity; when change occurred; and the legal, social, and economic meanings of such concepts as *entrepreneurship*. Challenging assumptions is particularly relevant when women of different races and cultures are taken into account. The presence of businesswomen at all periods of our history also suggests that women's historians should not ignore this important economic venue in their analysis of women's legal, social, and economic status. *Incorporating Women* assumes that women have been important historical actors as consumers and workers, managers and executives, and entrepreneurs and family members in the history of business development.

In 1991 Louis Galambos, who was then president of the Business History Association, laid out a program for integrating business history into the mainstream. At the same time, he suggested ways that historians of business could work toward a new narrative synthesis of the broad sweep of U.S. history. He argued, not surprisingly, that to be relevant to a wider audience, business historians would need to respond to issues being raised by historians in other fields. In addition, their questions should focus on power and on business's role in creating and using various power structures—not only political parties and corporations, which business historians have long recognized, but churches, schools, universities, and voluntary organizations as well.

Galambos further noted the persistence of two related myths that shaped most business histories. One he called the "myth of rationalization," which was the notion that businesses and businesspeople did not suffer from the same human emotions as the rest of us. Histories of business were often peopled by actors without prejudice, greed, or even positive traits such as empathy and caring. Worse, many histories of business had no people at all, merely "companies" that "operated" in an emotionless, apolitical void. The other myth Galambos termed the "myth of corporate hegemony"—the notion that power and cultural dominance were solely in the hands of corporate leaders and that business development takes place in a political vacuum. It was as though there were, as he put it, "no losers in business history, only winners over the long term."[1] The fundamental difficulty with these myths, Galambos asserted, is that they obscure the workings of power. The "who did what to whom" that students sometimes hide by using passive verbs business historians hid by using flawed assumptions.

Business histories that address Galambos's concerns are growing in number. But we have yet to formulate a coherent critique of the myths he identified. In taking on the task of writing this history of women in business, I have been forced to think about narrative structures and questions of relevance. The project immediately raised for me the difficulties of bringing together a history steeped in the fundamentals of power with a history that effectively ignores them. Women's history was born in concerns over how sex, gender, ethnicity, race, and class have shaped the lives of both women and men. Business history usually assumes white, male, and middle class as the neutral and—for the most part—uninterrogated standard. To "incorporate" women into a synthesis of business history, I would have to deal with Galambos's questions of irrationality, inequity, and mythology. And I would have to redefine the terms, conditions, and moments of change in business history in light of such social categories. The first problem demanded a theoretical approach; the second involved redefining the topic of study, redefining *business*. It would be useful to speak briefly to each of these issues.

Though power, as Galambos emphasized, is important, we need to define what power is and how it is supposed to operate. At the most obvious level, it refers to struggle, but over what is less clear. Scholars have argued that power—the process of asserting and ascribing meaning and the process of contestation over resources—is rooted in difference and the way we attribute hierarchical values to forms of difference. In essence, difference comes in the contrast of one thing with another: male/female, white/black, light/dark, good/bad, and high/low. Such contrasts are often coupled with inequities, to link opposition with "otherness." Some have argued that this tendency to see the world as a series of hierarchical contrasts, as a series of "others," is rooted in language, in some cases even a biological tendency to use certain linguistic forms. Others have argued for the role of culture in constructing this sense of difference. Still other scholars posit that all forms of socially constructed difference grow out of observable physical phenomena, primary among them sex and race.

Although scholars and theoreticians debate the degree to which sex, race, language, or culture is the most basic category of difference (a largely unresolvable debate since it is ultimately based on political choices), many agree that both race and gender are fundamental classifications of meaning and experience. Often those meanings and experiences are ambiguous and filled with contradictions, ironies, paradoxes, unresolved dilemmas, and layered implications. To understand a social category such as *race* rather than see merely black and white or race in isolation from other social categories, we could imagine a spectrum of shades and gradations that would encompass a variety of ways in which people identify their social realities. Several examples come to mind: the choice people of mixed racial inheritance must make about to which racial category they belong, the racial and ethnic categories adopted by the state for purposes such as the census or affirmative action, and the gradations of ancestry that construct whether one is Native American and the differing notions about that status advanced by federal Indian policy and Indians themselves. There also are the relations between class status and the phenomenon of lighter-skinned individuals "passing" for white among some racial groups or, finally, the different meanings of "sexual virtue" constructed around whiteness, coloredness, or class status.

To view difference as a continuum is not to deny the obvious material reality of sexual organs or skin coloration. Rather, it is to suggest that these physical phenomena are less useful in understanding historical experience than are the *significance* we have attached to them and the historical trappings that have led certain cultural categories (such as race and gender) to become so filled with contradictory meanings. The choices individuals make in constructing their identities, as well as their social, economic, and cultural relations, grow out of the dynamics of difference. The importance of difference to identity underlies the reason for studying that loose collection of social categories—race, gender, class, and ethnicity—that unfortunately has come to seem too much like a mindless chant. However, if we think of their shared premise in difference and its relation to power, we can perhaps understand why discussions and debates over the nature of these categories and their relation to historical change force us to raise questions about power in business history.

How, then, do we proceed to incorporate "otherness" into business history? One place to begin is to rethink our definition of the subject— what a discipline chooses to study and how it defines itself—since one of the fundamental aspects of power is the ability to include or exclude. Modern dictionary definitions of *business* and business his-

tory textbooks usually focus on such things as entrepreneurship (and
its consort nouns *initiative* and *risk*), professions, trade (meaning to
engage in buying and selling), commerce, and various forms of management.[2] Textbooks in business history, for example, often privilege
innovation, management structures, individuals, and small entrepreneurs in their narratives of American business. Before the nineteenth
century the term *business* referred as well to the idea of a calling, or
vocation. These definitions promiscuously mingle active verb forms
with descriptive nouns. They are coupled with a progressive, capitalist, and liberal (in the nineteenth-century sense) economy. They also
suggest certain behaviors related to business, some of which are
inherently economic (buying) and others of which are socially and
historically constructed economic or behavioral values (risk and initiative).

This book uses a broader definition of *business*, one that is as value
neutral as possible. It defines *business* as engaging in economic activity
in a market to seek profit. We can interpret the terms of this definition
as expansively as possible. This definition allows us to rethink what we
consider to be businesses and how we go about understanding their
histories. A hotly contested question, for example, remains whether
the family farm qualifies as a business and therefore as a topic of
study. Yet with the exception of those involved in subsistence farming,
family farmers take economic risks by selling or trading goods in markets. In general, they operate much like small businesses. Business
historians willingly embrace large-scale agriculture (agribusiness),
but when it comes to the family farm, they see something other than a
business enterprise, an entity better left to economic or social historians. In addition, business historians have handed over to historians of
women or race the discussion of the business role of farm women or
the differential impact of race on farmers' business possibilities.

A second issue addressed by redefining business history lies in the
narrow way business historians have used concepts such as *success,
innovation, risk, entrepreneurship,* and *profit.* Definitions of business
"success" that focus on growth and longevity exclude most women's
small businesses, which have tended to remain small and be individually short-lived. Yet they operate in the commercial marketplace,
employ many workers, and have been critically important to the material well-being of their female owners.[3] Historians also circumscribe
their vision of economic activity by focusing on cash or credit
exchanges and excluding noncash-based economic transactions, such

as barter. Yet barter has historically been, and remains today, a widespread phenomenon. One source estimated that in 1995 350,000 companies bartered around $1.2 billion in goods and services. Some of these trades were made locally and informally. Others went through an estimated 500 barter networks in existence nationally and even internationally.[4] How one defines business and economic activities is particularly important when constructing the history of women's and minority businesses, since small businesses and informal economies have been important niches for groups outside of the mainstream.

In fact, women's experiences undermine the notion that older forms of economic exchange disappeared with the development of liberal capitalism, industry, and corporate organization after about 1750. Barter and the provision of domestic services are two important examples. Women's role in barter has been amply documented although consistently undervalued by business historians. In the colonial period barter remained important to economic exchange even in the presence of cash transactions. Native American women involved in the fur trade interjected barter into the international economy in their dealings with the Hudson's Bay Company. Colonial women in North America engaged in a complex "woman's economy," bartering goods and services among other women. Barter relations continue in the twentieth century, particularly among rural and poor women, who trade services or goods (e.g., child care, transportation, sewing, and cooking). Professionally trained African-American midwives in the South in the 1920s exchanged their skills for foodstuffs and cloth. In terms of services, throughout our history women have played an important economic role as managers of households, mistresses of servants or slaves, and providers of domestic and support services in rural and urban areas. Despite the existence in the twentieth century of public-sector service providers such as fast-food chains, grocery stores, and mass-produced clothing factories, many women continue to provide services as household workers within the family. Business history has been interested in service industries on a large scale but has virtually ignored the economics of service production within the household.

A third area illuminated by redefining business is periodization, or how historians perceive moments of change. Most business history periodization is based on macrolevel technological and structural change—that is, revolutions in the market and industrial, corporate, and consumer relations. Actually, these first premises of historical change work better than standard political narratives for organizing the experience of women and minorities. Historical changes in the lives of women and other groups outside of the mainstream can often be traced to economic causes. However, their expressions and consequences can be different for women and minorities than for white men. For example, the introduction of a cash-based economy and the devaluation of unpaid labor (such as housework) is clearly connected to the segregation of certain types of businesses as "women's" and "men's." Further, economic change often must be interpreted in light of changes in the law. The status of slaves, for instance, had a bearing on the entrepreneurial opportunities available to free women of color, as Suzanne Lebsock demonstrated in the case of Petersburg, Virginia, in the mid-nineteenth century.[5]

Fourth, a more inclusive definition of business allows us to focus on business structures and their role in creating power relations. Current research on organizations emphasizes the part played by difference in constructing the workforce and large-scale organizations. The sociologist Joan Acker argues that organizations are gendered in that their "fundamental structure[s] of advantage and disadvantage, exploitation and control, action and emotion, meaning and identity are constructed through, and in terms of, distinctions between male and female, masculine and feminine."[6] In other words, organizations are not gender or race neutral but rather are premised on those fundamental contrasts and ambiguities embedded in the larger meanings of gender and race. Power exists as both direct authority and indirect influence. Outsider groups such as women and minorities traditionally have had better success wielding the latter. This finding suggests that people within organizations without direct sources of authority such as budgetary control may operate very differently from those who have such sources. These distinctions could be useful in exploring the way difference operates in relation to gendered and racialized bureaucratic lines of authority and their impact on women and minorities.

Finally, and perhaps most challenging to the field of business history, is the way the cultural dimensions of gender and race in business confront and undermine notions of economic rationalism. For example, at the turn of the twentieth century, most white-owned life insurance companies refused to sell their products to African-Americans. They based their neglect of this market on actuarial tables. However, the reality of high mortality rates among African-Americans was a function of living and working conditions, the stresses of living in a racist society, poverty, and limited opportunities. Without questioning the discrepancies in their actions, white-owned companies took as part of their mission the education and provision of health services to their white customers to improve their longevity. Similarly, managers in the electrical and automotive industries during World War II resisted efficiencies that would have meant hiring women to do men's jobs. They also restructured job descriptions to conform to preexisting notions of appropriate behavior for men and women. These are only two instances that suggest business rationalization has been a myth. Social categories such as gender and race have been an important force shaping how businesses approach markets, make hiring choices, and create organizational forms. The basic tenet of neoclassical economics—that markets are rational and always operate according to neutral "laws" of supply and demand—breaks down in the face of powerful nonrational forces such as gender.

Revising definitions of *business,* then, allows us to address the issue of difference and thereby the workings of power. One of the first questions about power raised by gender and race in relation to business activity is the nature of independence and autonomy in a business context. Can a person who has been defined as a dependent act to assume risk and engage as an individual in economic activity? Is a slave who produces food or furniture, sells the items in the marketplace, and uses the proceeds to purchase the freedom of family members an entrepreneur?[7]

Throughout most of our history, women have been bound by what one historian calls the "family claim."[8] Law and economic and social theory have defined women primarily as family members: as daughters, wives, sisters, mothers, or grandmothers. The common law, which is the basis for most aspects of our legal system, assumed women were relatives of men rather than individuals. Until quite late in the nineteenth century most married women had no right to control their earnings or property. After about the middle of the eighteenth century, with the growth of a liberal, individualistic society for men in the United States, women's status as dependents became even more glaring. Theoretically, someone who cannot legally execute a contract cannot operate a business. Yet we know women have done so throughout our history. The best recent estimates are that between 10 and 25 percent of the female population of North America in the colonial period engaged in some form of entrepreneurship and that as many as half of all Anglo-American urban retailers in the eighteenth century were women.[9]

Women have traditionally operated businesses because of their status as the relatives of men. As widows, as wives, and as mothers women held the family properties intact until a son or son-in-law was able to take over. This type of activity has been so consistent over time that it suggests the way we define *entrepreneurs* and *risk takers* in a liberal, capitalist economy must also accommodate those who act not as individuals but as dependents and economic caretakers who engage in "risky business" not for individual gain but for family prosperity and survival. This model is similar to that used to understand family businesses.

Incorporating others into business history could help bridge the disciplinary specializations that sometimes prevent us from sharing useful insights. For example, among the most promising avenues for incorporating women in business are recent works that analyze the family firm and small businesses. Although these types of businesses are not necessarily the same, they share certain features. To some extent, the myth of corporate dominance has obscured the persistence of business forms such as small firms, family firms, and barter and trade, all of which are especially important to groups outside of the economic mainstream. Although *individual* small firms or family partnerships may not have survived for long periods, these *business forms* have remained crucial to the larger economy as well as to individual entrepreneurs and families. Given that, historically, most women's and a great deal of minority business activity has taken place in the context of the family and in small businesses, this history provides a ready-made window into the way gender, ethnicity, and race raise questions about power in business.

However, as promising as these forays have been, much of the work on family firms is really the study of male family members. Rarely are women's activities—economic or otherwise—analyzed within the family. Nor are the inherent tensions of family-based business relations explored adequately. With a few exceptions, business historians have also overlooked the different economic meanings of families to different social or racial groups at different times. Families, like corporations, can be treated as monoliths. To do so, however, means sacrificing precisely those human interactions that reveal power struggles and compromises.

To some extent this tendency to overlook the component parts of business enterprise is related to the intense myopia of historical fields in general. Trained in one field, we are often unaware of or uninterested in the theoretical premises or research questions of another. The essays in a 1993 special edition of *Business History* devoted to "family capitalism," for example, ignored completely the vast historical and theoretical literature on the family, situating arguments about family businesses solely within the history of business.[10] Business historians often ignore the actual work that goes on in firms, the workers who do it, or the people who make up the markets where firms sell their goods. But business historians are not alone in this narrow view. Many labor historians pay little attention to the way businesses are structured or to the motives and methods of those who operate businesses, except to depict them as labor's enemies. Women's historians, although more sensitive to the economic dimensions of women's unpaid labor, generally have failed to link women's production to entrepreneurship or organizational changes in business. We have pretty much ignored business as a location for racial expression, class struggle, or women's economic activity.

This book, then, also argues for the importance of business to women's history. Business history illuminates a diversity of experience and blurs distinctions between women's public and private lives. For example, women who managed servants and slaves were the precursors of women (and men) who managed colleges, defined the professions, and ran businesses. Free and slave African-American women operated small businesses of cooking, sewing and weaving, or selling goods out of their homes. The connection between public-sphere economic relations, slavery, and capitalism clearly is rendered more complex when slave women purchase their own and their family's freedom by competing in the marketplace.

This book is an attempt to bring into a dialogue the two important fields of women's and business history. To do so, I have used two organizing themes: Each chapter focuses on the legal and economic environments within which women have participated in various types of businesses. The first deals with the relations among women's business experiences, broadly defined, in light of a diversity of economic relations. Rather than the one, progressively modernizing economy of most business history, this book looks at several business and economic forms. In addition to the types of economic issues normally found in business histories—such as growth, inflation, employment, and credit—I add economic relations among women, among families, and among women and men outside of family contexts. The second theme is the importance of the legal and social condition of women to their business opportunities. The legal and social status of women shapes their possibilities and limitations in relation to family, to their definition as citizens or public actors, and to their economic status as individuals. The law includes different historical traditions (common and civil law, for example), changes in constitutions and statutes, and court decisions. Since both the law and the economy also have played central roles in the evolution of business development, the overlapping of these two areas can help us to encompass an otherwise hopelessly complex history.

To explore these two themes, I emphasize the business experiences of diverse women in four areas related to the history of business. The first, and most obvious area, is as entrepreneurs. In this arena, women have made some surprising contributions and faced unique possibilities and limitations. Second, and less traditionally studied as an aspect of business, is women's economic role as family members. This discussion includes the issues of women as members of family businesses and the economic importance of domestic goods and services. Third, I describe the business aspects of professionalization, encompassing women managers and executives and the entrepreneurial dimensions of such fields as medicine, religion, and philanthropy. Finally, even when not directly assuming the risk-taking and profit-seeking role of entrepreneurs, women have been crucial to business history as slaves, laborers, wage earners, and managers. Often overlooked by business historians concentrating on the firm, workers add an important dimension to understanding the history of women and business.

As a final observation, in studying women's lives, we need to keep in mind that throughout our history women have lived with two— sometimes paradoxical—realities. On the one hand, all women share the experience of structural inequities and institutionalized discriminations. Deep-seated notions about "women's work"—that is, what work is appropriate for women or uniquely women's—have shaped the job possibilities, wages, and business opportunities of all women. As we shall see in the chapters that follow, the notion that women are weaker or more driven by biological and domestic urges than men has been professed in some form to all American women. On the other hand, women are divided among themselves by social realities of race, class, and ethnicity. In other words, all women do not experience the same general historical conditions in the same way.[11] There are "histories of women" as well as a "women's history" and as a result enormous variation in women's business experiences.

Chapter Two

Female Economies: Women and Business in Preindustrial America, 1550–1830

Whenever any husband . . . shall neglect or refuse to provide for his wife, or shall desert her, she shall have all the rights and privileges secured to a feme sole trader. . . . That creditors, purchasers and others may, with certainty and safety, transact business with a married woman . . . she may present her petition to the court of common pleas . . . setting forth, under affidavit, the facts which authorize her to act . . . and if . . . the court be satisfied of the justice and propriety of the application, such court may . . . make a decree . . . that she shall be authorized to act, have the power, and transact business. . . . And such certificate shall be conclusive evidence of her authority, until revoked by such court for any failure on her part to perform the duties . . . made incumbent upon her.

—*Feme Sole Trader Law, 1715*

When the former slave Coincoin died in Louisiana in 1816, she left behind a farm of nearly 1,000 acres; 16 slaves; a *vacherie,* or cattle grazing grant, of almost 800 acres; 14 free children (several purchased by her earnings); and numerous grandchildren. She had already turned other large land grants over to her heirs.[1] Several things are remarkable about Coincoin's achievement. She began with only a small tract of about 80 acres that had been given to her by Claude Metoyer, with whom she had lived for 20 years and had 10 children.

Through hard work, knowledgeable and ambitious use of colonial French law, and the help of her children, Coincoin left an estate that by 1830 had become one of the richest in the country belonging to an African-American family. The Metoyer clan owned more slaves than any other African-American family, as well as impressive homes, fine silver, and its own Catholic chapel. Coincoin was a former slave who used the boundaries and conditions of race, sexuality, and the colonial economy to reshape her own and her children's lives. However, Coincoin's legacy is less unusual than we might imagine. If its extent and longevity are remarkable, it nonetheless suggests the possibilities available to colonial women shrewd enough to make use of them and the importance of the legal and cultural context to early American women's business endeavors.

In this chapter I discuss several aspects of women's involvement in the colonial and early national American economy. Women were active in all types of business during this period, as farmers and herders, managers and producers, artisans and entrepreneurs, and traders and self-employed businesswomen in small operations. The absence of adequate records means it would be impossible to count exactly how many women were involved in business activities throughout this nearly 300-year span. However, historians estimate that from 10 to 25 percent of the female population was engaged in entrepreneurship during the preindustrial period. Evidence drawn from newspaper advertisements, tax lists, mercantile accounts, and private papers suggests that as many as half of all eighteenth-century Anglo-American urban retailers were women. If we use our broad definition of business activity to include such things as barter and market farming, the number of women engaged in economic activity probably would nearly equal that of men.

Business and economic historians have focused on the Atlantic economy and the fur trade; the introduction of slavery; the importance of agriculture; the growth of local businesses; the relations between urban and rural economies; and the development of capitalism, consumerism, industrialization, and a market economy in this period. Throughout preindustrial America, most people made their living by exploiting the natural resources of farm and forest. People were tied to their locality and governed by family and local relationships to a great degree. Most production and exchange took place within a household context. Formal trade and markets were dominated by urban merchants, who depended in turn on products grown, manufactured, or gathered by farmers, traders, trappers, and artisans throughout the colonies. The largest portion of gross colonial production (the gross national product, or GNP, in current terminology) came from plantation slave agriculture. However, agricultural production in general—of foodstuffs, textile resources, and countless other products such as candles, beer, and soap—dominated most people's everyday lives. As late as 1800 more than 90 percent of all Americans made at least part of their living from agricultural production, a figure that essentially was unchanged from the fifteenth century. Further, most enterprises, whether farms or merchant houses, were based on personal or familial financial and social ties, and a firm and its owner/operator were virtually synonymous. Some of this agricultural production was subsistence oriented and not connected to markets. However, the links among farms and local, regional, and international markets grew in importance throughout the colonial and early national periods.

By 1830 the long, slow adaptation to a capitalist economy was fully visible. Although scholars fiercely debate the precise point at which the United States began the transition from a precapitalist and preindustrial to a capitalist, market, and industrial economic system, most agree that evidence suggests the shift was fueled in part by the exploration and conquest of the Americas and became increasingly apparent by the middle of the eighteenth century. By the 1830s (depending to some extent on the region of the country), the United States was fully committed to liberal capitalism, a market economy, and burgeoning industrialization.[2] The new economic relations had several aspects. Regional, national, and international markets increased in importance. Populations grew, and cities became more prominent centers of increasingly complex financial networks. More people had the ability and desire to accumulate capital for investment. At the same time, more financial resources were available to spend on goods used to display status rather than simply to survive. Thus consumer spending on nonessential items such as silver tea services and imported silk increased. Finally, the gradual replacement of human and animal power with technologies led to an increasing specialization of work and new types of workplaces in factories outside of the household.

This developing economy went hand in hand with other changes, such as the need for better transportation systems, cheaper products, a more literate population, and the introduction of cash-based exchange and monetary standards rather than a predominant reliance on barter and informal understandings of value. As economic relations gradually extended beyond villages and neighbors to incorporate strangers in far-flung mercantile exchanges, writing skills and careful accounting procedures became more important. The court systems of the colonies, and later the states, began to follow stricter procedures as the need for standardized legal approaches in the face of diverse financial practices replaced the more informal relations of local exchange. Historians refer to the cumulative impact of these changes as the first industrial revolution, or market revolution, and by 1830 the dominance of preindustrial relations had given way to expanded regional transportation networks, industrial development, increased consumerism, and new social and economic relations.

In the following I explore the legal and social environment for women throughout this period and discuss the impact of the market and industrial revolutions on women's ability to do business. (Some of the issues raised here—such as industrialization—are explored further in chapter 3.) Women's preindustrial economic activities to some extent continued as the context for and meaning of those activities altered. Women's direct access to financial resources declined even as their participation in business continued. One result of the new demands for literacy and more formal legal interactions was that in New England by 1760, for example, it had become increasingly difficult for women to gain access to credit. However, in some businesses opportunities expanded for women, and new entrepreneurial arenas opened up. Thus, although the importance of women's economic activity was central to the market and industrial revolutions, the legacy of those changes for women remains ambiguous.

The Business of Colonization

Historians continue to debate the degree to which European exploration and settlement of North and South America was driven by religious conviction, materialist imperatives, or adventurous curiosity. Whatever the case, there is no doubt that economic relations and rationales infused the experience. Even the religious colonies of the Puritans relied on joint stock companies to fund their experiment and were expected to turn a profit for their investors. The "business of colonization"—the economic motives, structures, and imperatives behind the conquest and settlement of North America—helped fuel the Western world's shift to a capitalist economy and the market revolution.[3] However, women's experience makes it clear that the advent of capitalism and the market revolution did not represent the complete triumph of new economic relations. Consumption and capital accumulation became increasingly important but did not replace barter or trading. The seemingly monolithic Atlantic *economy* that united Europe, Africa, and the Americas in complex trading networks actually was comprised of many different sets of *economic relations:* one based on gender, another on the family, another on trade and consumption, and still others on geographic areas (local, regional, and international). Women's business activities are most visible at the smallest of these divisions. However, the impact of their participation extended to the largest, and their cumulative influence was enormous.

The Atlantic economy involved North and South American colonies closely in trade with Europe and Africa, uniting the Western world for the first time. By the mid-1500s, European contact with native peoples in North America was well established, and economic relations among the Old and New Worlds had an impact on both sides of the Atlantic. In northeastern North America, French, English, and Portuguese fishing expeditions expanded into more sustained and direct reciprocal trade in furs and European goods. In the South and Southwest, the French and Spanish had built forts that operated as military outposts and trade centers. Africans had already been imported as slaves in large numbers into the West Indies and Central and South America. By 1550 three generations of mixed-blood peoples had blended native and European societies. This mixing created distinctive new cultures in the Southwest (mestizo), South (creole and maroon), and Northeast (*métis*). By 1790 the reciprocal trade in furs, slaves, gold, sugar, tobacco, and manufactured goods had generated new wealth and raised the standard of living for many but also decimated indigenous populations, enslaved thousands, and changed forever the cultures of both the New and Old Worlds. The fruits of the colonial economy had created a market revolution that made capital accumulation and consumption increasingly important to economic growth and sustenance, as well as to people's way of life.

Women and ideas about gender were central to these changes. In their roles as traders, entrepreneurs, producers, and service providers, women of various ethnic and racial groups were important links in the colonial Atlantic economy. Women's involvement in networks of trade and barter, and as tradeswomen, retailers, and entrepreneurs, was one of the most persistent aspects of their business dealings. Among the earliest of North American businesswomen were Native American women of the South, Southwest, and Northeast, whose roles in trade and production antedated and survived the arrival of Europeans and Africans to North America. Without Indian women's work as translators, and their economic expertise and desire for goods, the European companies involved in the Atlantic trade would have had a difficult time doing business.

The fur trade was one of the most important bases of the Atlantic economy. The gender division of labor, women's general importance to group survival, and their control over some resources encouraged indigenous women to step into this trade with Europeans. Many of the fur trade forts employed indigenous women to provide domestic services such as cooking, to construct buildings and freight-carrying canoes (some of them as long as 32 feet), and to process and package furs. It was the negotiating skills and exchange networks of the Ojibwa, Micmac, Assiniboine, Chippewa, and other women that gave the Hudson's Bay Company and Northwest Company access to furs and other native goods. Traders' journals reveal that women brought items to trade almost as often as did men and that European traders (some of whom were French and Dutch women) had to negotiate with Indian women for some staples such as wild rice and maple sugar. Many of the items included in the trade were women's tools, replaced women's labor, or acted as ceremonial or ritual goods—copper pots, shirts, knives, and crackers and other foods—making Native American women among the first North American consumers. Native American women creatively adapted European goods to their own needs. For example, they incorporated blankets and glass beads into a new type of clothing, used metal tools in the preparation of animal skins, and employed copper pots as religious ritual objects.[4]

Unfortunately, Europeans also brought new diseases, overhunting, warfare, and racism to their contact with Native Americans. Indigenous populations were decimated by war, smallpox, and cholera. Fur-bearing animals such as the beaver disappeared from some areas of eastern North America by the late eighteenth century. Native women sometimes found themselves torn between their loyalties to the tribal group or Indian families and their European families and relationships. Some native women traders refused to adopt European ways, preferring to keep separate their private lives and trade with Europeans. Further, population decline, the slaughter of animals, and the coming of white women undermined native cultures and compromised Native American women's economic roles within tribes. The

appearance of white women in trading posts often signaled the imposition of new standards of behavior, made mixed-race liaisons less
socially acceptable, and encouraged adoption of the social and economic hierarchies of Euro-American civilization.

More broadly, the importance of women to trade relations was a
widespread pattern in the colonial world. The women of western Africa,
who made up the majority of female slaves imported into the Americas,
like many native women, came from matrilineal kinship groups and
tribes wherein women were producers and traders.[5] They controlled
the local exchange markets in agricultural goods, pottery, baskets, and
other items. Like the Native Americans and Africans, Europeans had a
tradition of women traders. In fourteenth- and fifteenth-century London and early modern Germany and the Netherlands women emerged
as dealers in bread, ale and beer, lace, ribbons, and fish. French and
Dutch women were among the most active fur traders in the Atlantic
economy. Like many of the native women, they also intermarried,
shoring up economic ties with social ones.

Ideas about race, gender, and sexuality informed the business of
colonization from the beginning. We can see this influence not only in
the presence of women in business transactions but also in the way
colonizers and the colonized thought about their actions and the
process of colonization itself. Sexual relations among male European
settlers and indigenous women supported colonization in complex
ways. The most famous example of this was Pocahontas's marriage to
John Rolfe in 1614. Sexual intercourse between Europeans and native
peoples was common throughout this period. Relations occurred
between European men and native women in part because there were
relatively few European women in the New World in the early years.
As important as numbers, however, was the intent behind European
and native actions. Spanish soldiers in 1598 interpreted their first
encounters with the Pueblo people as the sexual conquest of women,
later admitting to killing Pueblo men in order to subjugate the people
by raping women without interference. Further, state policy sometimes encouraged sexual relations between Europeans and natives,
recognizing the sexual element implicit in conquering a people by
making a new "race." In New Spain, Crown policy encouraged sexual
intermingling in the early years of settlement. For their part, many
indigenous groups also incorporated sexuality into their notions of
personal and tribal power. The Pueblo cosmology used sexual acts to
influence a complex relationship with the spirit world. Like the Euro-

peans, tribes such as the Pueblo and many East Coast groups used sexual intercourse to bring Europeans into their families, cement political and economic alliances, or borrow strength from contact with powerful beings.

These attitudes toward sexuality and power were also part of the vivid language of cultural encounter. For example, images of the American landscape were often based on analogies between female bodies and geographic phenomena. One English explorer provided a typical description when he spoke of the land as a *"Paradise* with all her Virgin Beauties." Sir Walter Raleigh, in 1595, referred to Guiana as "a countrey that hath yet her maydenhead, never sackt, turned, nor wrought." Thomas Morton described New England as *"Like a faire virgin, longing to be sped, / And meete her lover in a Nuptiall bed."* Streams were like the veins of the human body and mountains and hills fertile female forms. Even critics of the colonization process used gendered metaphors. John Hammond, in his 1656 attack on the spoilation of Maryland and Virginia, developed an elaborate comparison of the two colonies as fond mistresses, now ruined by "an indigent and sottish people." The end result, Hammond charged, was the rape of a generous mother earth by her own "sons," the English settlers.[6]

Precisely because of its newness and vast, seemingly untouched resources—to Europeans at least—the "virgin land" promised an undreamed of abundance of "commodities," natural resources waiting to be plundered. And if the "faire virgin" did not go willingly to her "Nuptiall bed," then Europeans believed they were justified in taking what they could. Since men were the primary landowners in European society, the notion of a female earth as men's property coincided with the legal emphasis on men's property rights in women's sexuality (hence the general importance of female virginity). Virginity promised an individual man exclusive ownership of earthly as well as fleshly bodies.

European settlers often interpreted economic and political relations with the indigenous peoples as romantic entanglements. They understood native women's willingness to have sex with them as an inherent generosity rather than as a part of cultural expressions of hospitality and economic exchange or as an effort to propitiate potential enemies. Native women sometimes provided feasts for Europeans in the early years of contact as part of the effort to incorporate explorers and settlers into local trading and defensive networks—what we could call the politics of accommodation. Europeans saw this political generosity as personal affection, an interpretation that lingers on in the romanticization of the Pocahontas story.

The notion of a "virgin land" and its related image of rape, as well as actual consensual and nonconsensual sexual relations, propelled conquest, shaped Native American-European relations, and influenced the legal and economic approaches to resource use, land tenure, and property ownership. The gendered landscape and sexualized power relations were embedded in the language of popular treatises; travelers' accounts; native societies; European beliefs; and village, crown, and corporate policy. Both women as traders and cultural intermediaries and ideas about gender, sexuality, and race were central to the business of colonization. In fact, these attitudes toward people, the land, and its commodities were of a piece with the legal and economic status of women in this period.

The Legal and Economic Status of Women

Within the gendered climate of conquest, ownership, and power exchanges, the status of women shaped their economic opportunities and their manner of engaging in business enterprises. Business activities took place in a legal, social, and economic context that simultaneously constrained complete freedom of action and permitted women to be economic actors. To assess women's potential involvement in the market, it is crucial to understand their legal status and their access to economic resources.

Although it is not appropriate to talk about a legal system among Native American groups, it is possible to describe native women's position as it related to control over economic resources. In most indigenous populations, men and women had more or less equal access to and control over group resources. Native people, however, practiced a strict gender division of labor, with men hunting large animals and fishing with nets or spears and women gathering, raising crops, hunting small animals, and fishing with weirs or small nets. This division led to gender cooperation for tribal survival and provided both men and women with important economic roles. In matrilineal agricultural groups such as the Seneca and Ojibwa, women controlled production and distribution of agricultural goods. In most tribes, since women produced and processed food, they had the right to the fruits of their labor. Ojibwa men who killed deer had to consult with wives or mothers over how to divide the meat, hides, and other by-products since it was these women who would render the carcass usable. In groups such as the Micmac, women's work included the preparation and storage of hunted and gathered items, and women may have had some responsibility for distribution. Thus indigenous women, as tribal members and producers, had numerous rights to group property.

In European North America two legal systems, derived from different legal traditions, provided somewhat varied legal situations for women in the colonial period. *Civil law* grew out of the Roman legal system and was based on codes of laws enacted by legislative bodies (statutes). All western European countries (except Great Britain) followed some version of this system. Civil law assumed that the basic unit of society was the family, particularly the married partners. It tried to regulate social relations in ways that would ensure the continuity of patrilineal families. Under civil law, property rights were held in common by married partners, and the marital partnership itself was the basis for rights to property. *Common law,* in contrast, grew out of the British system of feudal privileges and followed custom, tradition, and the decisions of judges. Feudal privileges were based on military obligations men owed other men, and only a man's lord, or baron, could confer rights to property. Thus under common law women could not have an absolute right to real property because they were outside of the feudal relationship of male obligations and duties. In common law, judges sought out previous judicial decisions in comparable cases—the doctrine of stare decises—and built their evaluations of current cases on those prior decisions.

In general, civil law afforded women more access to property and financial resources than did common law. In Hispanic America (under the civil law) a wife could inherit half of any real or personal properties accumulated during the term of her marriage because she was a coequal partner in that property. This status as a partner gave a wife rights to "community," or marital, property. Community property laws recognized a wife's economic contribution to the marital partnership, whether her labor was essentially domestic, managerial, or occurred outside of the family circle. In Anglo-American common law, on the other hand, married women had clear rights only to their personal property—such as clothing or jewelry—and to the *use* of marital property during their lifetimes. A woman could not inherit real properties outright, and restrictions could be made even on personal property acquired while she was married.

It is important to emphasize that despite these differences, both legal forms existed within cultures that were, at the core, *patriarchal* and *hierarchical*. European culture took men and maleness and relative wealth or family background as the standards by which everyone was evaluated. Under both legal systems, the law treated women differently than men, and free, slave, African-American, and Indian women differently than white or Hispanic women. Whether under the common law of Anglo America or the civil law of Hispanic and French America, in general the law saw women as dependents of men and relatives of citizens rather than as independent legal, social, civic, or economic actors. Men could assert their power in numerous ways, from their superior claims as public citizens to their right to regulate individual behavior within the family. In Anglo America, for example, a wife's earnings were automatically her husband's property under the common law principle of coverture, wherein a woman's legal existence was "covered" by that of a male relative. In New Spain, law granted the father *patria potestad*, or absolute authority within the family. No woman could ever possess this authority and its fundamental legal powers (including the right to keep a second household, or *casa chica*). Women, in short, were always subject to what one historian has called the "family claim."[7]

Throughout colonial America, the law assumed women were dependent on men for their economic support, and laws governing dower rights reinforced that notion of dependence even as they attempted to protect women from improvident husbands. Dower rights, which existed under both civil and common law systems, were a crucial economic tool in women's efforts to maintain economic viability. Common law designed dower rights to protect widows and children from destitution if a husband and father died intestate. It thus encouraged a man to shield his wife from financial difficulties should he die by setting aside as her dower right a life interest in one-third of his real estate and part of his personal property. At a husband's death, wives were entitled to their dower right, as well as any other inheritance their husbands chose to leave them. Dower existed, however, only as the right to *use* one-third of a husband's property *if and when he died* and for the widow's lifetime only. A woman could not "alienate" (sell or bequeath) her dower right, although she could trade it for another means of support—an annuity, for example. At her death any rights to dower reverted to her former husband's heirs.

Under civil law, the *dos*, or dowry, was property women brought into marriage, as an economic contribution to the maintenance of the family. Dowry could be real estate or movable goods such as jewelry, linens, bushels of wheat, or domestic tools. Dowry was not mandatory, but it was a widely accepted custom among people of all classes who could afford it. Throughout North America by about the middle of the eighteenth century, the notion that women could bring property into the marriage—the civil law's notion of dowry—had become widespread even in Anglo America. Husbands could use women's dowry, but women could bequeath any dowry properties as they saw fit. Combined with the community property rights of widows under civil law, in Hispanic and French America married women enjoyed more rights to property than their Anglo-American sisters.

The *dowery*—dowry and dower rights together—recognized a woman's economic contribution to a marriage. People often used dowery as security for loans, to start up businesses, or to make investments. For example, Sarah Todd's $300 dowry enabled her husband, John Jacob Astor, to go into business in the 1790s. From small beginnings selling pianos and flutes, they moved into purchasing and processing furs. (Marriage to Sarah Todd also brought Astor business and investment alliances with her relatives.) By the time Sarah Todd died in 1832, the Astor fortune was probably the largest in the United States. In addition to dowery, in Hispanic America women sometimes were entitled to an *arras*, a sum equal to 10 percent of their future husband's value at the time of the marriage. The *arras* was both an additional measure of financial security and a groom's token of respect for the good character of his bride. Both the dowery and the *arras* were protections for widowhood. Women generally did not have control over their properties during their husbands' lives, but dowery could provide start-up capital for a widow's business enterprise to enable her to be self-supporting.

However, married women generally were not legally independent economic actors, free of restraint and able to sign contracts in their own names or even write wills disposing of their property. Although the actual legal enforcement of women's property rights varied throughout the colonies, the essential point remains that dowry, dower rights, and the *arras* all tended to reinforce women's economic dependence on men. In addition, what was a legal protection for some women was destructive for others. Husbands could use the doweries during their lives, and some were better businessmen than others. In some cases, doweries increased due to good management; in others, women inherited only debts. Slave women were often included in white women's dowries or bequeathed as a portion of dower rights, which helped to cement the economic status of a white woman's family even as it undermined the families of slave women.

Since women's legal status throughout colonial North America also depended on their familial status, it was only as *family* members that the laws recognized women as potential economic actors. Both civil and common law prohibited married women, and single women before they reached their "majority," or legal adulthood, from issuing any legal document without the permission of some male member of the family, be it father, brother, husband, or guardian. Given such permission, however, they could act as individuals under the law. This status, called *feme sole* in the common law system, permitted married or single women to make contracts, buy and sell, and control any business enterprise. Widows and women who had reached their majority (or been "emancipated" in the Spanish system) also could operate as *femes sole* within the marketplace. In Hispanic America, never-married single women older than 25, who were not prostitutes (or, more vaguely, "loose" women), for all intents and purposes enjoyed the same social and economic privileges as men. Although they could not vote or hold public office and could not become priests, single women shared with men the right to inherit, to bring lawsuits, to act as witnesses in court cases, to loan and collect money, and to administer any property under their care. Widows had all of these rights and privileges, as well as the duties and benefits created by marriage: caring for children and the family estate. In Hispanic America, as in Anglo America, widows were some of the most active businesswomen.

Ethnic differences were also important to women's control of property and could alter their status even within legal communities. For example, the Dutch of New York until about the mid-eighteenth century continued to follow the civil law pattern of community property in marriage despite New York's general adherence to common law. Dutch men and women shared equally all property brought into and earned during a marriage, and women inherited equally with children. However, by the late eighteenth century, the Dutch use of the community property standard had given way to the English common law system in New York.

The development of equity rules and courts to administer them also greatly affected women's access to marital property. Equity rules evolved outside of the common law and were administered in Chancery Courts in England and, from the seventeenth century, in some colonies.[8] Equity developed to deal with issues of fairness not covered by common or statute law, and equity rules relating to property and inheritance superseded common law and statute. Under equity, married or engaged couples could create separate estates for husband and wife. Antenuptial agreements—contracts between husband and wife executed before marriage—effected this legal separation of property. Since not all North American colonies adopted chancery courts or developed equity rules, and since equity was extremely complex, many women did not have access to this legal remedy (a legal means for righting a wrong). However, by the eve of the American Revolution, equity had become an important aspect of marital property relations.

Women could use antenuptial agreements to assure that they would maintain control over any property they brought with them into a marriage. In 1760, at the age of 34, Elizabeth Murray Campbell married her second husband, James Smith. Before the marriage, Elizabeth and James executed an antenuptial agreement giving Elizabeth broad powers over her economic activities and preserving her separate estate. She received a settlement of £10,000 instead of dower (which would have been tied to her husband's management), and she could administer the substantial property she brought into the marriage and write a will to dispose of her property. The agreement further stipulated that if she died before her husband, her heirs would inherit as if "she had died sole and unmarried."[9] Elizabeth Murray Smith, in short, maintained her status as a *feme sole* despite her marriage. That women valued control over their own finances is suggested by the fact that more antenuptial agreements were signed in second than first marriages. In addition, antenuptial agreements signed before first marriages usually gave women only passive use of their properties; that is, women could give their consent to their husbands' management but could not themselves manage their property. Antenuptial agreements signed before later marriages more often incorporated active use, whereby women could operate as *femes sole*, managing their properties themselves.

As family members, women not only had the power but also the responsibility to assist in family businesses. Women could engage in a variety of male-defined occupations when acting for their husbands as protectors and enhancers of the family's economic resources—as "deputy husbands" or "agents of necessity." In some cases, women declared this status legally. In others, they merely acted within their community's understanding of the custom. A man whose wife signed contracts, loaned money, or made investments was bound to honor her actions so long as she was acting to protect her family's resources.

Laws in South Carolina and Pennsylvania specifically recognized that some women needed to operate businesses. In 1718 Pennsylvania passed a law according full legal rights as independent traders to wives of "mariners and others, whose circumstances as well as vocations oblige them to go to sea." South Carolina passed two laws, in 1712 and 1744, pertaining to the rights of married women to act as *feme sole* traders. On the surface, these laws would seem to confirm that colonial governments recognized and supported women entrepreneurs. However, the rationales behind these statutes, and their limitations, paint a more compromised picture. The Pennsylvania law accorded *feme sole* trader rights *only* to women whose husbands were out of the state engaged in occupations. It did not clarify the rights of wives with husbands at home, widows (even of mariners), or other single women. The South Carolina statutes were passed in response to the fact that women were evading creditors by pleading the laws of coverture. In short, the statutes were designed to regulate economic activity rather than to undermine women's dependent status. The only other colony or state to pass such legislation in the eighteenth century was Massachusetts, which essentially followed the Pennsylvania rule. Other colonies, and then states, operated with common law backing for *feme sole* status until about the mid-nineteenth century.

Women's preindustrial business activities occurred in the context of this legal marginalization. In some cases governmental regulations prevented women from entering entrepreneurial arenas. In early-nineteenth-century Mexico (and probably earlier), Hispanic women and mestizos were legally forbidden to operate *pulperías*, or small grocery stores.[10] It was also difficult for women to find capital to start up or sustain businesses. Credit was always a problem because of women's ambiguous legal status but also because they often had few resources or skills to offer as collateral. Many women sold to neighbors, friends, and acquaintances, making debt collection a potentially worrisome personal confrontation. The legal system made it difficult to sign contracts or conduct cash transactions. As a result, many continued to operate on the barter system, including shopkeeper Ann Elizabeth Schuyler, who collected a new roof in exchange for dry goods or had customers' servants do odd jobs for her.

To solve the problem of capital shortage, some successful women very consciously became supporters of other women's business endeavors. Sometimes it is difficult to sort out which investments were based on economic self-interest, which were more philanthropic, and which were designed to strengthen social or kin networks. Most transactions were probably impelled by a mixture of motives. Elizabeth Murray Smith, for example, invested in women's businesses. She set up a small shop for two orphan sisters, Anne and Betsy Cuming, and introduced them to other well-off Bostonians for whom they taught young girls fancy needlework. She gave money to start a school to Janette Day Barclay, who had an illegitimate daughter and thus had become a social outcast. She loaned start-up money to three young female artisans who became partners in a shop making and selling mantuas (shawls) and millinery. She assured that her own nieces received good educations, including the increasingly necessary writing and accounting skills. A number of Pennsylvania widows who had run family businesses created trusts for their married daughters, perhaps to act as start-up capital for a shop or other business in case the daughters also lost their husbands. Other female shopkeepers gave part or all of their estates to women retailers or extended credit to daughters, friends, or women who were good business prospects. In late-eighteenth-century Philadelphia at least five partnerships were composed of sisters and another between brother and sister, pooling family resources or inheritances. In New Spain, convents commonly acted as banks, loaning money to women as well as men, and particularly to elite women as a way of strengthening relations with the upper class.

However, not all women in business faced identical possibilities. Class status, racial background, ethnicity, and even age shaped the fields open to female entrepreneurs. Slave women tended to be less literate than nonslave women. Poor women began with fewer and shallower economic resources than did middle-class women and thus had a harder time getting credit or amassing enough capital to move out of the small shopkeeper or petty trader class. Racial prejudices and class status often dictated the types and locations of women's businesses. Many poor women, for example, simply sold goods out of their front rooms or made and sold things such as beer or cider in their backyards. Much of poor women's business was neighborhood business in small, homemade domestic items or foodstuffs that required little capital investment. The various types of lodgings run by women catered to different types of clientele and suggested the importance of economic and material resources as well as class status. Boardinghouses could be respectable establishments catering to wealthy single women or merely rooms in someone's home. One Philadelphia boarder in the late eighteenth century described the building's owner as "a very fashionable fine woman . . . tho' the house is hers and we her boarders, we have no connexion with her only as we meet her at table as we should any other Lady."[11] Other women ran boardinghouses near the docks for sailors or took in day laborers.

Because of their status in relation to men and the unspecialized nature of the preindustrial economy, women's businesses were characterized by their eclectic approach as well as their emphasis on "women's work." Women often operated many different businesses at the same time or consecutively. In Charleston, South Carolina, Sarah Singleton made and sold baby linens, took in boarders, made drawings for money, and taught school. Frances Swallow at different times operated a boarding school, a millinery shop, and a tavern. Coincoin raised cattle and pigs, leased land, and packaged and shipped bear grease (a popular mosquito repellent).

Women often went into business out of necessity. Poor, female-headed households were numerous in the colonial period, although death rather than divorce was usually the cause. In Hispanic America in the late eighteenth century, female-headed households comprised between 25 and 45 percent of all households. In some areas, female-headed households were more common than any other type of headship. Throughout Anglo America in the last half of the eighteenth century, approximately 10 percent of adult white women were widows, and by that period widows often did not remarry quickly if they remarried at all.

Women's Economic Activity

Women were in a special category as economic actors, yet their activities took place within identifiable sets of relationships. Briefly, women participated in three general sorts of economic interchange. The "female economy"[12] consisted of both the production of goods and services and the trading or bartering of goods and services *primarily* by and among women. The *household* or *family economy* encompassed women's economic role as producer of domestic goods and provider of services within and for the family. Local and more distant markets constituted the *public* or *market economy* of formal economic relations such as shopkeeping. Each of these layers overlapped and intersected throughout women's lives.

Within these broad divisions, women's activities encompassed three major aspects of business: They produced goods, they provided services, and they profited (or foundered) as "middlewomen" in trade, barter, and wholesale and retail merchandising. These economic activities were not as distinct in the preindustrial period as they are in our world. For example, women who produced goods also often acted as traders or retailers. However, we can identify the elements of these business activities by exploring in some detail the variety of women's economic dealings.

Barter was the most pervasive way in which women participated in the preindustrial economy. Barter retained its economic importance throughout this period, particularly in the exchanges that shaped the female economy. Cash seldom changed hands in the female economy even as late as the early nineteenth century. Women's trading activities were part of economic interchanges that included as well their production of goods and provision of services. These activities were woven into a series of economic connections that linked the female economy of trade among women and households to the public economy of local and distant markets. Women produced and traded food, textiles, beer, and cider; shared child care services; acted as midwives and doctors; and "loaned" servants or daughters to households that needed a temporary infusion of female labor. Barter could take place simply as a way of exchanging goods and services for needs, or it could provide a way of calculating the value of goods and services. In fact, these exchanges involved often complex reckonings among women and among women and men. Some women kept account books in the form of diaries. Martha Ballard, of Hallowell, Maine, wrote in her diary on April 15, 1788: "Mrs. Savage here. Shee & I made a settlement on account of her spinning and the wolen wheel, my being with her when sick & 1 pair of shoes & medicine I let her have when her children were sick & we wer Evin in our accounts. I lett her have 4 lb of flax which she has not paid for."[13] This is not double-entry bookkeeping, but it is a concise record of the exchange value of goods and services.

The female economy was a result of the gender division of labor and the absence of professionalization and specialization typical of all of the various ethnic and cultural groupings of colonial North America. Men and women learned different kinds of skills, both of which were often needed to complete an entire production process. Women's economic role derived from their domestic duties and production and encompassed tasks and skills believed to be inherent in the female condition. In Anglo, French, and Hispanic America this division marked the difference between men's agricultural production for the cash market and women's home production for domestic barter and consumption. In New England men worked "abroad," cutting trees, plowing and sowing grain, or milling lumber. Women worked the home farmstead: growing vegetable gardens, raising swine and poultry, providing medical care, supervising children and servants, and making the products necessary for a functioning household, such as candles and soap. Among the Pueblo, women tended, prepared, and distributed vegetable foods and built the houses. Men were responsible for the hunt, raising grains, weaving, and community protection.

Women's domestic responsibilities entered directly into economic relations when products not consumed by the family were traded for other goods, depending on an individual woman's skills and available domestic tools. Not every family owned an oven or loom, for example, and women could barter the products made with these tools, or the use of the tools themselves, for other goods and services. Skills ranged from a knowledge of the complex chemistry of beer making to the preparation of animal carcasses, the preservation of food, weaving, knitting, butter making, and herb lore.

Women's medical skills were an important element of exchange in the female economy. Specifically, women provided nursing, midwifery, and doctoring services learned from other women in this period before licensing and medical specialization. Such services performed in the public sector grew directly out of similar services women provided for the family without pay. Different levels of training and commitment shaded the class or status connotations of doctoring, and the income from these activities varied considerably depending on a woman's skill and involvement. Many women could supplement their incomes by watching at a sickbed, medicating those who were ill, or concocting and selling medicines. Traveling nurses often moved from family to family, living with one family for several weeks or even months to care for the ill or incapacitated or to free up family members for other duties. The range of nursing commitment varied from those who merely helped out on occasion to women who moved continually from house to house. Skills also ranged from the untutored to those more broadly knowledgeable in plant and disease lore. Nursing, however, was often the choice of widows, older women, and other single women who had nowhere to live, no resources except time, and no talents but the ability to nurture.

Midwifery, on the other hand, required specific skills and normally was a midwife's major source of income. It was a field dominated by women until well into the nineteenth century. Midwifery required no medical school training and was not licensed in this period, and women with a knowledge of herbs and birthing techniques could present themselves as midwives and make a substantial living. Janet Cumming of Charleston earned an average of £400 a year in the 1770s from midwifery, a sum equal to the earnings of lawyers and merchants. Mrs. Dennis of Newport, Rhode Island, claimed that in 1774 she had delivered about 350 of the 430 babies born in town during that year. Janet Alexander was so widely sought after that when some people in New York City tried to lure her away from Boston, a group of women raised $1,200 to keep her. Slave and free African-American women also practiced midwifery; slaves sometimes were able to keep part of the earnings for themselves.

The female economy was integral to the family's economic well-being. It was one component of the household economy that included other family members and servants whose products were used for family consumption or the market. The production of linen fabric in New England is a good example of how the household economy worked. Men plowed the fields, sowed, tended the flax plants, and reaped and separated the ripe seeds. Women helped with the weeding and then performed the approximately 11 other tasks necessary to produce a piece of woven linen, including combing, spinning, bleaching, and boiling the thread. The resulting fabric could be traded locally or sold in more distant markets.

Although some household trading activity occurred only among women, in other cases men entered into women's networks. Men sometimes recognized women's exclusive claim to certain products. For example, when Thomas Vose wanted to start a potash works in 1789, he had to find women willing to divert ashes from the neighborhood trading networks of the female economy and the home production of soap. Further, women's products were not merely part of local trade networks. Martha Ballard, who between 1790 and 1799 was home less than half the days of the year, traveled as a nurse, midwife, and trader throughout surrounding communities. Some bartering networks stretched all the way into the Atlantic economy. A woman who paid a medical bill in sheep's wool or cotton cloth was a local dealer in trading networks that went from Britain to the West Indies to the northern colonies.

Because women were part of the household economy, a family's life stage influenced women's business involvement. Like a person's life stage, a family's life stage could be young (with a newly married couple and small children), mature (with several children capable of work), or old (with the children gone to start their own families). The respect and high status accorded to older people in the preindustrial world, as well as the centrality of the family rather than the individual, meant older women could command the labor of younger people to further the interests of the family. Older women in large and successful households at their peak of production (when all of the family members were mature but still young enough to be healthy and at home) managed a number of servants, slaves, or neighbors' daughters "put out" to learn housekeeping skills. Martha Ballard, for example, in the late eighteenth century managed several "servants" (who were the daughters of local families), brought her own daughters into housekeeping tasks, oversaw the production of a range of domestic items, and operated as local doctor and midwife.

This reliance on family and neighborhood labor exchanges ensured generational continuity and constant, low-level production but also meant that a woman's ability to specialize in a particular area of production was in part a factor of her age and the life stage of her family. During a family's peak earning years it was possible for the senior woman in a household to engage in work that required more concentrated effort or long absences. During the years when her daughters were at home and old enough to help, for example, Elizabeth Wildes was able to weave and market cloth coverlets. Martha Ballard's peak years as a midwife came while her daughters were still at home and able to maintain daily domestic tasks, allowing her to travel and be away from home for days at a time. With a senior female householder specializing in a particular product, there was more domestic work for others, and more work for others meant a family could take on outside help. As families began to shrink because daughters married, it became harder to sustain a high level of domestic production, and outside help became relatively more "expensive."

Women were involved not only in the female and household economies of local domestic trade and subsistence activities but also in the public or market economy as entrepreneurs. Everywhere in eighteenth-century North America, women ran small shops. Between 1740 and 1775 more than 400 women were engaged in commerce in New York, Boston, and Philadelphia alone. As previously noted, half of all eighteenth-century Anglo-American retailers may have been women. Most, such as Mrs. Benedicta Netmaker of Boston, sold dry goods or catered to women consumers. Netmaker advertised in 1742 a long list of materials and furnishings, including "black Shammy, and Girl's flower'd Russel Shoes, black Velvet, white Damask, . . . Women's Black and Children's Red Morocco Pumps, Women's Worsted and Thread Hose, . . . Silver, Paduasoy and other Plain Ribbons, Fans, Necklaces, Earrings, Masks, Wires and all other millinary and Haberdashery Wares." Others, such as Mrs. Sheaffe of Boston, sold foodstuffs such as flour, currants, rice, "Choice Hyson tea, . . . Coffee by the hundred or less, Very fine Mustard, Pepper Allspice," hair powder, snuff, corks, olive oil, and oatmeal.[14] Women retailers also offered furniture, books, china, seeds, spectacles, pharmacological supplies, and beauty and hygiene products. Elizabeth Murray Smith, one of the most successful businesswomen of the colonial era, began selling millinery and dressmaking supplies in Boston at the age of 23. Some women's shops were quite long-lived, even in the unstable economic climate of the eighteenth century. In Philadelphia 35 women shopkeepers ran their businesses for 10 years or more, and 6 of these businesses operated for 20 or more years. In Hispanic America *comerciantes* ran small neighborhood stores, where they sold groceries and dry goods. In eighteenth-century Mexico, Micaela Carrillo, a mestizo widow, supplied homes and trades for two legitimate sons and provided for three illegitimate daughters. She became fairly wealthy by producing and selling pulque, a potent alcoholic brew made from the agave plant.

Although the import-export business was dominated by men throughout colonial North America, some female merchants were successful. Of these, a few operated independently in male-dominated retail areas. Others became merchants because of their family duties or entered economic arenas seen as the province of women. Around 1630 Catalina de Erauso began running mule trains loaded with European and Mexican goods between Veracruz and Mexico City. She was a formidable businesswoman not afraid to protect her trade routes with her own sword. Her competitors accused her of unfair practices and of monopolizing the use of the royal road. At her death in 1650, she left a prosperous business and a reputation that spawned a play and the first Mexican novel, *La Monja Alferez*. In eighteenth-century Boston, Elizabeth Peck Perkins imported china in a ship of which she was part owner and maintained a thriving business in an office separate from her home. Although she had had a hand in the family business throughout her marriage, she began running it by herself when widowed at the age of 42. As in most fields, women usually became merchants because their husbands had been merchants. At least one never-married woman, however, built and ran her own business all of her life. Ann Bent of Massachusetts, at the age of 16 in 1784, was apprenticed to an import firm in Boston that dealt in china and dry goods. When she turned 21 she opened her own successful shop. Even women who did not actually operate a business could provide capital, knowledge, and contacts, as Sarah Todd Astor did.

As with merchandising, other tradeswomen were not limited to entrepreneurial activities based on the gendered division of labor. Some pursued occupations that were considered the province of men. Throughout colonial North America, a few women were involved in male trades, such as tinsmithing, cobbling, coach making, and silversmithing. They did so, most often, as widows, wives, and daughters— again, as family members and contributors to the household economy. In Boston in the eighteenth century, for example, most (two-thirds) female shopkeepers were widows continuing in a trade begun by their husbands.

Widows were prominent as shopkeepers for several reasons. As an acceptable women's activity, running a shop could alleviate the poverty caused by the loss of a male breadwinner. Further, a wife may have been running a shop herself before her husband's death, but her activities may have been hidden because she was operating under her husband's name. Additionally, a widow could take over a family business operated by her husband because, as a family member, she would have participated in craft production or customer relations, thus acquiring skills or business "goodwill"—a business's regular clientele, credit, and stock—to use if her husband died. And shopkeeping was risky but potentially more lucrative than many other businesses. In Hispanic America, for example, licenses (*estancos*) to run tobacco shops were routinely given to widows of civil servants and considered advantageous since they were potentially more profitable and dependable than an often erratically paid pension. Government licensing of soldiers' widows occurred in some Anglo-American colonies as well.

Women were usually found in less physically demanding skilled trades or occupations. A good example of such a trade is printing: a number of colonial women took over their husbands' or families' businesses and made a name for themselves while sustaining their families. We know more about women printers than other female entrepreneurs in the eighteenth century in large part because of the important role printers played in the Revolution. As professional word-smiths, printers were among the most literate of the population and left more historical documentation than most entrepreneurial women.

The first known female printer in colonial North America was Dinah Nuthead, whose husband, William, began a print shop in 1686 in St. Mary's, Maryland. When her husband died around 1694, Dinah inherited the business, transplanted it to Annapolis, and made a living at that seat of the colonial government by printing forms. She ran the business except for setting type, for which she hired a journey-man printer. The first known colonial woman to publish a newspaper was Elizabeth Timothy, the wife of a newspaper publisher who died in 1738 and left her the *South Carolina Gazette*. Her son Peter took over in 1741, but after his death *his* widow, Ann, continued to publish the paper, became the official printer for the state government, and ran the printing business until her death in 1792. The official Declaration of Independence was printed by a woman, Mary Katherine Goddard, who learned the printing trade from her brother, William. Mary Katherine's mother, Sarah, was the widow of a physician, and she set her son up with a printing business after his apprenticeship. William, however, became interested in politics and left his mother and sister to run the newspaper. In addition to setting type and managing the paper, both mother and daughter wrote editorials and humorous essays. Anne Franklin, the widow of Benjamin Franklin's older brother, con-tinued to run the family print shop after her Loyalist husband left the colonies during the Revolution. She took on a male partner and oper-ated the business with the help of her two daughters and a female ser-vant.

Many types of businesses welcomed women precisely because they were domestic managers with household skills. In Hispanic America, nuns managed convents, which often involved investing funds, mak-ing purchases, and overseeing secular employees. Convents, in fact, were important banking institutions in Latin America, loaning money to merchants and property owners. Older women who needed an income managed apartment houses for absentee landlords. Middle-class women ran charitable institutions, such as municipal hospitals and poorhouses that sheltered women. Typically, women's managerial skills were called into play when managing other women, as in the case of hospitals, rather than for the general population.

Women's household managerial skills also found an outlet in running homes away from home. Women frequently operated boarding-houses, taverns, inns, or roadhouses, particularly in port towns or other urban areas, providing services for money that women usually performed without pay for their families. In late-eighteenth-century Boston, 12 of the total 34 licensed inns were run by women, and 17 of 41 alcohol retailers were women. Women could rent out rooms in their houses or own and manage hotels for travelers, as did Mary Withy, a Chester, Pennsylvania, widow. Mary Burke of Boston offered food, rooms for dancing, and sleigh rides to her hotel patrons in 1793. Mrs. Hudson of Schenectady, New York, managed an inn that also did duty as a stage stop and dry goods store in the same building. Most innkeeping was oriented to business travelers. However, some women operated spas or furnished rooms for people who migrated out of the city during the summer. Southern women ran stagehouses or merely offered rooms to travelers in their homes since there were few towns in the South and houses were far apart. In Hispanic America, as well, women operated taverns (sometimes without a license), ran restaurants, or took in boarders.

In addition to managing households or taverns or operating as artisans and shopkeepers, women were also property owners and landlords, managed plantations and farms, and speculated in real estate, again often acting as widows. Farm households could be complex affairs. Their management encompassed dealing with hired and slave labor, loaning and borrowing money, keeping accounts, and trading in a wide range of commodities and services. Abigail Adams, who modestly referred to herself as a "farmeress," was largely responsible for running the family farm while her husband, John, was running the Revolution. The historian Jonathan Chu has argued that Adams had a sophisticated economic knowledge and such wide-ranging business interests that she amounted to a "conglomerate."[15] Eliza Lucas Pinckney introduced indigo production to the colonies in the 1740s; she claimed to "love the vegitable world extremely."[16] At the age of 17 she began managing her father's extensive plantation in South Carolina. Later returning as a widow to direct the family lands, she supervised three plantations of more than 5,000 acres, including feeding, clothing, and training numerous slaves. Indigo was only the most spectacular of her crop experiments. She also planted fig trees to export the fruit and was constantly introducing new vegetable and grain crops to her farms, seeking those that would be most successful. Martha Logan, less spectacularly than Pinckney, ran a plantation near Charleston, and also sold seeds and operated a boarding school in her house. Elizabeth Digges was the richest woman in Virginia in the late eighteenth century and owned more slaves than anyone else in the state. South Carolina's Sarah Blakeway rented and speculated in land, bought and sold slaves, and leased houses. Elite Southern white women, in fact, may have been better trained than Northern women in managing large landholdings since in general they had a greater hand in the day-to-day management of plantations and estates. Of course, as was true of all slave enterprises, wealth for whites built on the labor of unfree men and women.

In Hispanic America, women frequently supervised large estates, family mines, or rural manufacturing establishments such as *molinos* (flour mills) or *trapiches* (sugar mills). Some women inherited and managed large parcels of land on the deaths of their husbands or took over from incapacitated or improvident husbands. Graciana de Velasco, a wealthy member of the nobility, managed lands worth more than half a million pesos. Women also ran medium-sized estates, or *labradoras*, beginning in the sixteenth century. Like Anglo-American women, Hispanic women could purchase land directly through their own labor. In addition, in some areas inheritance laws allowed mothers to leave their estates to their daughters. In Latin America the practice of entail (limiting inheritance to particular family lines) kept properties among siblings and sometimes enabled daughters to inherit if there were no sons.

The numerous wars of the eighteenth century, particularly the American Revolution, both reinforced women's economic importance within the household and provided new opportunities for women to engage in economic activities. Women sometimes participated in war as consumers, boycotting imported goods and replacing them with homemade products. In this sense, women's household production took on political, as well as economic, dimensions. Wars disrupted the usual trade networks, often took men away from home, and brought many women acting as "deputy husbands" into business or active management of family enterprises, farms, merchant houses, shops, and artisanal establishments.

Some women found that they enjoyed running a business or were better at it than their husbands. Mary Fish Silliman was forced to take over management of the family lands when her husband, Gold Selleck Silliman, went to fight the British in the Revolution. He came back a man broken in health and spirit, unable to resume his duties with his former insight. On his death a few years later, Mary discovered deep debts and disarranged finances. By 1800 she had paid off the debts, accumulated some U.S. stock, and enrolled her two sons in Yale College.

For other women, however, acting as "deputy husbands" in this way was a burden. When Christina Barnes was left in charge of the family's Marlborough, Massachusetts, store in 1770, she negotiated the business world with difficulty. She wrote to her friend Elizabeth Murray Smith that "To one gentleman I write for insureance [sic] to another to secure freight to a third to purchase Bills and all this is done in such a Mercantile Strain that I believe many of them think me a Woman of great capacity."[17] She learned quickly, but like many women unfamiliar with the intricacies of notes, credit dealings, contracts, and interest rates, suffered through that learning process. Many women probably scraped by, struggling to find enough sources of income to support themselves and perhaps children, elderly parents, or incapacitated spouses. The Revolution especially disrupted the trade in luxury goods, an important market for female retailers. However, although colonial wars made women's economic lives more complicated, they did not fundamentally challenge or restructure their ability to do business.

The Market Revolution and Women's Business

The expansion of capitalist markets and consumption after the middle of the eighteenth century, combined with the gender division of labor among men and women, probably contributed to women's ability to engage in business. At the same time that these shifts in the economy opened up opportunities to women, however, they tended to constrict the arenas open to female entrepreneurs, devalue women's household labor, and increase the importance of cash and credit transactions that often constrained women's access to capital. These changes increasingly distanced the preindustrial world of the female economy and household production from the male-dominated, cash-based entrepreneurial economy of nineteenth-century liberal capitalism.

Because of the market revolution, more people had more discretionary income to use for nonessential items. By the mid-eighteenth century, the colonial economy was shaky and many large American merchant houses were deeply in debt to their British suppliers. To bypass the large houses completely, many British companies began to deal directly with small shops. This shift created room for numerous smaller establishments, precisely the kind most conducive to women's business. The rising standard of living of the eighteenth century, visible in the increased consumption of luxury goods, broadened the possibilities for women as artisans in the millinery business or as shopkeepers in dry goods (lace, hosiery, cloth, perfume, books, and seeds), imported foods, and household goods.

By focusing on these retail products, women shopkeepers sold items that were merely an extension of their role within the family economy as providers of food, clothing, domestic services, and household goods. Their primary market was urban women who were well enough off to substitute store-bought goods for domestic products or to purchase manufactured items that could not be made at home. Women consumers increasingly made decisions regarding household purchases using their knowledge of household management ("huswifery")—and the market—to make informed choices. Despite economic growth, shopkeepers could still operate on a combination of cash and barter, or "in-kind," payments, a system with which most women were familiar. No special bookkeeping skills were required, although some education was clearly necessary.

Because of the history of artisanal independence, and the gender separation of men's and women's work and cultural roles, some women involved in market economic activity were female artisans trained to produce goods for female consumers. The growth of consumer markets after the 1750s expanded this sector of women's business. Young girls could apprentice to milliners, dressmakers, hairdressers, embroiderers, and artificial flower makers to learn these trades. Millinery and dressmaking were the highest-status female occupations and required a great degree of skill. Ultimately, an expert milliner or dressmaker could become a shop owner and manager, relieving herself of the actual work by taking on apprentices while keeping for herself the trickier managerial tasks of dealing with customers and suppliers, finding credit, keeping up with styles, and cultivating the social networks that would bring in the wealthiest customers. African-American slave women less often became artisans, perhaps because slave owners reserved for African-American men training in skills such as carpentry and blacksmithing. Slave women were set to work weaving, however, and could use that skill to earn income.

Millinery and dressmaking, in turn, supported several other female trades that demanded varied levels of training and skill. Seamstresses (and sometimes dressmakers) worked out of their homes or traveled to their clients' homes, where they might remain for weeks, sewing, making alterations, or retrimming dresses and other garments. Dyeing and glazing kept clothing looking fresh, and dyers and glazers needed a knowledge of chemical interactions and specialized equipment. At the bottom of the retail clothing trade's entrepreneurial scale, laundering employed many women, particularly those who needed to work in their homes because of family responsibilities (then, as now, child care was a problem for working women) or who had no specialized skills beyond those belonging to all women as part of their domestic education. Laundering was a business particularly open to slave and poor free women because of its low status and simple equipment needs. Poor Hispanic women also worked within their homes, producing goods for the millinery trade: washing and spinning cotton and making lace, ribbons, and even shoes. Millinery and dressmaking establishments also fed customers to other, usually female, shopkeepers for the trimmings and dry goods that were part of fashionable dressing. In New Spain, female artisanal trades were also common. To further encourage women's involvement in production, a royal order of 1798 permitted them to engage in any occupations commensurate with their strength and status. Although designed in part to weaken the power of artisanal guilds in New Spain, most of the enumerated areas were those traditionally assigned as women's domain: hair stylists, lace makers, and wool weavers.

The growth of cities in the eighteenth century also expanded trading opportunities for women, reinforcing this traditional form of women's economic activity. A rural-urban trade network, created and sustained by women, was economically significant to both individuals and local markets. In the Hispanic Southwest, Florida, and Mexican territory, Native American, European, and mestizo women brought agricultural goods and other manufactured items from the countryside to the city or village. *Corredoras* sold jewelry, combs, stockings, and other small items door-to-door. In central Mexico, Juana Roldán, the daughter of a *cacique*, or chief, created an estate as a petty trader. In Mexico City by the late eighteenth century, markets were dominated by female traders, as Native American women from surrounding villages brought fruits, flowers, and vegetables to female vendors in the city market. In some areas of Spanish America, Native American women essentially controlled the preparation and distribution of food, except for grain, meat, and imported goods.

Wherever they were present in North America, African and African-American women operated as petty traders or participated in city markets. Rural women produced fruits, vegetables, chickens, eggs, and baked goods and then bartered or sold these items to urban women, who in turn ran stalls, wagons, or hawked goods on the streets. By 1750 Charleston, South Carolina's Lower Market was the largest and most economically significant open-air market in which African-American women participated. These market women had earned a reputation as shrewd traders, one customer complaining that they routinely made profits of more than 100 percent. In Philadelphia African-American women pushed carts filled with prepared stews kept warm by charcoal fires. Women and girls sold hot corn, crying their product through the streets. Once their duties for the master or mistress were completed, some slaves were free to grow food on small patches of land, take up a stall in the city market, or sell on the street. They usually paid a percentage or fee to their owners for this privilege, but the rest of their earnings were their own.

In a sense, these women were operating on the fringes of society. They were poor, slaves, and/or members of racially stigmatized groups. However, their poverty and low status do not negate the fact that their trading activity was an essential element of the growing market economy. They linked the countryside and cities and villages, as well as producers and consumers in rural and urban areas.

In addition to growth in these traditionally female niches, entirely new areas opened to women to provide important services for the expanding market economy. The need for literacy, made necessary by more complex and distant economic interchanges, led to a demand for schools and teachers. Women's schools in the colonial period catered almost exclusively to a female clientele. For middle-class widows or daughters with few skills and economic resources, opening a school—often with boarders—was a simple matter of advertising in the newspaper. "Dame schools," as these were called in the Anglo-American colonies, covered a broad range. The simplest taught young girls plain sewing and reading. The more sophisticated offered instruction in fancy needlework, music, drawing, reading, writing, dancing, and other skills necessary to "finish" a young middle- or upper-class girl for marriage. Sometimes a husband-and-wife team operated a school: he taught the boys and she the girls. In Hispanic America before the

middle of the eighteenth century, teaching was less socially acceptable but was an attractive position for Native American or mestizo
women since it was one of the best-paid occupations open to them. But
the marginalized racial status of *amigas* who taught young children
meant that teaching was a less attractive position for Hispanic middle-
class widows or daughters. In the mid-eighteenth century the Company of Mary began training women who had taken religious vows to
teach, which somewhat improved teaching's status.

Other new entrepreneurial service areas included the provision of
entertainment and the organization of alternative religious establishments. These entrepreneurial fields experienced exceptional growth
after about the middle of the eighteenth century with the advent of traveling theatrical troupes, theater companies, and a plethora of nondenom-
inational religious organizations. The juxtaposition of these two fields is
not as odd as it might appear. Although different in some of their aims,
both religious activities and theaters required of their leaders some skills
that linked them as business endeavors. Both demanded a high level of
managerial ability in fund-raising, payments to service providers, and
investment decisions. Both placed women before audiences at a time
when most middle- and upper-class women were not allowed to speak in
public to mixed- or opposite-sex groups. Both theaters and the evangelical or protestant ministries with which women were involved were fringe
activities. They flourished beyond the cultural mainstream, where the
usual rules of female decorum could be suspended, allowing women to
establish income-earning organizations. Female religious leaders, stage
actresses, and theater managers relied on their charisma, intelligence,
and organizational skills to found theater groups, establish ministries
and churches, and build theatrical or religious organizations.

Jemima Wilkinson, who referred to herself as the "Universal
Friend," started a ministry when in her mid-40s in 1775 in New England. She purchased land with donations and planned to create a head-
quarters in Pennsylvania. Her ministry continued until her death in
1819. Ann Lee, the founder of Shakerism, left a more enduring legacy.
When she and her followers arrived in America in 1774, they purchased land and began a community in New York. Lee presented herself as the female version of divinity, a counterpart to the male Jesus
Christ. Her organization survived long after her death in 1784. In addition to these more ambitious spiritual leaders, women preachers
sprang up with each revival in the mid–eighteenth century, including
Mary Neale Paisley and Catherine Payton Phillips, who were traveling

revivalists between 1753 and 1756. Barbara Heck was responsible for founding the first American Methodist church, in 1766. Other women, clearly more marginal if no less "inspired," operated as fortune-tellers and spiritualists in the seamier neighborhoods of large cities.

Actresses led highly visible lives in the eighteenth century as part of the world of popular entertainment. Some were partners in family theater troupes; others were independent artists. Women such as the then-famous Mrs. Melmoth acted in stage plays, gave dramatic readings, performed in concerts as musicians or singers, and sometimes taught music and singing on the side. In addition, several women in the eighteenth century operated traveling curiosity shows or waxworks. These businesses also included apprenticeships and room and board for young women interested in learning the trade.

Finally, the growth of leisure and literacy, particularly among women of the upper and middle classes, and the availability of new printing technologies that lowered production costs, opened up a new profession for literate women. Although writing as a profession would not become extremely lucrative until the early nineteenth century and no women writers in the eighteenth century were able to support themselves solely by authorship, the profession first appeared in the mid-eighteenth century. Women wrote and sold both fiction and nonfiction, poems, novels, histories, travelogues, religious meditations, and dramatic accounts. The best-known Anglo-American female poet of the colonial period (and the first American poet), Anne Bradstreet, published her pieces in London, as did Phyllis Wheatley, an African-born slave in mid-eighteenth-century Boston and the first African-American female poet. Hannah Adams of Medfield, Massachusetts, wrote several histories, including *A History of New England*, that were widely circulated. Because, like many scholars, Adams had trouble supporting herself by her scholarship, she also wove straw hats. Sarah Knight published lively, popular travel narratives. Mrs. Morton, the author of the novel *The Power of Sympathy, or the Triumph of Nature, Founded on Truth*, was one of 26 women writers who published works of fiction between 1789 and 1830. These early inroads into publishing opened an important professional niche for literate women.

Conclusion

Several sometimes contradictory patterns emerge from this exploration of women's business activities during the transition to a market economy and liberal capitalism. First, women's involvement in business usually occurred in the context of their families' needs rather than for personal autonomy or individual satisfaction (although those things may have followed). The nineteenth-century liberal model that defines entrepreneurship as individualized endeavor does not fit women's preindustrial business role, which everywhere in North America was based on either a communal or familial model. Most women were seen first as family members and then as individuals (if they were seen at all).

Second, because the economy remained decentralized, and local and regional markets maintained their importance into the early nineteenth century, women were able to operate in a variety of business roles that would disappear or change radically after 1830. The wives of artisans, for example, had opportunities to learn their husbands' trades, which allowed them to continue the household business if widowed.[18] In other words, although the family claim prohibited some activities, it encouraged others. *As family members,* women had responsibilities that could lead to economic activity. The legal status and social definitions of Anglo-American women entrepreneurs as *femes sole,* and the importance of the family as an economic unit, laid the groundwork for female artisans, shopkeepers, farmers, and landlords. *Feme sole* status allowed married women, normally considered to be without legal identity, to act as *if* they were single. *Feme sole* could make contracts, buy and sell, obtain credit or loan money, and generally perform in the marketplace as if they were men.

Third, not all women were the same. Ethnic, class, and racial differences influenced entrepreneurial opportunities and rewards. The variety of laws, customs, and beliefs found in various regions of colonial North America and the early United States meant women had different cultural, legal, and social conditions for their economic activity.

Finally, despite this diversity, the cultures of North America all divided labor by gender and had traditions that supported women's economic activity. Slave and free African and African-American women such as Coincoin, for example, worked for their freedom and that of their families by building on a familiarity with trade brought from western Africa. The importance of women's provision of goods and services to their families and communities remained even as the development of a cash-based economy obscured their direct economic impact.

We find in the following chapters that some elements of these patterns—such as the tendency to locate women within a family context and the importance of ethnic or racial difference—remain viable even into the twentieth century. At the heart of the history of women and business since 1830 has been the effort to bring women's opportunities and the meaning of their business endeavors into the modern world. But this discussion has also made it clear that preindustrial women's business activities ran the gamut. If there was money to be made, an entrepreneurial possibility to be seized, or a trade to be founded, women were there to take advantage of the opportunity. But if some were entrepreneurs who would stand out in any crowd at any time for their shrewd financial dealings—such as Coincoin, Catalina de Erauso, or Elizabeth Murray Smith—most never achieved such spectacular results. Colonial businesswomen at all levels operated in a cultural and legal climate that first disadvantaged them and then allowed them to make the most of their disadvantages. That so many did, and did so well, seems testament to both women's financial need and their economic resourcefulness.

Chapter Three

Mills and More:
Women's Business and the First
Industrial Revolution, 1830–1880

*I went into the [textile] mill to work. . . . [The work] tried my patience
sadly at first, and does now when it does not run well; but, in general, I
like it very much. It is easy to do, and does not require very violent exer-
tion, as much of our farm work does.*

—Susan [Harriet Farley], 1844

"The difficulties of the times throw a gloom over everything," Rebecca
Pennock Lukens (1794–1854) wrote to her cousin Hannah Steele during the Panic of 1837. "All is paralyzed, business at a stand. I have as
yet lost nothing but am in constant fear. . . . I have stopped rolling for a
few weeks—and set my men to preparing the [mill] race, dam, &
heavy stock manufactured already. I . . . shall take the first gleam of
sunshine to resume." Rebecca Lukens's ironworks, the first documented rolling mill owned and operated by a woman in the United
States, survived the Panic intact. In fact, Lukens's astute management
over a period of 22 years led the works from the deep debt it was in
when her husband died in 1825 to regional prominence and financial
stability. By 1847, when she handed over the helm of the business to
her son-in-law, Andrew Gibbons, and retired at the age of 53, Lukens
had navigated her company through the treacherous shoals of the
Jacksonian marketplace. She had engaged in legal battles over water

rights, fought off her mother's attempts to wrest control of the company from her in favor of her brother, survived widowhood, and raised two children.[1]

This chapter explores women's business activity between 1830 and 1880. During this period, most Americans continued to earn some portion of their living in agricultural production, and the nation remained predominantly rural. As in the preindustrial world, women's business activities bridged the female, household, and public economies. Rebecca Lukens's business life followed the preindustrial pattern of a small, family firm inherited and maintained by a widow for the next generation. The economic structure of America also underwent profound changes, which are reflected in Rebecca Lukens's experiences. In fact, between about 1820 and 1880, many of the modern meanings of terms such as *business, profession,* and *occupation* first appeared.[2] In this period, which historians have called the first industrial revolution, or the market revolution, local markets integrated with national and even international ones, methods of finance and credit became more specialized, and machine power gradually replaced muscle power.

Other diverse areas, some of them closely related to economic change, also had important implications for women's involvement in business. The advent of a women's rights movement, the shifts in inheritance and property law, and the growth of female literacy opened up new possibilities. The continued growth of cities, the increasing use of corporate business forms,[3] the development of a new middle class, and the midcentury upheavals of civil war all contributed to new social and business roles for women as producers, consumers, managers, and workers. At the same time their ties to domesticity limited women's engagement in the birth of bureaucratic rationalism and professionalism, the development of new technologies, and in some entrepreneurial ventures. The acquisition of territory in the West and Southwest created opportunities for some women on the frontiers while placing new limits on the activities of Native Americans and Hispanics. Older social and economic roles limited women's participation in business activities even as new areas opened to female entrepreneurship and managerial skills.

Changes in Women's Status: Law

Probably the most important development in women's status in the mid-nineteenth century was the passage of state legislation designed to regularize and codify the rights of women. The debates about women's legal status—especially women's right to property and access to capital—were important in business development and women's business role between 1830 and 1880. Over the course of the nineteenth century, incremental changes in state laws brought women's status closer to that of men.

In part these laws were the heritage of the Revolution, which increased women's importance as the mothers of citizens and thus encouraged women's educational and moral development. In part they built on the complex of attitudes toward individualism and open access to markets emblematic of the early years of the industrial and consumer revolutions. The Revolutionary generation had promoted the notion that a successful state was based on an educated and independent white male populace. This view led to the expansion of the white male electorate after 1800. By the end of Andrew Jackson's second presidential term in 1836, all free white males over the age of 21 could vote, regardless of their property holdings or social status. Political rights went hand in hand with economic rights in the expanding capitalist markets after 1790. Economists define *laissez-faire* as the notion that individuals are the basic unit of market relations and that individual economic choices should be the foundation for those relations. Political and economic individualism was (in the early nineteenth century as now) supported by efforts in the legislatures and the courts to shape and constrain the market. A purely unregulated, individualistic market has never existed. That fact, however, does not make the construct less compelling.

From a legal standpoint, one of the most vital aspects of doing regular business has been the ability to act independently: to make contracts; obtain credit; borrow money; and apportion products, capital, and credit in response to the market. As we have seen, colonial North American society circumscribed this ability for women in various ways, such as the "inalienability" (the inability to freely buy or sell) of dower rights. The common law and equity courts had accorded women rights as traders through *feme sole* status and antenuptial agreements. However, in the years after independence and the Revolution, all of the former colonies and new states codified various changes in the common law and equity. These changes either developed before the Revolution itself or sprang from its social and economic consequences. This codification was a general process, initiated to regularize rather than revolutionize legal practice.

Historians, however, are divided over the impact of codification on women's legal status and economic possibilities. In some ways, these changes advantaged women. All states except South Carolina, for example, passed or reinforced legislation allowing for absolute divorce rather than the usual divorce *a mensa et thorough* (from bed and board). Absolute divorce, such as we have in the twentieth century, means completely severing all legal and economic ties. Divorce *a mensa et thorough* was a formal separation that ended a couple's financial and sexual "duties" but did not allow remarriage. Before the Revolution, only New Englanders had the right to absolute divorce. Primogeniture had been challenged before the war;[4] at war's end, changes in the inheritance laws of every state abolished the practice. As we have seen, equity courts in some colonies provided legal alternatives to coverture (see chapter 2). The practice of women leaving personal estates to daughters also to some extent circumvented coverture. Abolition of primogeniture, however, guaranteed daughters, for the first time, the same rights of inheritance as their brothers. Such inheritance allowed for access to all family property including land, often the most valuable portion of a family's estate and in a market economy an important financial resource. All of these changes brought women's legal status closer to that of men, giving them more control over and responsibility for their own economic activities.

In addition to these general changes, some states legislated various other rights that affected women's ability to act as individual agents. In most states *feme sole* status expanded. In South Carolina and Connecticut alterations in inheritance law gave husbands and wives equal shares of each other's estates. Both were allowed to either alienate or dispose of any form of property as they saw fit. After 1788 women in Connecticut could not only dispose of personal property including clothing and jewelry—long allowed under colonial law—but also any rights they had in real estate. These changes gave women more access to family financial resources and meant women could mortgage property or sell it, perhaps to acquire capital for other ventures.

However, the new laws also presented new difficulties. In some cases they removed legal protections without equalizing women's status in other ways. For example, most states gave husbands the right to usurp married women's earnings, even if the couple no longer lived together. Further, dower rights, a protection for women against profligate behavior by male relatives, eroded substantially after the Revolution. One response to this problem was to reinstitute legal protections for women to make up for their loss of dower rights. Laws in states such as New York, Pennsylvania, and Arkansas passed in the 1830s and 1840s primarily codified equity procedures. In 1839 Mississippi gave property rights in slaves to married women but maintained a husband's right to manage or control slave labor and its profits. An 1844 Michigan statute protected a wife's property from debts incurred by her husband. This legislation was a clear attempt to defend women's traditional dower rights from changing credit laws. These were modest changes, essentially shielding women from economic risk according to traditional assumptions about women's subordination to their male relatives.

The problematic nature of the legal situation is clear in the case of *married* women's control over property. This issue was tied to the changes of a developing market and industrial economy. Concerns about married women's status came from fears about family instability and the growing uncertainty of a market economy. The Panic of 1837, for example, stimulated a widespread debate over the way dower rights impeded the flow of credit, market relations, and real estate transfers. So long as families were tied to the land by agriculture and primogeniture, estate debts were typically paid first out of personal property in order to leave enough real property to support widows and children. But the onset of industrialization and the intrusion of international markets at the local level by 1800 meant that the inability to freely buy and sell women's dower properties hindered the settlement of debts and the smooth generational and market transition of family assets.

Partly in response to these issues, from the 1830s to the 1880s every state passed married women's property acts or laws dealing with marital community property.[5] Such laws would seem a liberating step since they made women's legal status closer to that of men. These laws for the first time in Anglo America permitted all married women to keep their own property and earnings gained during marriage. Women could freely negotiate contracts and buy and sell without acquiring the legal status of *femes sole*. The first of these laws was passed in Pennsylvania in 1832. Married women's property clauses were added to the constitutions of California (1849), Oregon (1857), and Kansas (1859). Other states, such as New Mexico, Louisiana, and Arizona, favored the civil law system of their Hispanic and French heritage and formalized the community property tradition. This tradition treated all marital property as equally owned by husband and wife. On the death of either spouse, the survivor had a half interest in the deceased's estate. Evolving laws ultimately gave married women more access to family property. By 1880 90 percent of states had laws respecting separate estates, and 63 percent had enacted legislation giving women the right to their own wages during marriage.

However, historians remain divided over precisely what impact the married women's property acts had in this period. On the one hand, the effects of these legal and ideological changes were fundamental to women's economic status. Freer divorce, access to marital properties, control over earnings, and the shift to support women's individual property rights all eventually bore fruit. Some women were able to not only do business but also profit individually from entrepreneurship and enjoy legal protection for their earnings. Women's status in regards to men—of their own class and race—was equalized. The legal climate for women's access to *family* assets, in other words, more closely resembled that of men, and thus women became over the course of the mid-nineteenth century potential *individual* players in the economic markets of the day.

On the other hand, women lost traditional legal protections and were left to the mercy of the notoriously unpredictable nineteenth-century economy. In exchange for this loss of legal protection, women at first did not receive more equitable access to family properties. In addition, the impact of inheritance and property laws that would have made family assets more available were uneven until after at least 1880, depending on the region of the country, its ethnic traditions, and the class or race of the woman under consideration. In 1830 only 13 percent of states automatically granted *feme sole* status to women who had been abandoned, and only 33 percent gave widows legal access to the personal estates of their husbands. As late as 1860 only 46 percent of states gave women the right to execute wills. Most likely the full benefits of these laws—none of which were retroactive—did not make themselves felt until a generation later, when the wills of women who were young when the laws were passed began to be probated in the 1880s.

Further, the disappearance of dowery undermined women's economic value in marriage. As the corporate form of business organization became more prominent toward the 1880s, family assets were less critical to business success since corporations could borrow capital from banks and be shielded from debt laws. The historian Carole Shammas has argued that this situation undermined some of the economic reasons for keeping families together.[6] The shift to corporate capitalization beginning in the 1860s made it more difficult for women to access capital since financial markets became more formal, restrictive, and driven by the need for long-term creditworthiness. In part because of women's unequal access to credit, most women's businesses remained small and often were more managerially conservative than men's businesses.

In addition, given the enormous disparity geographically and over time in the passage of legislation relating to women's property, any benefits or disadvantages in the laws were uneven. The existence of community property laws in New Mexico in 1860, for example, could favor an upper-class Hispanic woman. The same woman would have been at a legal disadvantage if she lived in a state (such as Utah) without community property. Further, between 1830 and the Civil War, free African-American women in the South managed to accumulate and hold property even in the face of increasingly constricting slave codes after 1830. Perhaps 15 to 30 percent of Southern African-American women owned real property on the eve of the Civil War. Ironically, black women's property ownership declined after the war as more African-Americans were entitled to and chose legal marriage, which subsumed married women's property into that of the family in most Southern states.

The ragged and sometimes treacherous impact of these changes contributed to a far-ranging debate over women's place in society. They spurred a movement for enfranchisement, increased educational opportunities, support for the expansion of credit and property rights to women, and a wider public voice and arena for women's activities. In fact, the economic dimensions of the nineteenth-century women's rights movement far outweighed interest in suffrage. Most important in evaluating the impact of legal changes on women's lives was the degree to which women could achieve parity within a patriarchal system. The women's rights platform of the 1848 Seneca Falls Convention (the official start of the women's rights movement) contained a statement on the need for married women's property rights. Women's rights leaders such as Susan B. Anthony lobbied throughout the nineteenth century for equalizing women's access to credit. Other advocates of women's rights, such as Lucy Stone, saw access to credit as a fundamental tenet of liberal democracy and a basic right that should be available to all women. Before the 1890s, in fact, more supporters of

women's rights advocated economic opportunities than believed
women should have the vote.

Changes in Women's Status: The Ideal Woman

One of the most important aspects of the mid-nineteenth-century economic environment was the elaboration of new gender, class, and
racial differences. Specifically, a new and predominantly white middle
class began to appear in urban areas by the middle of the eighteenth
century and had established itself as a cultural authority and economic
leader by the early nineteenth century. This group distinguished itself
from the upper and lower classes in part by emphasizing social distinctions of gender, race, class, and ethnicity. In middle-class, or bour-
geois, ideology, men and women, people of color and whites, and the
immigrant and native born inhabited "separate spheres" of influence
and experience. White men's sphere, for example, was the public
realm of business and politics, while white women's was the private
realm of family and domestic interests. Whites were the dominant
race, and blacks and others were subordinate.

However, these divisions were more fluid in practice than in the
ideal. So long as men or women justified their activities on the fundamental premise of gender, racial, or ethnic distinctions, men could
have an important familial role and women could participate in public
life. A small free black middle class existed in areas such as Philadelphia, New York City, Charleston, and New Orleans. Blacks and whites
shared in achieving and maintaining middle-class status. Both groups
educated or apprenticed sons in various sorts of clerical, managerial,
or professional work. In white and black middle-class families wives
and daughters stayed out of the workforce altogether. They had fewer
children so that each child could receive more of the family's emotional and financial resources. And they carefully selected, consumed,
and displayed luxury goods. Class status, in other words, derived from
a series of decisions about the use of household or family resources.
The black middle class in the antebellum period shared concerns with
whites about respectability and education, with the difference that
racial betterment took a more insistent place.

To some extent divisions of labor and status in middle-class America built on traditional preindustrial assumptions of gender difference.
Women were dependents of men. The new ideal, however, elevated

women's social and moral position at the expense of their economic one. The "cult of domesticity" emphasized women's roles as home-makers, mothers, and dutiful wives and stressed women's essentially private and domestic functions. Unlike the colonial and early national period, when women's labor was recognized as economically impor-tant, the advent of a waged workforce undermined the value of non-waged domestic labor. Much of women's work became hidden in the home; the tasks changed little, but their meaning was altered a great deal.

However, the white middle-class ideology of domesticity also afforded white women an important public role as the mothers of citi-zens—as "republican mothers." Republican mothers were responsible for the moral education of sons and daughters. It was their duty to oversee the ethical integrity of family life, even as the family's financial integrity was men's responsibility. For the numerically small African-American middle class, women's role emphasized racial betterment. As moral overseers, both black and white middle-class women engaged in a variety of social reform activities, arguing that as moth-ers they were bound to protect their children from the hazards of the world. The hazards included those that most obviously threatened family life, such as intemperance, gambling, venereal disease, prosti-tution, and, for blacks, slavery. But some women reformers used their responsibility as moral guardians to define family protection even more broadly. The white interest in the abolition of slavery and the general movement for women's rights, educational and health reform, and informed consumerism also were based on the logic of republican motherhood.

The new awareness of gender emphasized that to be male or female was an important part of one's most intimate identity and that the social expressions of gender were tied to class status and racial privi-lege. For example, the emphasis on female domesticity assumed that white, middle-class women were less sexually active and had fewer physical desires than lower-class women or women of color. Although the relationship between ideology and action is not entirely clear, the white birth rate did decline over the course of the nineteenth century, from about 7 children per married couple in 1800 to 4.24 children by 1880. Information about existing birth control methods was made more widely accessible by the advent of inexpensive printing tech-nologies after about 1820. But since no new contraceptive technolo-gies were available, most of this decline probably derived from abstinence. Some historians have argued that the assertion of the ideal of female "passionlessness" enabled white women to have more control over their reproductive lives by legitimizing marital celibacy. Fewer children meant each one could receive more of a family's resources. The fact that smaller families could foster capital accumulation engaged men's interest in abstinence within marriage. Thus the urban middle-class family as a whole benefited economically from having fewer children. Of course, this construction denigrated other women and justified the existence of prostitution and the sexual abuse of poor, slave, and free women of color. In fact, given the nineteenth-century assumption that all men, unlike some women, were inherently lustful, marital celibacy went hand-in-hand with the increase in commercialized prostitution that also took place in the course of the nineteenth century.

Continuities in Women's Business Activities

It is not possible to make exact comparisons between the colonial period and the first industrial revolution. Federal and state census categories shifted, as did the nature of retailing, wholesaling, and the content and form of many types of work. For example, artisanal trades were moving toward divisions into unskilled labor, even as textile production left the home for the factory. However, local studies of Boston, Albany, New York, and the state of Ohio help outline a sketchy profile of women's businesses in this period. That profile suggests a great deal of continuity with the earlier period.

Within the new legal and ideological atmosphere, the reasons why some women engaged in business in many ways remained those of an earlier period: widowhood, inheritance, and the need to support families. The ability of women to act independently as entrepreneurs, while expanding in law, remained bound by older traditions. Widows operated family farms and grist or saw mills, keeping the family estate "in trust" until their children came of age and the family assets were parceled out among them. Eveline Rieger Wallace, for example, inherited the family farm in Illinois from her husband in 1854 and ran it until her youngest child married and the property was distributed in 1864. Pauline Poley Rauch operated the family grist mill with her brother's help for several years in the 1840s after her husband died.

Women's endeavors continued to be hedged in by beliefs about appropriate avenues for women's and men's business efforts. Women tended to dominate in business areas related to their role as house-keepers, mothers, and wives—food preparation, textiles, and women's and children's clothing. The federal census of 1870, for example, noted that 98 percent of all "milliners, dress and mantua [shawl] makers" were women. Dressmakers and milliners were the fourth largest female occupational category in 1870, surpassed only by domestic servants, agricultural laborers, and seamstresses. Like most middle-class men's businesses, women's businesses were small, with fewer than five workers. Unlike men's businesses, however, they often were undercapitalized, more ephemeral, and short of credit. They were, as one historian puts it, "penny capitalists."[7] Most women business owners were probably older married women or widows.

We have no firm comparisons with the colonial period in terms of women's percentage of the retail sector. The constriction of women's sphere kept women-owned businesses in a feminized niche, but that niche grew between 1830 and 1880. The increased consumption of nondurable goods (such as clothing) and luxury items may have allowed female retailers to keep pace with the general growth of the economy. Historians estimate that women's earnings as a percentage of men's increased substantially between about 1815 and 1850, from 29 to 50 cents on the dollar (table 1). In addition, the family farm economy maintained the traditional divisions of labor and inheritance even in the face of the growing market economy. Some of women's agricultural activities—such as butter and egg production—fit smoothly into patterns of urban consumption and involved women directly in the market economy.

In spite of gender divisions that emphasized female domesticity and built on the traditional gender divisions of men's and women's work, women's nineteenth-century business enterprises and public economic activities were quite varied and extensive. Businesswomen, in fact, owned and operated many types of companies. One study of Albany, New York, between 1840 and 1885 found hundreds of women—married, single, and widowed—engaged in business. They owned and managed bookstores, small manufactories, shoe shops, dry goods stores, grocery stores, and ornamental hair businesses. Some operated under their own names, and others used those of male relatives. Elizabeth Keckley, a former slave, became Mary Todd Lincoln's milliner. She produced and sold products, trained apprentices, and kept accounts. Her business required that she maintain networks of customers and suppliers in small towns as well as big cities. In 1870 in the Midwest almost 31,000 women—10.5 percent of gainfully employed women—owned and operated shops, ran boardinghouses, or sold professional skills. In New York City at midcentury, African-Americans Phebe Cills and Catherine Ferguson owned, respectively, a toy store and a confectioner's shop. Businesswomen could make a

TABLE 1
Median Weekly earnings of Full-Time Wage and Salary Workers, by Sex, 1815–1999 (in 1999 dollars)

Year	Median Earnings		Ratio of Women's to Men's Earnings
	Men	*Women*	
1815			29.0
1850			50.0
1900			55.0
1920			56.0
1930			58.0
1950			54.0
1960			53.0
1980	312	201	64.4
1984	391	265	67.8
1986	419	290	69.2
1988	449	315	70.2
1990	485	348	71.8
1992	505	381	75.4
1994	522	399	76.4
1999	618	473	76.5

Source: Figures for before 1980 are adapted from Claudia Goldin, *Understanding the Gender Gap: An Economic History of American Women* (New York: Oxford University Press, 1990), chapter 3. Figures after 1980 are adapted from table 1–7, Cynthia Costello and Barbara Krimgold, eds., *The American Woman, 1996–97: Where We Stand, Women and Work* (New York: W. W. Norton, 1996), 63; and Department of Commerce, Bureau of the Census, "Table 696, Full-Time Wage and Salary Workers—Numbers and Earnings: 1985–1999," *Statistical Abstract of the U.S.: 2000* (Washington, D.C.: U.S. Government Printing Office, 2000), p. 437.

respectable living, earning more from their businesses than skilled male artisans in the same period. Many remained in business for more than five years, a mark of success in the volatile economic conditions of the nineteenth century. Other businesswomen owned, operated, or managed nationally and internationally prominent companies. Some contributed innovative techniques to the development of marketing and new technologies. Although female tycoons were relatively scarce during this period, they did exist. Some women headed, managed, or participated as family members in large and extremely lucrative business endeavors.

In some cases women's traditional roles propelled them into the industrial economy rather than keeping them out. Like many businesswomen before the twentieth century, Rebecca Lukens inherited her business from male relatives. The ironworks was one of several properties her father had developed in the Brandywine Valley between 1810 and his death in 1824. Her father left Rebecca an interest in the works as her portion of his estate. It is not clear whether he actually expected her to operate it, and her husband began running the ironworks several years before her father's death. Rebecca's husband, Charles Lukens, became a partner in her father's various businesses in 1813 and by 1824 had introduced a then-experimental rolled boiler plate process, the first in the United States. On his untimely death in 1825, however, Rebecca inherited the works in addition to control of their joint properties—now an experimental and thus shaky investment. It is not certain whether she had any commercial experience in the business before taking over the manufactories in 1825. But her quick and seemingly assured decisions suggest she had spent time with her father at the ironworks when she was young or had worked with her husband. The fact that the Pennock family was Quaker, and had ideas about women's capabilities that were more liberal than most, also contributed to Rebecca's ability to step into the business. Also helpful, no doubt, was the early-nineteenth-century expansion of women's education. She was literate and skilled in mathematics and accounting.[8] As with many *femes sole* before her, Rebecca Lukens apparently dealt easily with merchants, agents, suppliers, and customers; executed contracts; took out loans; gave orders to the workers; and generally ran her business with confidence.

As Rebecca Lukens's case suggests, training for business could still occur within the family. Operating a business with family members remained an avenue for female entrepreneurship during the nineteenth century probably because this flexible business form could be easily adapted to new economic conditions. Ellen Demorest's case is illustrative. The daughter of a New York hat manufacturer, she started her own business life as a milliner and later became a partner in the leading women's fashion company of the mid-nineteenth century. In the 1850s, when the corporate form of business was gaining wider currency, Demorest, her husband, William, and her sister Katherine Curtis developed Katherine's system of pattern making and dress cutting into a million-dollar business with 1,500 franchise agencies in the United States, Canada, Cuba, and Europe. The Demorest empire sold its products to hundreds of milliners and dressmakers, who displayed garments made from Demorest patterns in their shops and took orders for completed garments. They launched several publications (with a circulation of 60,000 even during the Civil War) and revolutionized the paper pattern industry with aggressive home marketing to housewives. Ellen Demorest handled the buying trips, operated the agency system, and made design decisions, while her sisters, Katherine and Nell, designed garments and wrote articles for the Demorest publications. They undertook all of these tasks without changing the organizational structure of their family partnership.

An absent, ailing, or incompetent husband still brought many women into business because of the need to support a family. Lydia Pinkham founded a dynasty in 1874 that lasted into the twentieth century with her medical compound for "female complaints." The company's initial impetus, however, sprang from her family's financial troubles. Pinkham's husband, Isaac, could not make a good living from any of the several endeavors he undertook. Never prosperous, the family was completely ruined by the Panic of 1873. Company tradition has it that Isaac received a recipe for medication in partial payment of a loan he had made. Whether this story is true or whether Lydia invented the formula herself, in 1875 the family began selling her compound. She cooked, filtered, and bottled it in the kitchen, using kitchen tools, while her husband and sons traveled the country selling the product. Pinkham's use of domestic tools, skills, and space to manufacture a marketable product was typical of women's businesses. At a time when women made and administered home remedies rather than seeking a physician's care, home "receipts" (recipes) were highly prized and widely traded, sometimes as items of commerce.

The tradition of *feme sole* traders remained especially important to

African-American women, both slave and free, before and after the
Civil War. African-American women, in fact, used *feme sole* status to
carve out an important economic niche in difficult times. In general,
free African-American men had fewer economic opportunities and
were limited by racial divisions to low-paid labor. The business efforts
of African-American women therefore supported the women and their
families. Slave women operated within the market economy with the
same vigor as slave men, raising and selling garden products, live-
stock, and fowl and peddling prepared foodstuffs. Slave women likely
were more active than men in retail trade, running market stalls, vend-
ing from pushcarts, or selling door-to-door in urban areas. Free black
women, although fewer in number, were equally active entrepreneurs
despite a restricted legal context for all African-Americans throughout
the period. They owned property and rented buildings or rooms in
boardinghouses, one of the more lucrative business endeavors of
black women. Some free women of color acquired slave labor, although
most operated their businesses themselves or with the aid of their
families. Confectionery and coffee shops, bakeries, millineries, and
hairdressing shops constituted the most frequent small businesses
run by African-American women in the South.

Suzanne Lebsock's study of Petersburg, Virginia, in the antebellum
period suggests that free black women were more likely than white
women or black men to own property and be engaged in business
dealings.[9] From the perspective of Petersburg's blacks, in fact,
African-American women's wealth was an extremely important
resource and may even have afforded black women a measure of independence from men of their class and race. Probably because they
held more property than Petersburg's black male population, they
tended to marry less often than white women of the same class. Black
women property owners in at least some cases seem to have been
familiar with the legal system and used it to their advantage: bringing
suits in court for broken contracts or to collect on loans or outstanding
debts. A small minority of free black women in the South became
extremely wealthy and operated in areas normally out of bounds to
blacks. One of the wealthiest African-Americans in the United States in
the antebellum period was Madame Cecee McCarty of New Orleans,
who owned many slaves and in 1848 had an estate valued at more than
$155,000. She made her living in wholesale and retail dealings, send-
ing her slave sales force into the hinterlands of Louisiana to sell goods.
She was also a powerful money broker. By far the largest concentra-

tion of wealthy African-Americans in the antebellum period was in Louisiana, no doubt because of the former French colony's relatively generous civil laws regarding slave-holding and women's right to property.

New Directions in Women's Business Activities

Household-based market agriculture remained the dominant type of business for most Americans between 1830 and 1880, retaining its economic importance even as industry grew. On the eve of the Civil War, fully 80 percent of Americans still lived and worked in rural areas. Most farms were family farms, and men and women continued to work their fields, dairies, and truck gardens much as they had before 1800. But the shifts to national and international markets and new technologies were changing the production of farm goods in subtle ways.

Cheese making is a good example. Before 1860 women produced most of the milk, cheese, and butter products consumed in the United States and exported to other countries. The complex process of cheese making required the labor of numerous women. At least one woman needed to understand the whole process to coordinate its various steps and on smaller farms to do the labor herself. On larger farms one or more "girls" milked the cows (which had to be done twice a day, every day, no exceptions); separated the cream, butterfat, whey, and milk; worked the presses; and turned and wiped the cheeses as they aged to prevent the growth of unhealthful molds. "Girls" could be daughters, unmarried aunts, sisters, or hired women (local people or immigrant servants from Ireland), but cheese making was women's work. In some families women also handled the marketing, although male cheese "factors" (usually local merchants) often coordinated that aspect of the process. Skill, careful management, and much intensive labor were necessary to produce tasty cheeses that were free of potentially deadly contaminants. Cheese makers were known by their product, and a good reputation could command a higher price.

After 1860, however, cheese making (like dairying in general) began to be industrialized. The attractions of mass production for profit, combined with new mass-production technologies such as steam-power boilers and gang presses, introduced factory production into some rural areas by the mid-1860s. At first women continued to make cheeses, but in factories rather than at home. Some even owned factories themselves, as part of a husband-and-wife team. Gradually, however, men took over ownership and production. This process of industrialization and revised gender roles was typical and happened in a variety of areas where women's labor moved out of the home and into the public world of factories and mills.

Textile making is instructive. The earliest textile mills, beginning with Slater's Mill in Rhode Island in 1790, were built near water power (streams and rivers) in rural areas to take advantage of the labor of farm women and children. It is estimated that children made up 50 percent of the workforce, women about 25 percent, and men the remainder. Men, who were paid more, usually worked as managers and supervisors, repaired machinery, or ran the larger machines. Some parts of the process in this early period were "put out" to women working within their homes on hand looms. Farm families found this opportunity to make money to supplement the annual round of crops and cows attractive, particularly as farm prices and the weather fluctuated as usual between good and bad. Mill work took advantage of labor nearly every woman and girl in America already knew how to perform, since making thread and weaving cloth traditionally had been women's domestic tasks. Particularly valuable were the skilled labor and tools of women who owned their own looms.

The lure of both markets for textiles and increased income for domestic work came together. By the 1830s mills were sprinkled throughout the Northeast wherever good sources of swift water and willing workers were found. Even the War of 1812 did not slow this industrial growth. In 1814 the Boston Associates, a family partnership headed by Francis C. Lowell, introduced sophisticated new machinery and built the first mills that integrated all parts of the textile production process under one roof. The Lowell Mills in Waltham, Massachusetts, brought their owners a 25 percent profit in one year. In addition to their innovative organization, the Lowell Mills created a predominately female workforce. The owners advertised jobs, enticing young rural women from distant areas to work by promising families they would be strictly supervised and well cared for.

The Lowell "girls" were among the first factory operatives in the United States. They were also the first group of young women to legitimately leave their families of origin without being married. In some cases, their wages went to their families or at the least relieved their families of their support. In other cases, the wages provided funds for education, personal items such as clothing, or a dowry (most mill girls

ultimately married). Women workers were not immune to the difficulties of mechanized labor in factory conditions, and the partnership
between mill owners and operatives was often problematic. The Lowell employees were among the first labor protesters in the newly
industrializing America, staging strikes for higher wages and improved
conditions.

Rural women were not the only ones to become caught up in the
industrial process. The wives of artisan shoemakers, who were predominately city dwellers, had long been engaged in the shoemaking
process. Since women learned the basics of sewing as part of their
domestic duties, it was easy to translate those skills into sewing
together the upper parts of shoes. Shoemakers' wives and daughters
frequently engaged in this part of the production process, leaving cutting, sizing, and final assembly to the artisan and his (usually male)
apprentices. Capitalists began industrializing shoemaking first by
"putting out" leather uppers for women to sew at home. Most of these
workers were not artisan's wives but simply women with the common
ability to ply a needle and thread. These women, or others like them,
soon became factory operatives, stitching shoe uppers outside of their
homes, earning wages, and sometimes striking for shorter workdays
and higher pay.

Clear patterns of early industrialization are observable in cheese
making, textiles, and shoemaking. Entrepreneurial capitalists or family partnerships stepped into women's domestic production, providing
materials for them to use to produce goods at home. Women used
their own tools and skills they already possessed. From the capitalist's
point of view, start-up and maintenance costs were lower since he (or
perhaps she) did not have to provide buildings, tools, and machinery.
However, domestic production was also a somewhat inefficient system
(from the capitalist's perspective), since workers might be called away
by child care, a gossiping neighbor, more pressing family responsibilities, or seasonal work on cash crops. There were added expenses
involved in transporting goods from myriad locations and the problem
of nonstandardized products. Thus, capitalists saw a need to bring the
various parts of the process, as well as the workers, to one central
location.

As markets expanded and new technologies became available, rural
women moved into nearby and later distant factories to perform the
same or similar labor in a factory setting. Some degree of labor specialization took place in the factory. Whereas before a woman might grow

her own flax, spin her own thread, dye it, and weave her own linen, in the factory she might find herself only minding the spindles or dipping cotton into huge vats of chemicals. Women did work for wages that they previously had done as part of a family agricultural or artisanal production process. They became workers in these industries, in other words, because the work that was being industrialized was already categorized as women's work. Factory jobs increasingly went to men as machines multiplied, the processes rationalized, and the labor required split into more parts that demanded different skills. These men were not necessarily former farmers or artisans but could be immigrants from Ireland or displaced agricultural laborers. Thus the role of women and gender in the industrialization of various types of business was complex but central to the development of a waged labor force.

The importance of women to waged labor is paralleled by the crucial role wages—or the lack of them—played in many women's lives. In that regard, no study of women's business activities in the nineteenth century would be complete without some attention to prostitution. The economic exchanges involved in selling sex for money bring together several important issues: the low wages of working women, the sexual double standard, commercialization and expanding markets, and traditional arenas of female entrepreneurship. Before about 1880 brothel keeping and its related activities may well have been the single most important type of female proprietorship, surpassing in numbers and capital investment even millinery and dressmaking. Further, after 1840, the demimonde of prostitution spawned a market for printed pornographic materials, which became a fast-growing segment of the urban underground economy. Because of the difficulty of uncovering information on activity that is not only illegal but connected to sexuality, we may never know its full extent and economic importance. However, we have some information on the commerce in sex.

In the eighteenth and early nineteenth century, most "prostitutes" were working-class or poor women who traded sexual favors for clothing, money, or food. Before the criminalization and commercialization of the trade beginning around the 1850s, many women who sold sex also went in and out of the workforce as factory hands or domestics or married respectably. Studies done in Boston at midcentury suggest that for many women prostitution was an economic choice rather than a question of lapsed morals. In 1855 48.6 percent of prostitutes had been domestic servants, the lowest-paid female occupation.

For some women, prostitution had traditionally provided an avenue to proprietorship, property ownership, and upward mobility. Adeline Miller, for example, started as a prostitute and after 30 years in "the life" owned a great deal of valuable New York City real estate, some of which she leased to other brothel keepers. In the 1880s in Helena, Montana, female brothel keepers provided most of the banking services—especially mortgage loans—and owned a fair portion of the new city's real estate. Before 1880 most brothels in the United States were owned and operated by husband-and-wife teams or by single women—widows or those never married—some of whom established homelike atmospheres. Well-known proprietors even attained a degree of celebrity, such as Julia Brown, who successfully ran several brothels and attended parties among the New York City elite in the 1840s.

Between 1830 and the Civil War, prostitution and its attendant market in pornographic publications became highly commercialized and more visible, which brought them to the attention of urban authorities and reformers. After the advent of professional city police forces in the 1840s in places such as Boston, New York, New Orleans, and San Francisco, prostitution was to some extent regulated; laws mandated health inspections, for example. Women engaged in prostitution, as either brothel keepers or prostitutes, became more likely to remain in the trade, treating it as a profession or career rather than as a temporary stopgap measure to supplement wages earned in other jobs. Commercialization was also evident in the growing existence of directories and other forms of advertising that brothel keepers used after 1850. The advent of inexpensive printing technologies and an urban mass market made brothel directories possible. They were part of an explosion of salacious printed material that included racy novels and cheap newspapers—the "sporting press"—that detailed the exploits and celebrities of the urban commercial sex trade.

After the Civil War, interest in reform waned as the nation became more concerned with returning to stability. Cities increasingly distinguished between keeping a brothel, in which various forms of vice were contained and could be easily regulated as businesses through liquor or gambling licenses, and streetwalking, in which individual women plied their trade standing on street corners. Brothel keeping went largely unregulated so long as operators maintained reasonable decorum by curtailing drunkenness and violence and obeying the health regulations. The police and court systems focused instead on streetwalkers, making sure they stayed away from respectable neighborhoods. By 1880 prostitution had gone from a casual business perhaps associated with a tavern or a small local brothel operated by a woman or husband-and-wife team to a highly organized business venture complete with middlemen (procurers), advertising, licensing, and payoff schedules for the authorities.

One area in which legal, ideological, and economic conditions came together to encourage new types of business endeavors was women's education. Economic opportunities, reformist zeal, and a willingness on the part of some to see women as individuals in their own right all encouraged female literacy. Literacy among white women increased during the first years of the nineteenth century as public education became widespread. Between 1830 and 1850 the nation witnessed the largest expansion in the number of female academies in its history. This growth created openings for women in education, which in turn gave them the skills to pursue other opportunities as teachers, managers, and entrepreneurs.

The first female seminary to incorporate elements of men's traditional liberal arts education recognized the fact that to compete with men, women would need to have access to the same training. Emma Willard's Troy (New York) Seminary opened to students in 1821. Others followed this experiment in women's education, most notably Mount Holyoke in 1837. Mount Holyoke funded some students in recognition of the fact that many families saw expending resources on a daughter's rather than a son's higher education as a waste. In 1831 Oberlin College admitted female students to a coeducational campus for the first time, although it trained its female students to be ministers' wives rather than ministers.

Professional training for women followed on the heels of more educational access. Although their numbers remained small, 525 female physicians, 67 female ministers, and 5 female lawyers (out of almost 2 million employed women) appeared in the federal census of 1870. The increase in literacy and access to collegiate and professional training also made more women more capable of managing or owning businesses than ever before. Most of the first few generations of women trained in female seminaries who used their education outside of the home were teachers. Some of them went on to found their own schools and colleges or to superintendencies. Betsey Mix Cowles superintended several Ohio schools and administered an entire school system. Anna Peck Sill created the Rockford Female Seminary in Illinois, using the Mount Holyoke model of providing funding for some of its female students to train as teachers.

Founding a school was a business endeavor. Creating female seminaries and women's colleges demanded entrepreneurial risk taking, superb managerial skills, a knowledge of the product and its market, and the capital to begin and the profits to continue. In that sense, early seminaries and colleges that sprang up around the country were small businesses. Since getting credit continued to be difficult, those who founded women's colleges employed innovative capital-formation techniques. They borrowed from recent developments in fund-raising for social reform organizations instead of modeling their approach after banks, corporations, or joint stock companies. Typically, a woman began by enlisting the aid of friends and family within her own neighborhood or kin circle, which could lead to the formation of an association, with paid subscribers. Women also became traveling speakers, addressing the topic of women's education and requesting funds to start a seminary or college. Mary Lyon, a graduate of a female seminary and a former teacher, founded Mount Holyoke by engaging in vigorous fund-raising around the country in the early 1830s. Many of the women who founded colleges were well connected in the abolitionist or women's rights movements and used those connections to move into promoting women's education.

The founding of colleges also demonstrates that women's businesses were sometimes started for social as well as economic reasons. Since most people expected that women would marry, and that marriage would be permanent, many believed education for women was unimportant or would ill suit them to be wives and mothers. However, the frequent incidence of widowhood and the increasing social awareness of spousal abuse, desertion, and family breakup suggested to some, more practically minded, individuals that marriage was not always a permanent or pleasant state. College founders recognized that one key to enabling women to make choices about the future lay in training for employment and the professions. Education would give women a fallback position if, for whatever reason, they found themselves without a male breadwinner.

The women's rights movement of the nineteenth century, which brought women into the public arena as fund-raisers, speakers, and political activists, similarly shifted the meaning and influence of women's traditional business networks. As in an earlier period, female entrepreneurs often helped other women to get a start in business. The women's movement of the mid-nineteenth century, however, sometimes gave that financial assistance decidedly political overtones.

The Demorests, for example, were active in various social reforms, including temperance, abolition, and women's rights. They made hiring women—especially widows—a priority. Ellen Demorest took her belief in the possibilities for self-support inherent in entrepreneurship one step further. Along with friend and fellow reformer Susan King, who had made a fortune investing in New York City real estate, Demorest created the Women's Tea Company in 1872. The company imported tea from Asia for women retailers. King and Demorest hoped by this means to give more women who needed economic opportunities an avenue to self-support. These links among social reform, women's economic status, entrepreneurship, and the "feminization" of certain types of business built on older connections among women and products. They made operating a business a protofeminist political statement.

These networks of capital were built with family and friends and with organizing skills learned in social reform contexts. They paralleled the evolving male managerial and entrepreneurial model based on apprenticeship as a clerk in an office. This is not to suggest that male managers or businessmen ignored family networks—they did not. But early in the century women lacked access to clerkship. When they did move into clerical work after 1860, beliefs about women's place in business kept them from most managerial tracks—a point to which we will return later.

Like education and social reform, the growth of interest in religion broadened for women another entrepreneurial avenue first visible in the late eighteenth century. Creating and managing churches provided both direct and indirect managerial and entrepreneurial opportunities. As with education and reform, many of these organizations had overt social agendas. The way to fulfill those agendas, however, was by making a profit and remaining in business. The Second Great Awakening, between the 1790s and the 1830s, and the increase in women's church membership over the course of the mid-nineteenth century allowed some women to make a living as preachers, ministers, and activists or to create religious organizations. Both African-American and white women preachers were popular in the early nineteenth century. Mary Livermore even spoke before the U.S. Congress, the first time in 1827 and the last in 1843. Female preachers established new churches, which then supported them, and converted hundreds to a variety of evangelical sects. Many also published books about their lives or about religious issues in general. These women were in a sense pioneers in the art of self-promotion, marketing a persona as well as a message, much like modern celebrities.

The true marketing geniuses of nineteenth-century religion, however, were the spiritualists. From the first "spirit rapping" heard by teenage girls in Rochester, New York, in 1848 to the appearance of Madame Helena Blavatsky in 1873, spiritualism captured the imagination of Americans of all classes. Spiritualism sought to prove that the spirit outlived the body by initiating communication between the living and the dead. Within that religious goal, however, was an egalitarian and heterodox social agenda that postulated the equality of men and women inside and outside of marriage, argued for a variety of health reforms (dress, temperance, and vegetarianism), and supported labor activism and radical abolitionism. Spiritualism afforded women important roles as *mediums* and *trance speakers,* first in public halls and later in the century in private homes. Women such as Achsa W. Sprague, Cora L. V. Hatch, and Emma Hardinge traveled widely on speaking engagements in the 1850s and 1860s. Spiritualism held several attractions for women, not the least of which were—as the historian Ann Braude puts it—"rebellion against death and rebellion against authority."[10] The movement's lack of an organizational structure and its assumption of individual experience, rather than office or formal training, as the source of authority facilitated women's leadership role in spiritualism.

One reason schools, reform organizations, and churches thrived can be found in the growth of an increasingly gendered national market for products of all kinds, whether spiritual comfort or herbal teas. Transportation networks linked disparate regions, creating a national economy. New technologies sped and standardized production of goods. The development of advertising attempted to shape and appeal to an increasingly diverse population. Women, particularly those in the middle class, had new discretionary powers over familial resources. In other cases women consumers had their own incomes to spend. The marketplace they entered continued to be based on traditional assumptions about women's appropriate business niche: products related to domestic needs or women's work. But this combination of gendered products and consumers, new technologies, and national advertising and shipping networks led to new developments within women's traditional business venues. Some female entrepreneurs began to consciously establish empires on the newfound spending power of middle-class female consumers. Ellen Demorest, for example, believed that women were best suited to selling feminized products such as sewing patterns to female consumers, and she built her fortune on the market for home sewing aids.

The success of Lydia Pinkham's elixir hinged on gendered marketing techniques and the growth in demand for nationally recognized products. The photograph of Pinkham's attractive, healthy, motherly, and dignified face that appeared on all of her products reminded consumers of women's venerable role as family nurses and caregivers. She represented a trusted female friend, speaking to other women about "female complaints." Hers was the first mass-produced product to carry a woman's likeness as an advertising ploy. It also was no accident that the compound hit the market in the 1870s, on the wave of post-Civil War prosperity. The substitution of apparently "homemade" consumer goods for real homemade items was a mark of status. With more discretionary income, both urban and rural women could purchase some items rather than make them themselves, thus saving time and labor. Pinkham's company was a big business by any standard, offering a product previously characterized by small-scale, local operations and minimal need for start-up capital.

Publishing provides additional evidence of the connections among consumption, the growth of the middle class, and the impact of changes in the economy and technology on women's business involvement. White female literacy increased the demand for literary works of all kinds, and new technologies sped the printing process and reduced costs. From the advent of sensationalistic and inexpensive newspapers in the 1830s and the introduction of women's magazines to the appetite for fiction, the growth of publishing after 1830 is one of the most remarkable phenomena of the mid-nineteenth century. The number of women writers swelled in the early nineteenth century. Female authors wrote for both magazines and the growing women's market for so-called sentimental, or domestic, fiction. In the antebellum period women writers were responsible for about 40 percent of all of the novels reviewed in periodicals. Nearly half of the best-sellers written before the Civil War were by women. Hundreds of women by the 1880s were "doing literary business," thanks in part to the expansion of female literacy and women's control over discretionary income. The two best-selling fiction authors of the nineteenth century were E.D.E.N. Southworth and Harriet Beecher Stowe. Stowe's megahit, *Uncle Tom's Cabin,* sold more copies than any other novel in the century.

The novel *Ruth Hall* provides a fictionalized account of these connections. It was written by the best-selling writer and women's rights activist "Fanny Fern." Fern, whose real name was Sara Payson Willis, was probably the best-known woman journalist in the nineteenth century. She made a household name for herself and a good living writing essays and novels. A sort of female Mark Twain, Fern's social commentary was so bold, satirical, and mordant that some critics thought she must be a man. *Ruth Hall,* published in 1855, is a semiautobiographical account of a young widow with two children who lost her naïveté and became a shrewd bargainer in the publishing business. In nineteenth-century publishing, virtually all authors were self-employed independent contractors, whether they wrote novels or magazine articles. Ruth became "a regular businesswoman" who could negotiate contracts and protect her own interests with the best of them: "She took up the contract and examined it; it was brief, plain and easily understood, *even by a woman,* as the men say. 'It is a good offer,' said Ruth, 'he is in earnest, so am I; it's a bargain.' Ruth signed the document."[11]

Lydia Pinkham's adaptation of home recipes suggests another new area of women's business involvement: technologies and product development. The federal Patent Act of 1790 said nothing about the gender of patentees, and women took advantage of this opening to patent their inventions. A good example of an early—but forgotten—"inventor" is Katherine Greene, who allegedly suggested to her plantation foreman, Eli Whitney, that metal wires might work better than wooden ones in his cotton gin. The first woman who took out a legal patent was Mary Dixon Kies, who in 1804 received a patent on a process for weaving straw that was used in the hat industry. Some of women's inventions had applications unrelated to "women's work," such as the underwater illuminating device patented by Sarah Mather in the 1840s and modifications of agricultural machinery such as reapers and mowers. But most women's patents up to the late nineteenth century involved processes related to women's domestic labor: weaving, sewing, cooking, and dairying. Among these patents were those for Nancy Johnson's invention of the now-classic hand-cranked ice cream maker and Ellen Demorest's "Imperial Dress Elevator," used to lift heavy skirts (*imperial* became the popular name for all such devices). Women were responsible for a wide variety of new processes (not all of them patented) for making butter. Their familiarity with butter making led to adaptations in the processes and tools used. The historian Joan Jensen has argued that these adaptations substantially increased production on mid-Atlantic farms before 1860. It was in fact this increased production that led male entrepreneurs to see dairying as a lucrative business and that encouraged men's increasing takeover of the industry after 1860.[12]

Women inventors faced particular obstacles made more difficult by their gender. Acquiring patents required elaborate models, scale drawings, and sometimes exorbitant legal fees to obtain and protect exclusive rights to inventions. The technical skills and high costs associated with patent applications presented challenges to women milliners, farmwives, and seamstresses whose work experiences provided them with ideas for improved production processes but not necessarily the funds or legal knowledge to protect their inventions.

Women and the Emergence of Business Specialization

Women also participated in and helped develop the organizational changes that so profoundly shaped American business enterprises in the nineteenth century, particularly management and clerical-sector growth. The introduction of professional managers by the 1870s in a variety of businesses was an aspect of the increasing specialization of production and the growth of bureaucracies. The rise of a new middle class with its attendant efforts to professionalize resulted in new avenues of opportunity for women as managers and entrepreneurs. In this early period management was as yet unspecialized and unregulated by professional organizations and did not exist within a body of theory about managerial behavior, prerogatives, and usefulness. Nonetheless, people "managed" businesses or people—that is, they ran companies: dealt with personnel, sought credit and markets, and coordinated myriad activities. Women nurtured managerial skills in two areas: moral and other reform organizations and productive enterprises. The gender typing of markets and products, as well as the fluid status of early managers, meant women had access to a variety of managerial opportunities.

Sarah Josepha Hale, for example, edited the influential *Godey's Ladies Book,* arguably the most important women's magazine of the nineteenth century. *Godey's* carried stories, articles, pictures of the latest fashions, and editorial columns on domestic matters. Initially a teacher and then a mother, Sarah was left at age 35 with the sole support of five children when her husband died in 1823. Like other middle-class women whose most marketable skill was literacy, she began her own magazine in Boston. It was so successful that a rival editor, Louis Dofgey, bought it to acquire Hale's editorial services. Magazine editing, in fact, was an increasingly important managerial avenue for women. Numerous publications had women editors; in the 13 western states alone in 1880, 58 women edited and managed a variety of periodicals and newspapers.

In addition, women also managed retail establishments. Margaret Getchell LaForge, for example, at the tender age of 25, became "superintendent" of Macy's New York City department store in 1866. She married a partner (whom she had hired as a buyer) and continued to manage the entire operation even during the partners' frequent European buying trips (including periods when she was pregnant) until her untimely death at the age of 38. Female managers such as LaForge were the precursors of what would become, after 1890, a flood of midlevel women managers in department stores, particularly as buyers (see chapter 4).

One especially lucrative avenue for female entrepreneurship and management came in the ownership and operation of theaters. Many female actors eventually became involved in theatrical management to gain more control over the material they performed and the profits they generated. Laura Keene's experience was typical. She first became a theater manager in Philadelphia in 1852 and went on to operate her own theaters in several cities until the late 1860s. During that time she continued to perform as well as manage. Managing a theater meant running a business operation: handling and often risking substantial sums of money; making contracts with a variety of suppliers (for costumes and stage props, for example); writing and placing advertisements; and casting plays, dealing with sometimes temperamental performers, and supervising the workforce involved in play production (carpenters, painters, and musicians). In some ways theater management was a welcoming field for women. Theater was part of the shady demimonde, where expectations about women's behavior were less strict. Women who had already lost "respectability" could find lucrative careers acting or managing. It was a profession that could be learned from the bottom up, by experience, or from husbands or fathers. Since the theater was, by definition, not a "serious" undertaking, there were few social pressures to thwart an unladylike ambition.

In other ways female theater operators were subject to unique pressures. Like most women entrepreneurs, it was difficult for female theater managers to obtain credit in the male-dominated commercial world unless they had a male protector, or patron—someone who could serve as a go-between. Further, their gender hampered female theater managers in dealing with the many unscrupulous people who inhabited the world of entertainment. Unless they had *feme sole* status, or a male protector, bringing suit against someone who stole receipts or rights to a play would be difficult. Women also had to fight for favorable attention from theater critics, who in this period clearly bent their praise to those who lined their pockets or provided other favors. The casting couch was not a Hollywood invention.

College-educated women also applied managerial skills in a variety of large and small institutions, mostly catering to areas designated as women's sphere. Educational institutions, hospitals for the mentally ill, homes for female indigents, and women's lying-in (childbirth) hospitals all used women managers and directors from at least the 1830s. One of the best examples of an individual who combined education, managerial skill, and women's sphere is Clara Barton. Her educational training led to a job in the federal patent office, and her practical experiences as a nurse during the Civil War gave her the skills to found and manage the Red Cross in 1881.

Even middle-class women who had no other occupation practiced household management, which extended beyond cooking and cleaning for the nuclear family in several ways. First, many people besides the immediate family lived or worked in households, such as servants and slaves, wet and dry nurses, cooks and laundresses, and gardeners and maids. Middle-class housewives hired and fired, bought and sold, trained and educated, negotiated pay, and resolved conflicts among these individuals. In fact, the numerous social reform organizations of the nineteenth century owed some of their organizational drive and know-how to women who learned management skills by running complex households. Second, women probably played a continuing role in the creation of familial and social business networks. Although we have yet to fully document this phenomenon for the United States, the British case suggests that women helped cement financial networks through marriage and sustained kinship ties, especially but not exclusively in the case of family partnerships. Finally, for families with small or growing businesses, women's domestic management did not always stop at the household door. Victorine du Pont Baudry's household account books from 1838 to 1842 contain a separate section detailing her oversight of work performed by household servants for the family's black powder mill. They "made and mended" mill operatives' sheets and clothing and sewed quilts and curtains. Victorine and some of the female servants in one month produced 70 cotton powder bags for the Hagley Yard. In fact, du Pont women and household servants appear to have produced all of the fabric goods used by the powder mill, including even the horse cart covers. In a letter written in 1861, Eleuthera D. du Pont Smith asked her friend Mary Wilkinson if she knew of a needleworker she could hire to sew for the household and mill. "We do the *mill work* here, making bags, sieves, bolting cloths, sheets, etc. and it requires a good hand to cut it out, and do it properly," she observed.[13]

Exactly what role women may have played in the genesis of professional management remains unexplored at this point. What is clear is that women were managing businesses, either as owner/operators or at the middle level in firms they did not own, mostly in fields related to their sphere. Consequently, they probably did not have much influence on the development of so-called industrial management, the managerial techniques that derived from the railroads and industry beginning in the mid-nineteenth century, or on scientific management, derived later from engineering. As we shall see in later chapters, however, this type of management was only one of the avenues managerial development took. Historians have tended to overlook managerial models of the late nineteenth century that probably had their roots in social reform, fund-raising, and educational institutions—women's arena. While business historians have charted business history by following corporate growth, the family partnership remained viable into the twentieth century. The family firm model of managerial strategies is only beginning to be explored. We will probably find that women's role within these firms was more extensive than previously thought. All of these issues, however, await further research.

We know more about women's role in business as office workers, one of the most important business developments of the nineteenth century. The late nineteenth century witnessed a major transformation in the nature of the middle-class workplace as businesses and government bureaucracies increased in size. Most middle-class men in 1860 were small shopkeepers, petty entrepreneurs, farmers, professionals, or clerks in small businesses. Most women engaged in middle-class businesses were milliners or "penny capitalists"—proprietors of small dry goods or grocery stores, owners of pastry shops or confectioners, or farmers. By 1900 most middle-class men and women in business were white-collar workers in large corporations or state and federal bureaucracies. The federal government, for example, employed only 1,268 people in its Washington, D.C., offices in 1859. By 1900 9,000 clerks out of a total workforce of 25,000 peopled the federal bureaucracy. The federal census reports that in 1880 144,000 men and 6,600 women were engaged in clerical occupations; by 1900 nearly half a million men and more than 200,000 women were so employed.

This "incorporation of America" reduced the autonomy of most middle-class men and women on the job, introducing job segmentation and specialization. The job category shorthand writer, for example, first appeared on the federal census in 1870; seven women were listed in this occupation. By 1880 5,000 men and women were stenographers and typists, 40 percent of those women. Stenography and typing were specialized positions. One took dictation using a system of symbolic writing; the other used the new typewriting machines, first introduced in the early 1870s, to do work previously done by hand by male clerks as part of a wide variety of other tasks. Despite their drawbacks, both positions opened up to unmarried middle-class girls and young women new avenues to economic opportunity in white-collar office work.

When the Civil War created a manpower crisis in the federal bureaucracy, and a shortage of male breadwinners within families, young, single, white middle-class women stepped in to fill the gap. In various executive departments of the federal government during the 1860s, young women began working as clerks and copyists. By 1870 52 percent of women in clerical work were employed by the federal government. These young women were the beneficiaries of the expansion of women's education. They were the vanguard of what would become, by the 1890s, a flood of women clerical workers as national economic growth stimulated the expansion of private-sector office work. For white middle-class girls, office work was clean and appropriate to their status. By the 1860s most factory labor had been taken over by immigrants and no longer appeared suitable for white middle-class daughters. Further, the incorporation of office machinery such as the typewriter, the increasing specialization of office work, and the fact that women would work for less than men all made the lower echelons of office labor less attractive to male white-collar workers.

Although most of these office jobs did not lead to managerial status for women, at least not in this early period, the general growth of the economy, combined with the continued conviction that women were more suited than men to certain types of businesses, provided new opportunities in business fields previously closed to women. (We discuss these developments in more detail in chapter 4.) By 1880 women began to appear as general agents for life insurance, as cashiers and bookkeepers in banks, and as stockbrokers and agents. The growth of white-collar work in large corporations and bureaucracies, especially after 1880, represented one of the most important changes for women in business in the preceding 300 years.

Western Expansion and Women's Business

Like the white-collar frontier, the expansion of the western frontier had important implications for women's economic roles. The rapid spread of Anglo America into the West and Southwest in the early nineteenth century provided both opportunities and difficulties for female entrepreneurship and business activities. The westward movement of Anglo-Americans repeated earlier patterns of trade, disease, and warfare and continued to push native peoples out of their homes or confined them to reservations. The annexation of Texas in 1845, the Mexican War of 1846–48, and the resultant settlement of large numbers of Anglo-Americans in the West and Southwest shifted the legal basis for some women in Hispanic North America from civil law to common and statute law. The acquisition of Texas, New Mexico, Nevada, Utah, California, most of Arizona, and parts of Colorado and Oklahoma brought approximately 900,000 square miles of land and thousands of Hispanic, Indian, and mestizo people into the United States. This shift to Anglo-American control created a new situation for the women of the West and those who migrated there.

As was true in earlier periods, the impact of westward expansion on native peoples was mixed. With the advent of widespread Anglo-American migration to the Southwest and West, and the imposition of U.S. federal law, western states and territories could choose whether they would adopt Anglo-American common and statute law traditions or remain attached to the Hispanic civil law tradition. Many western states chose to retain at least some aspects of civil law. For businesswomen, the most important of these were laws regarding community property, since they allowed both spouses a share of marital resources. In these western states, women had more rights to property as wives than almost anywhere else in the nation until 1880.

Western women had a good deal of economic autonomy. The colonial fur trade continued into the early nineteenth century, moving farther west as overhunting decimated the population of eastern fur-bearing animals. Much like the Ojibwa in the eighteenth century, Salish women of the western seacoast worked as partners with their husbands in trapping expeditions, preparing furs for trade as long as the animals and the market held out. The women of New Mexico, whether Hispanics, Indians, or mestizos and whether married or single, traditionally owned and operated businesses under their own names as independent operators. Women sold goods ranging from farm products to homemade whiskey in the plazas of the Southwest. They loaned and borrowed money to maintain businesses and operated a variety of enterprises with little regard for what Anglo-Americans considered to be respectable. For example, in the late 1830s the widow of a former governor of New Mexico territory "owned the only billiard table in Santa Fe [New Mexico], which she rented to gamblers for five to six pesos a week."[14]

As had occurred in similar contexts in previous centuries, contact with Anglo-American markets tended to erode Hispanic, Indian, and mestizo women's economic status over time. Women continued to own land in areas under civil law or within autonomous pueblos. Many also continued to write wills, leaving property to daughters as well as sons. But Anglo settlers used the (Anglo-controlled) court system, violence, and economic clout to wrest control of much of the land in the West and Southwest from Hispanic and mestizo ownership over the course of the late nineteenth century, reducing most of these populations to peonage by 1900.

Santa Fe, New Mexico, is an instructive example. In the 1850s Anglo merchants flooded into Santa Fe, introducing a market economy into a system of barter and exchange. Women's ability to engage in small business or farming declined once the economy shifted from a barter to a cash basis. With a deeper capital base, Anglo merchants and landowners invested in cattle and hogs. These animals were more expensive to pasture and feed but brought a higher return than the sheep and poultry of the indigenous female economy. Inflation aggravated the situation, and by the 1870s the number of poor in Santa Fe—mostly single or widowed women—had increased noticeably. The census of 1850 showed the Hispanic and mestizo female population working as midwives, farmers, confectioners, and petty traders. By 1870 women were rarely listed in these occupations; rather, domestic and cleaning services dominated women's work.

Many of the same forces that had structured their business endeavors elsewhere shaped Anglo women's experiences in the West. Since Anglo women did not suffer under the racial and ethnic stigmata of Hispanic and native peoples, however, migration often offered to Anglo women opportunities to earn more from their domestic (and sometimes sexual) skills than they might have elsewhere. As with agriculture for the previous 300 or more years, women's labor within the household was an important part of sustaining and spreading farming operations throughout the West. In addition to women's economic role in agriculture, areas where ranching and mining predominated provided opportunities for women to sell their domestic skills as small-scale entrepreneurs. These areas—such as New Mexico, Arizona, and the gold and silver mines of California and Nevada—were populated mostly by single men. Of the approximately 70,000 people who streamed to California between 1849 and 1852, for example, only about 11 percent were women.

Consequently, the far western frontier provided many opportunities for entrepreneurial women of all class backgrounds because scarcity augmented the cash value of their domestic skills. Besides panning for gold themselves in California, women sold liquor, cooked, chopped wood, and did laundry. Washerwomen, in the inflated economy of gold rush California in the 1850s, earned more than U.S. congressmen. One woman claimed to have made $18,000 baking pies in an iron skillet over a campfire. Women owned theaters or, like one African-American woman, charged admission for piano concerts and other entertainment. They were photographers, doctors, barbers, and dance teachers in the feverish economy of the mining frontiers.

The boomtown atmosphere of places such as San Francisco, and the commercialization of sex already under way by the 1850s, led to both opportunities and exploitation in prostitution. Prostitution in the West has received a great deal of attention, most of it more sensationalistic than realistic. The image of Kitty in the Longbranch Saloon on television's *Gunsmoke* is the usual stereotype: the dance-hall girl and fallen woman, who goes on to own her own establishment, over which she presides with sage wisdom and a "heart of gold." The reality of frontier prostitution was quite different.

The business of prostitution knew no racial or ethnic boundaries. In California the demand for cheap labor led to the importation in the 1850s of thousands of Chinese laborers, mostly men. The first Chinese woman arrived in 1848 as a servant in an Anglo household. Ah-Choi came to San Francisco with some knowledge of English and enough jewelry and other capital to pay her own passage from Hong Kong. Within two years she had opened a brothel, and her knowledge of the business suggests she had been a prostitute in China. However, Ah-Choi's example was not typical of other Chinese women, who began arriving in some numbers after Chinese men organized prostitution by 1854 and began importing hundreds of Chinese women. Some were lured under the pretense that they were to marry; others were kidnapped or sold into slavery or indentures by parents faced with poverty in China. Most of these women led short lives ravaged by hunger and disease. A few escaped to Anglo mission establishments or went on to become entrepreneurs: proprietors of their own houses or artisans. Most, however, died in their "cribs"—small rooms with barred windows where prostitutes serviced customers.

Although a few women engaged in prostitution became the proprietors of flourishing saloons and even real estate developers—including Sarah Bowman, discussed in a later section—many prostitutes in the Far West were marginalized and exploited. They operated alone or with their male "protector," selling sex for 25 cents in a small back room. Many were mothers, and a fair number were married—to husbands who as often as not pimped for them in saloons, dance halls, tents, or wherever men with money to spend gathered. Marriage was a fluid state on the frontier, and its absence never seems to have closed women out of business any more than its presence closed them out of prostitution.

The federal armies stationed throughout the West and Southwest in the years before the Civil War provided additional opportunities for women entrepreneurs, acting alone or within family businesses. Before the Civil War, civilian agents supplied army personnel with food, clothing, and services. They provided room and board for enlisted men and officers; accommodated horses, mules, and oxen with shelter and feed; coordinated laundry, sewing, and mending services; and sold entertainment, food, liquor, and sex in saloons and brothels. Most agencies, scattered throughout the West and Southwest, were husband-and-wife operations; however, some widows and single women ran agencies.

Sarah Bowman (ca. 1800–1866), nicknamed "The Great Western" after the largest steamship of her day—she was over six feet tall and weighed around 200 pounds—is a good example of the relationship of businesswomen to the U.S. Army in the antebellum period. Although the exact details are fuzzy, Bowman probably got her start with the army when she was recruited along with her first husband in the mid-1830s. This was common procedure, providing a camp with new soldiers as well as "respectable" (i.e., married) women who could nurse the wounded and ill, cook, and do laundry and mending. The army recognized laundresses, in fact, as an official part of military support; army regulations assumed they would be the wives of enlisted men. Enlistment sometimes hinged on whether a recruit could produce a wife willing to scrub uniforms. Since at this time the army did not provide anything but the bare necessities, both enlisted men and officers used their own money to purchase goods and services from independent suppliers. Female entrepreneurs furnished many of these goods and services, often under direct contract with the army. Such women sometimes were referred to as being in the army or as part of a particular company. They often maintained their connections to a particular army division for years over a wide territory as the division moved about. Some even successfully applied for federal pensions based on their service during wartime.

The nature of the federal contract system, educational limitations, and the place of women in antebellum society meant that women's businesses on the army frontier were short-lived, sporadic, and eclectic. They combined legitimate enterprises such as dining services with less legitimate endeavors such as procuring, profiteering, and gambling. Between the 1840s and the 1860s Sarah Bowman created saloons, boardinghouses, and restaurants in Saltillo, Mexico; El Paso, Texas; Yuma, Arizona; and other forts and towns in the Southwest. Her businesses catered to both enlisted men and officers and were popular meeting places for soldiers. Probably Bowman, and many other female operators, also procured women as prostitutes (and may themselves have traded sex for money or favors) and provided rooms in their establishments for prostitution. Many women on the frontier moved in and out of prostitution, pimping, or procuring; eschewed formal marriage; and frequently adopted or abandoned "spouses" (or were abandoned by them). Since the business of prostitution in the antebellum period generally was a family affair, husbands and wives running saloons, restaurants, and boardinghouses that shaded over into brothels, the dealings of someone like Sarah Bowman were less unusual than they might appear. Bowman, for example, operated numerous saloons and boarding establishments over the approximately 30 years she appears in the historical record. No one establishment survived for more than two or three years, but her involvement in these *types* of businesses was continuous throughout her adult life, regardless of whether she was "married" at any given time. She fine-tuned her knowledge of the ins and outs of federal contracting over years of working the system to her advantage.

An army officer's journal gives us a glimpse of Bowman's life in the 1850s, when she was in her 50s and had been supplying the army for 25 years and through several wars. The journal suggests she was a shrewd and even gifted entrepreneur. She bought and sold second-hand goods and ran the officers' mess and laundry at a level just good enough to forestall complaints. Hers was probably the largest business enterprise in Yuma, Arizona, in the 1850s. She convinced the major in charge of the fort, who woke up to her intentions when it was too late, to spend federal money to help her set up a new hotel across the river in Mexico. This enterprise placed her out of reach of federal authority, allowed her free rein in operating her various enterprises, and—with consummate political wisdom and a pork barrel strategy any business mogul could envy—let the federal government pay for the development in a foreign country of what became her private property. She "adopted" children and put them to work in her various enterprises, in the process providing them training as laundresses and cooks, teaching them her business savvy, and finding the girls husbands among the soldiers—in some cases after they had worked a stint for her as prostitutes.

Despite her talents, however, like many women in her position, Bowman was illiterate. She sometimes also was violent and abusive. Although her courage and generosity were legendary, and she had fought several times alongside soldiers in wars in Florida, Texas, and Arizona, she could be cruel, small-minded, and mercenary. She sometimes physically abused her servants, "knock[ing] them about like little children," according to one contemporary.[15] She contracted young women as prostitutes for the soldiers and rented rooms to them for sexual activities. Her gifts to soldiers usually were repaid with patronage and inside gossip on the army's movements (which allowed her to travel and set up business before her competitors). Bowman never retired and continued to move with the army throughout the Southwest until her death from a tarantula bite in 1866.

Conclusion

Rebecca Lukens and Sarah Bowman would seem to have little in common. One was a respected widow who operated an ironworks for 22 years and passed it on much strengthened to her son-in-law. The other was a woman of the shadiest reputation who moved about the Southwestern frontier starting and abandoning one enterprise after another. Women like Rebecca Lukens and Sarah Bowman often have been cited as exceptional: The Lukens Steel Company is proud of its female entrepreneur, and Sarah Bowman is the stuff of frontier mythology. However, the limited research on this period suggests that women such as Rebecca and Sarah, far from being the exceptional oddities of popular history, are firmly located on the spectrum of nineteenth-century businesswomen.

Traditional assumptions about women's domestic economic role maintained women's dominance in some types of businesses and allowed them to expand into others as consumption of mass-produced goods became more important, especially for the middle class. As was true in an earlier period, women could engage in virtually any business concern if their connections and justifications were familial or domestic. Widows could maintain family businesses in trust for their children, and over the course of the midcentury changes in the law increased the theoretical rights of married women to control their property, including businesses and earnings. For the poor or relatively unskilled, however, sex was often the only available commodity to offer in the marketplace. In general, women's individual businesses continued to be short-lived, even as their efforts to find a living had them trying their hands at a variety of products and services over time. Increasing literacy rates and the movement to larger and larger bureaucratic and corporate organizations by 1880 provided opportunities for women as white-collar workers for the first time in history. The women's rights movement inaugurated a debate over women's status that acknowledged the importance of their economic existence independent of men and their ability to participate in the public economy if they chose to do so. In these ways, the mid-nineteenth century witnessed the beginnings of transformations that carried over to the turn of the twentieth century and the advent of women's modern business roles.

Chapter Four

Personal Work: Women's Business in a Corporate World, 1880–1930

Although only 24 years of age and but a wisp of a girl, she has accomplished more in three years than most men do in an entire lifetime. [Bus company owner] Helen Schultz received her early business training as a clerk in a railroad office, and little did she think then that later she would have six powerful railroads fighting her as their keenest competitor in the state of Iowa. But . . . she knew how to fight—and won.
—On Helen M. Schultz, the "Iowa Bus Queen"

Maggie Lena Mitchell Walker (1867–1934) was a passionate and committed woman who lavished her impressive energies on the economic and social advancement of African-Americans, particularly African-American women. This daughter of newly freed slaves was born, not "with a silver spoon in mouth; but instead, with a clothes basket almost upon my head." When still a child the murder of her father thrust family responsibilities on Maggie, who found herself helping with her mother's laundry business and caring for her baby brother. Walker's fierce belief in the powers of self-help may have been born in these years. It was a belief shared by many of her generation and one that Walker (among others) brought to spectacular fruition. From her mother's trials and her own experiences, Walker also came to feel the special disadvantages and problems attendant on being black and female in America. "[My] great absorbing interest," she once said, "is the love I bear women, our negro women, hemmed, circumscribed with every imaginable obstacle in our way, blocked and held down by the fears and prejudices of the whites, ridiculed and sneered at by the intelligent blacks." Walker believed especially in the importance of women's "industry" and the need for women to engage in business for themselves as well as for their race. She held to this idea despite the fact that she believed—as did many—that women were not suited for the fiercely masculine business world. "The timidity and retiring disposition of women," she observed in one of her numerous public speeches, "unfit [women] for the strife, competition, and worry of business life. But, we must do something. We are up and doing, working and suffering because our needs and necessities and our ambitions force us to enter the world and contend for a living."[1]

Walker put her beliefs about women's business abilities to the test by herself becoming the first female bank president in the United States. She founded the St. Luke's Penny Thrift Savings Bank in 1903 in Richmond, Virginia, as a spin-off from an African-American mutual aid society started in 1867 by another woman, Mary Prout. The bank furnished a way to invest the funds gathered by the mutual aid society. It allowed African-Americans in Richmond to—literally—deposit their pennies and nickels into savings accounts. Walker especially had in mind as customers the black women who made up the majority of domestic servants and laundresses in Richmond, as well as nationally. So effective was the bank that by 1920 almost 650 local African-Americans had purchased homes financed by mortgages drawn on St. Luke's. Walker continued to run the bank until she retired in 1932, and it was financially and administratively strong enough to survive the Great Depression.[2]

Maggie Lena Walker was in many ways an exceptional woman. But her life also illustrates an important point related to women and business at the turn of the twentieth century. African-Americans born at the end of the Civil War came into a world that seemed to offer limitless possibilities. Slavery was gone, and the federal government had given the vote to black men. All of the fruits of freedom in a growing and prosperous nation seemed within grasp: education and literacy, economic possibilities, and social justice. That sense of optimism had unique overtones for blacks such as Walker, but it was more generally true for all American women. Given the economic depression and the world wars that followed, it is often hard to imagine that for many Americans entering the twentieth century—the modern age—everything seemed possible.

That sense of optimism sprang from very specific roots. The increase in female literacy between 1880 and 1930 was greater than at any previous time, and women had better access to higher education and professional training. Particularly after slavery, African-American women such as Walker had new avenues to basic literacy. This educated female population found job opportunities in entirely new occupational categories, including as typists and social workers, that called for a high school or college education. The wider acceptance of the notion that women were capable of acting in the public sphere, combined with the availability of paid work and careers, meant that for almost the first time some single women had a choice of whether to marry. In 1920 the federal government amended the Constitution, enfranchising white women for the first time since 1807. (The effective enfranchisement of black women had to await the Civil Rights movement of the 1950s and 1960s.) Economic power, political clout, and the rights of citizenship all seemed to point toward limitless vistas for personal growth and social betterment, particularly, but not exclusively, for middle-class white women. Recognizing that a generation of women approached the future with that sense of possibility is important to understanding the direction of their efforts and the results they obtained.

Women's engagement in various aspects of business at the turn of the century was a decisive element in creating the modern business world. Conversely, business developments were important to the lives of women. In almost no other area, besides perhaps politics, can we see so clearly the changed nature of women's lives in the early twentieth century. Understanding women's involvement in business requires a closer look at several issues. Women in general, and women in the business world particularly, heard conflicting messages about their latent chances for individual entrepreneurial success and career or job fulfillment and their capabilities for negotiating the public economy. Adjustments in divorce, inheritance, labor, and citizenship laws affected women's economic status. The ascent of big business and professionalism opened up some arenas such as the so-called women's professions even as they blocked others. New technologies diversified women's relationship to entrepreneurship, professionalism, and even housework. Finally, the federal government's response to the increased presence of women in the workforce highlighted women's role on the national economic stage.

The Incorporation of America

The years between 1880 and 1930 witnessed a kind of revolution after several hundred years of incremental change in the structure of businesses and in women's relationship to business opportunities and involvement. What historians have variously called modernization, the culture of professionalism, or the incorporation of America delineated the growth, nationalization, and even internationalization of big business and of business organization. In the 12 years between 1895 and 1907, an average of 266 firms a year disappeared because of absorption by bigger concerns. By 1904 large firms dominated core mass-production industries. For example, 318 companies held 40 percent of the nation's manufacturing assets in that year. Several things fueled these changes after 1869. Industrial growth, the creation of nationally and internationally unified markets, mass communication and transportation, and a population increase encouraged consumption and the consolidation and expansion of firms in the industrial, consumer, and service sectors. America's economic center turned away from small-scale agriculture and businesses and toward large-scale banking, insurance, manufacturing, retailing, and bureaucratic corporate structures. By the late nineteenth century the reliance on machinery, standardization, and mass production first visible in the mid-eighteenth century became the normal form of industrial fabrication. In the 1850s the most important industrial concern was cotton milling, and even the largest manufacturing or service organizations employed no more than about 500 people. In contrast, by 1910 firms such as the United States Steel Corporation (created in 1901) were capitalized at more than a billion dollars and routinely employed more than 100,000 workers. In banking and insurance, five or six firms prevailed in the market whereas before hundreds of smaller family partnerships, mutual aid societies, and local banks had provided financial assistance; fire, casualty, and life insurance; and capital for mortgages or business development. The Metropolitan Life Insurance Company, for example, went from a staff of 6 at its genesis in 1867 to nearly 2,000 office workers, managers, and support personnel by 1910. By 1930 the home office in New York City alone employed more than 40,000 people. After 1890 the expansion of national markets in the retail sector encouraged the development of large-scale retailing through department stores and mail-order firms.

As numerous historians have observed, the new structural and legal forms of corporate America had diffuse dimensions. In particular, both incorporation and professionalism were influential approaches to social and business organization. Corporations are legal entities that effectively manage a business, as well as economic entities that consolidate and circulate capital. The concern technically is "owned" by stockholders, each of whom purchases a paper interest in the corporate profits, which supplies the capital to begin and maintain operations. Incorporation had been increasingly important since the early nineteenth century, but after about 1870 it was coupled with extremely large, fully integrated industries. Incorporation was a liberating business form that strengthened the American economy in the late nineteenth century. It limited the amount of liability for which each investor was responsible and provided continuity more effectively than did family partnerships. Most importantly in the business environment of the late nineteenth century, it was an effective way of raising the large amounts of capital demanded by businesses such as railroads, utility companies, and heavy industry. Incorporation, coupled with the economic growth it both fostered and built on, promoted the centralization of business in urban areas, where access to labor, transportation, and other services was easier.

But incorporation also abetted corrupt practices, such as overselling stock or making stock available to insiders. It was difficult to pin down a large corporation when it came time to take responsibility for its actions. Many Americans saw the corporation and the social changes it made possible as a major threat to public health, welfare, and economic well-being. For example, although the corner butcher shop still existed well into the twentieth century, the butcher's meat came from increasingly farther away, unfamiliar, and unregulated sources. Whereas before 1900 a butcher might purchase wholesale beef from a regional supplier, after 1900 most beef came from a corporation such as Swift or Armour. Meat packers and suppliers in Chicago and Kansas City purchased cattle from sources all over the United States (and even other countries), processed the meat in huge, unsanitary packinghouses, and shipped it. In *The Jungle,* novelist Upton Sinclair documented the abuses of these large corporate suppliers: the processing of long-dead animals, the corruption of local meat inspectors, the dangerous working conditions in the plants, and the questionable additives (and sometimes human body parts) that found their way into processed meats.[3]

An educated native-born middle class, mostly but not exclusively white, set itself up as the gatekeeper of these changes. They believed that the burgeoning economic and social power of America should be guided by well-trained, objective, scientifically minded men and women who could place the interests of all above their own individual gain (and maybe gain individually in the process). To some extent this culture of professionalism was an updated version of the older notion of stewardship. In other ways, however, it took that traditional attitude in new directions. Professionalism advanced the value of specialized higher education and the importance of finding a public-spirited, full-time, paid occupation that offered expertise in a particular field. Practitioners created local and national organizations that policed entrance into a profession through licensing and certifying boards. Professionalism encompassed everything from organized team sports—baseball's National League, for example, was formed in 1876—to theology, law, medicine, dentistry, and academic disciplines such as history, anthropology, and sociology. Extreme specialization marked some fields. By the 1880s, for example, medicine had more than 10 national associations devoted to different specialties, including ophthalmology, neurology, dermatology, and pediatrics.

The corporate culture that supported professionalism was also modern culture: anonymous, fragmented, unregulated, and often frightening in its impersonality. Small offices once staffed by five or six men were replaced by large rooms filled with 50 or 100 female typists and male bookkeepers. "Positions" that promised (even if they often did not deliver) upward mobility for men were replaced by "jobs" that offered only dead ends. Giant manufacturing and service companies attempted to make the workplace more familial by offering lunches, sewing classes, paid vacations at company resorts, or even—as the Pullman Company did in the 1880s—creating entire "company towns" for their workers. The family metaphor, however, usually was just that: a metaphor. Job specialization extended beyond wage workers such as typists or stenographers. A class of managers evolved who were specialists in the art and science of running large corporations or bureaucracies, motivating workers, making investment decisions, purchasing supplies, and generally performing the myriad tasks that involved no actual physical production of goods or services. Managers received training in a variety of ways, including through business colleges, apprenticeships, and courses offered by employers or professional organizations. Most managerial areas by the 1920s had their own national professional organizations. Insurance agents, for example, created the National Association of Life Underwriters in 1890.

The problems associated with the rise of corporate Goliaths sparked responses from a variety of groups. One of the most common responses was counterorganization. Some founded alternative institutions such as settlement houses. Others worked within established institutions including churches and universities. Still others invoked state or federal government assistance in controlling some of the excesses of corporate America. The agrarian Populist movement, for example, sought federal help in regulating railroad shipping rates in order to lower the cost of moving agricultural products to market. Urban Progressives—middle-class professionals, social reformers, and government bureaucrats—sponsored legislation to break the strangle-hold of monopolistic practices and allow the federal government to regulate the meat-processing industry. Labor unions, such as the American Federation of Labor and the Industrial Workers of the World, brought workers together to strike for higher wages, shorter hours, and safer working conditions.

Women in business came together to organize the National Federation of Business and Professional Women's Clubs (BPW) in 1919. It lobbied state and federal governments on issues of concern to professional and businesswomen. This association of hundreds of local clubs encompassed teachers, typists, personnel managers, female entrepreneurs, and white-collar occupations. Clubs were active in their communities in a variety of ways such as occupational education, career development programs, attracting new businesses and promoting business growth, and grooming women for public office.

Not everyone was dissatisfied with businesslike approaches, even though they might decry the problems big business created. New methods of financing, capitalization, and operating efficiency even made inroads into that traditional bastion of female management: philanthropic work. Protestant mission societies, for example, attempted to alleviate the problems of corporate America by adapting business organizational forms to their welfare endeavors. To provide social services, Protestant women used traditional fund-raising techniques—many small donations from numerous individuals—to finance the creation of orphanages, asylums, and training schools. These were not businesses in the technical sense since they were not designed directly to profit the "investors"—the thousands of individual men and women who donated money. But the women running these organizations used the tools of legal incorporation, administered annuities, borrowed against future income, and strove for efficiency and longevity in managing portfolios that amounted to millions of dollars at the height of their efforts in the early twentieth century.

Women's Changing Status: Law and Education

Along with the continuities, however, there were important shifts in women's status between 1880 and 1930. Women's efforts as professionals, workers, and business reformers were pivotal to the new corporate culture of America. Women's role in business and their status as economic and civic actors were among the era's most hotly debated topics. The historical patterns in women's status we have observed in earlier periods were repeated to some extent after 1880. New definitions of women's place stretched but ultimately did not break traditional notions of the differences among men and women.

The nature of the debate over women's place in politics and the economy combined both the nineteenth-century liberal women's movement emphasis on men's and women's sameness and the need for shared civil rights with a renewed stress on women's essential differences from men and their need for protection. These two facets of the nineteenth-century women's movement had come together in 1890 under the umbrella of the National American Women's Suffrage Association (NAWSA). The organized women's movement emphasized the vote in its campaign to expand women's rights. In 1905, led by its new president, Carrie Chapman Catt, NAWSA began a concerted effort toward passage of state and federal suffrage amendments. Several states adopted women's suffrage between 1900 and World War I. The philosophical differences that underlay the two versions of womanhood, however, were difficult to bridge and led to the formation of rival organizations with different goals.

Alice Paul, a Quaker social worker, formed the Congressional Union (CU) to work broadly for women's equality. Like Susan B. Anthony before her, but unlike the new NAWSA leadership, Paul believed that men and women were more alike than different. Anthony and Paul argued that women should have the vote because they were citizens in a democracy, just like men. NAWSA claimed instead that women should have the vote precisely because they were different from men. Women's more moral and empathetic nature, they believed, would ensure honest politics and bring some heart into public policy. It was very much a Progressive argument, and an appealing one. Many people by the end of World War I believed women should have the vote because they had served loyally as nurses, ambulance drivers, and war workers during the conflict. But very few saw men and women as having the same basic nature.

Paul was more aware than most feminists of the problems attendant on emphasizing women's uniqueness.[4] Carrie Catt also recognized that in stressing the vote, feminists had turned their back on other important issues. Women worked in sex-segregated jobs. They were subject to protective labor legislation and a lower wage ceiling than men. They did not have equal access with men to professions, higher education, and capital. And while the federal amendment enfranchised white women, because of Jim Crow laws in the South black women were still not able to vote.[5] No national feminist organization took up the banner for black women's vote between 1920 and the 1960s. But organizations and individuals continued to push for improvements in specific aspects of women's status. NAWSA became the League of Women Voters in 1920 and worked to educate women about the responsibilities and benefits of citizenship. Harriet Stanton Blatch (Elizabeth Cady Stanton's daughter) forged effective alliances with working-class unions to address issues such as wages for female workers. The National Woman's Party (NWP) succeeded Paul's CU and introduced the Equal Rights Amendment (ERA) to Congress in 1923.

However, there was broad support for treating men and women differently in the workplace and little support for the notion that men and women should have the same rights and responsibilities under law (which helps to explain the failure of the ERA throughout this period). The most vociferous debates focused on issues such as whether married women should work outside of the home and whether women's status as mothers meant they needed special protections in the workplace.

The controversy concerning wages was a complex public debate with several aspects. One centered around the relative value of men's and women's work. The belief that men were and should be the major breadwinners had been around since the early days of waged labor. It had been part of the debate surrounding the family wage during strikes in the shoe industry in the 1850s and 1860s. The family wage was a "living wage": enough for a man to support a wife and children who stayed out of the labor force. Most working men and women believed in the appropriateness and justice of the living wage. When women began working for wages in larger numbers in the late nineteenth century, discussions of their living wage focused on single women.

Another controversial issue surrounding working women's wages was the question of how much income was necessary to live. These debates made implicit judgments about what living meant for single women. Budgets included in legislative discussions of a woman's living wage were set at near-starvation level. As the historian Alice Kessler-Harris has remarked, "to live alone [in such conditions] required the strictest exercise of thrift, self-discipline, and restraint. The budgets warned fiercely against expectations of joy, spontaneity, pleasure or recreation." A woman's wage was enough to keep from starving but not enough to make leaving home attractive. That businesswomen and women workers disagreed with the budget makers about the relation between living and earning is clear in their efforts to maintain both children and a career outside of the home, in their need to support dependents in the absence of male breadwinners, and in the strikes and passionate demands of female laborers for a living wage that would allow them roses as well as bread.[6] (The question of a woman's wage survives in the form of debates over equal pay and comparable worth; we return to these issues in later chapters.)

A related debate over women's place in business and on the job led to a series of state and federal protective labor laws and U.S. Supreme Court decisions. These laws and rulings restructured the parameters of women's involvement as workers in many occupations. They assumed that women were physically frailer than men and that biological and social motherhood, and not economic production, was women's most important role. The landmark 1908 U.S. Supreme Court case *Muller* v. *Oregon* allowed employers to curtail women's hours, prohibited women from working in certain jobs and at night, and mandated provisions for things such as chairs so that female workers could sit rather than stand at the assembly line. Included in this decision was a 113-page brief written by Louis D. Brandeis, who represented the state of Oregon. The Brandeis brief contained two arguments. One was based on statistical documentation provided by Florence Kelley's National Consumers' League in support of the notion that long hours had a negative effect on both male and female workers. The second argument, however, persuaded the Court and shaped legislation dealing with working women for years to come. It used traditional gender roles to argue that even though working conditions affected both men and women, women were in a special category because they were physically frailer than men and because of their reproductive function. Like the justifications for slavery made in *Dred Scott* in 1857, the Brandeis brief advanced the case that women were a special category of citizens and thus subject to government protection.

The call for protective legislation initially came from among middle-class reformers. And it must be granted that they were addressing severe problems in the workplace: long hours, unsafe conditions, low pay, and sexual harassment. Reformers such as Kelley also acknowledged that protections needed to be accompanied by mandated salary increases, as working-class women pointed out. The Supreme Court was willing to institute protections, thereby stepping into business relations at a time when the courts in general were loathe to curtail any of business's rights to freedom of contract. Traditional notions about gender rules apparently overrode laissez-faire economic theory in this case. The courts and the legislatures, however, stopped short of instituting a minimum wage to accompany the new mandates for shorter hours. A minimum wage would have violated the "right" of labor to contract freely with management for wages. It could also undermine the notion that women ideally were dependents of men.

Not enough research has been done on this period to fully evaluate the impact of changes in inheritance and property laws. Preliminary evidence suggests a mixed bag. Throughout the course of the nineteenth-century most states passed laws allowing women to be testators, meaning they could write their own wills to dispose of their own properties. Increasing numbers of women took advantage of these laws, leaving their properties to the heirs of their choice—to the profit of daughters, nieces, and granddaughters. Also, by the 1880s, middle-class male testators increasingly tended to treat sons and daughters equally as heirs; this more equitable treatment benefited girls and women. In the area of married women's property rights, by 1880 all states had instituted some form of protection, and married women in some states took advantage of legal protections for their earnings, whether wages or property. But those laws were compromised by their erratic and uneven nature, their selectivity, and the fact that women still made less money than men from their training, skills, and labor. For example, as late as 1900 12 states still did not protect married women's wages, among them California, Virginia, Nebraska, and Florida. In states with earnings acts, protections were sometimes uneven. Earnings acts were designed to secure women's wages from their husbands and in many states represented an alternative to more inclusive property acts. Arkansas and West Virginia passed earnings acts in 1868 and 1879, but they only protected married women not living with their husbands. As forms of capital became more liquid—stocks and bonds rather than land—West Virginia amended its property law in 1891; Arkansas had not done so by 1900. Particularly after 1880, when stocks and bonds began to replace land on a large scale as investment property, women became less likely to manage the family properties than they had been when agricultural land was the primary form of familial wealth.

Less-stringent divorce laws and the growing willingness of courts to grant divorces, especially after 1880, gave women increased flexibility in constructing their lives. The U.S. Census Bureau found that between 1887 and 1906 the national divorce rate jumped from about 1 in 50 to about 1 in 15. Most women who sought divorce (about 60 percent) cited grounds such as desertion and cruelty, and women initiated 66 percent of all divorces. By 1928, on the eve of the depression, about one in every six marriages ended in divorce, and women brought 71 percent of those suits. Divorce rates were higher among African-Americans, whose economic marginalization aggravated desertion, adultery, and abuse. Divorced women, like widows and women whose husbands merely deserted them, struggled to make a living. Many turned to the traditional avenues open to unskilled, undereducated, or racially marginalized women: taking in boarders, doing laundry, selling prepared foodstuffs, or entering into complex familial and neighborhood networks of barter and trade.

Although some women's legal status had improved by 1930 in areas such as married women's property, better access to divorce, and the right to vote, in other ways women still suffered under the limitations of second-class citizenship. It was not until 1931 that the passage of the Cable Act overturned the principle that a woman's citizenship followed that of her husband. American women who married citizens of other countries before the passage of this act automatically lost their citizenship according to mid-nineteenth-century laws that were reaffirmed in 1907. The federal constitution after 1920 gave all women the right to vote, but segregation, racism, and Jim Crow laws barred many black women from exercising that right until the 1960s. These changes and continuities in women's status were closely related to their roles in business development.

Women's Changing Status: Business Opportunities

The years between 1880 and 1930 witnessed the beginnings of what has in the twentieth century proven to be long-term change for women's position in businesses and in their entrepreneurial opportunities. In terms of their sheer numbers as employees and professionals, women's presence made them a force with which to be reckoned. In 1870 15 percent of women over the age of 15 were gainfully employed; by 1930 that figure had risen to 25 percent. Women's presence also forced changes in the gender dimensions of jobs and professions. Positions or jobs that had been dominated by men, and had taken much of their meaning from ideas about manhood and men's responsibility for family support, had to adjust to the presence of women. The clerical sector, for example, saw women go from 2.5 percent of all workers in 1870 to 53 percent by 1930. These two phenomena were interrelated and came ultimately from growing prosperity, urbanization, governmental expansion, and the purchasing habits of turn-of-the-century consumers.

Women entered the new business world in larger numbers than ever before for several reasons. Inadequate child care, low wages, and traditional female employment in the domestic service sector remained facts of life for women workers well into the twentieth century. Many women who had to work to support themselves or their families continued to fall back on old standbys such as running boardinghouses, doing laundry, and preparing food. But some began to have genuine opportunities to operate outside of the family claim that had structured women's economic and social interactions for hundreds of years. Despite fears of "race suicide," the white birth rate continued its nineteenth-century fall even as many of the tasks of social motherhood were taken over by schools, peers, and the media. In addition to shrinking domestic responsibilities, some women had better access to higher education and professional training. For the first time in American history some women could choose a paid career or occupation rather than wifehood and motherhood as their life work. Some could even attempt to combine the two.

The demographic profile of the workforce suggested important shifts in the backgrounds of economically active women. First, unlike in previous years, the numbers of married, divorced, and widowed women in the workforce increased. According to census returns, the proportion of economically active married women doubled between

1900 and 1930. Census methods no doubt concealed an even greater portion of women who had been married previously and had returned to the workplace but were listed in the census as single. Second, despite the numbers of working women (or perhaps because of them), their wages continued to lag behind those of men. In 1920 the average wages of female and child factory laborers together were less than the average wage of male factory workers. The same was true in service industries among stenographers, typists, secretaries, and office clerks. Third, between 1890 and 1900, the largest gains in the percentage of women engaged in occupations came in areas associated with service industry growth. For example, the numbers of stenographers and typists increased by 305 percent during this period. Fourth, the phenomenal growth in the numbers of working women was followed closely by increases in the percentage of professional women: clergy, journalists, architects, educators, designers, draftspeople, and lawyers. The number of women in these categories increased by 222 percent overall. This expansion is even more striking when placed in context: the numbers of women engaged in economic activity increased overall by only about 35 percent during this period.

Within these larger categories, however, the gains were distributed unevenly among women according to race and ethnicity. Foreign-born white women experienced the largest expansion in the professional service category, 242 percent. Native-born white women witnessed an increase of 68 percent, while African-American women experienced only about a 3 percent gain in the total number of women in these occupations. However, the number of African-American professional women grew a substantial 77 percent. In some business-related areas African-American women's involvement in clerical and managerial positions increased more than all women's share of these positions. For example, in 1910 when the percentage of all women bookkeepers and cashiers in banks was only 5.6 percent, African-American women made up 24 percent of all blacks in these occupations. African-American women also were well represented as stockbrokers, clerks, agents, and managers through 1930.

Not only were women important to business, business was important to women. A striking feature of turn-of-the-century America was the sense that business offered special, perhaps even unique, opportunities to women. Many saw business as almost a panacea for women. Evidence for this attitude appeared in a new genre of popular nonfiction literature: business advice. After 1880 hundreds of books, magazine and journal articles, and novels and short stories dealing with women in a variety of business roles appeared. Some spoke specifically to issues of etiquette in the heterosocial office. Others offered advice on the different types of businesses women could own. For example, in *How to Make Money Although a Woman* (1895), Irene Hart suggested that women expand butter and egg production; purchase a milk cow; grow flowers; invest in beekeeping to produce honey for market; take up writing; sell piano lessons or singing talents; learn shorthand, typewriting, or manicuring; or become a "professional wakener," electrician (a new field not yet dominated by men), dressmaker, or embalmer. Hart told the story of one woman who had started a business collecting, sorting, and reselling bottle corks to saloons.[7] The appearance of numerous books and magazine articles dealing specifically with the job of private secretary constituted a field of business advice in itself.

In the 1920s the federal government finally began to collect statistics and publish studies of women workers, including those in professional areas. The formation of the federal Women's Bureau in the Department of Labor in 1920 demonstrates the intense interest in women's business role. This office gathered statistics on a range of topics, including wages, professional status, child care, and working conditions. This information was published in reports that circulated among reformers, professionals, civil servants, academics, politicians, and the general public.

All of these types of publications, whether advice books or statistical tables, recognized both the need many women had to earn a living and the possibilities the growth of the business world opened up to women specifically. Much of it argued for emphasizing and building on areas in which women already had a large presence: as farmwives, teachers, or homemakers. Many advice authors echoed the arguments of contemporary feminist theorists such as Charlotte Perkins Gilman and Olive Schreiner. They asserted that women's greatest need was financial autonomy and that the potential for developing that autonomy was enhanced by business growth. Gertrude de Aguirre, for example, in her 1894 *Women in the Business World or Hints and Helps to Prosperity,* contended that business involvement would enable women to fulfill their individuality by making them less dependent on others. Like many advice authors, de Aguirre observed that financial independence granted power and self-confidence and that the business world offered unique avenues to that independence.[8]

Gendering the Professions

Some of the suggestions made by advice authors required no special training beyond what women were normally exposed to as homemakers, wives, and mothers. But some positions demanded training, particularly in areas such as teaching, writing, and professional careers. Better access to higher education created a generation of highly trained women, many of whom sought to put their training to work for either their individual economic betterment or the benefit of society as a whole. In 1870 11,000 women were enrolled in colleges and universities in the United States—21 percent of all students. By 1910 more than 140,000 women attended postsecondary institutions, and in 1930 women made up about 44 percent of all college and university students.

Many of these women graduated and went on to a variety of careers. Most (75 percent) spent some time teaching, regardless of what they did later. As in the early nineteenth century, writing and editing remained viable options, although newspaper journalism still resisted the entrance of large numbers of women. By the mid-1880s only about 500 women performed some sort of editorial work for newspapers, usually on so-called women's pages dealing with topics such as clothing, child care, food preparation, and other feminized subjects. In 1930 news journalism remained a male-dominated field. Few college women went on to become business executives in major male-controlled corporations. As was true in the early nineteenth century, however, women managers and executives could still be found in family-owned and ethnic businesses, such as Maggie Walker's bank. Still others opened schools to train the new army of women clerical workers; one of them, Katharine Gibbs (1863–1934), started her prestigious Schools of Secretarial and Executive Training for Educated Women. In fact Gibbs herself attended Simmons College in Boston at the same time she and her sister were operating their first secretarial school.

In the face of these enormous changes, however, the traditional image of women's place remained strong. As a result, the process of professionalization in general did not facilitate women's entry into areas such as medicine, the clergy, or law, which remained male-defined and male-dominated domains. In fact, professionalization often drove women out. Between 1870 and 1920 training in law left behind the apprenticeship model wherein aspiring attorneys started as clerks in law offices and learned the law from other attorneys. Instead, law schools offered specialized training courses, and national and state professional organizations controlled licensing and admission to practice law. In medicine, school-trained "regular" physicians gradually pushed out most midwives, doctoresses, and homeopathic doctors by 1900. The formation of the American Medical Association (AMA) in 1847 to regulate entrance into the profession and standardize medical knowledge further cemented regular physicians' hold over medical practice.

In battling for control over medical decisions, the AMA specifically targeted female doctoresses and midwives because in the nineteenth century, as now, women made most health care decisions. AMA physicians saw pregnancy and childbirth as central to convincing women to choose medical-school-trained physicians over female lay practitioners. At midcentury physicians had little more to offer than what midwives and doctoresses could provide. Anesthesia was not part of their arsenal. In fact, physicians helped spread puerperal fever, a deadly staphylococcal infection that was nearly always fatal. Physicians usually were present only for an actual birth and attended to several women in one day. Since germ theory remained unknown until the 1880s, hand washing was not a part of their routine. Midwives, in contrast, normally attended to one woman throughout the process, remaining after the birth to care for the mother and child. They treated fewer women at any given time and thus were less likely to spread infection. With no spectacular technologies or special treatments to offer, physicians had to find something that would set them apart in positive ways as professionals from midwives and other female health care providers.

Physicians focused on the medical aspects of abortion. They argued that since pregnancy was a life-threatening condition for women, only *professionally* trained physicians should be involved in any life-and-death decisions surrounding it. Thus abortions, which threatened the life of the mother, were critical to making their case to the public.[9] Abortions were fairly common in the nineteenth century, as in previous times. There were no medical tests for pregnancy, and it was impossible for anyone but the woman to tell for sure if she was pregnant—by the onset of quickening, or intrauterine movement. Before that time, abortion easily shaded into miscarriage. Herbs that could encourage menstruation and thus cause miscarriages or aborted pregnancies (abortifacients) commonly were advertised in both medical journals and church newsletters. Laws regarding abortion protected the pregnant woman from untrained or inexperienced midwives or other abortion providers. The laws also focused on substance regulation since some abortifacients were dangerous poisons.

By the mid-nineteenth century abortionists were doing a thriving, public business, thanks to the growth of inexpensive print mediums. One of the best-known was New York's Madame Restell, who reportedly spent $60,000 on advertising in 1871. Like many abortion providers, Restell sold pills and potions through the mail and provided on-site care at her clinic. Abortion remained a profitable business venture into the 1870s. However, in their effort to take control of all medical aspects of pregnancy, regular physicians succeeded by the 1880s in making abortions provided by "untrained" persons illegal and themselves regulating who received legal abortions. Thus medical professionalization undermined the entrepreneurial efforts of midwives and abortion providers.

In all of these movements to professionalize, women's access to medical training and licensing grew difficult. Medical schools were late opening their doors to women. At midcentury the first two regular female physicians in the United States—Elizabeth Blackwell and Harriot Hunt—were rejected by medical schools and received their training initially as apprentices with sympathetic physicians. Once trained as doctors, women found the profession slow to license them. Law schools evolved in a similar pattern, opening their doors first in state schools (such as Michigan in 1870) and later in private universities (such as Yale in 1886, Cornell in 1887, and Stanford in 1895). A law school degree, however, did not guarantee admission to the bar or employment in a law firm. Most women lawyers worked with husbands or fathers. The independent female practitioner was rare. In addition, even the finest female lawyers had difficulty gaining complete access to professional privileges.

Belvah Lockwood is a case in point. Lockwood was one of the first women to graduate from the National University Law School in Washington, D.C. But the school refused to award her degree. Not to be thwarted, she contacted President Ulysses S. Grant, also the school's ex officio president, who pressured the school into awarding her degree. However, once a member of the bar in the District of Columbia, she was refused permission to practice before the U.S. Supreme Court. The 43-year-old Lockwood attacked this problem by fiercely and successfully lobbying for federal legislation that would give all female lawyers access to the Court. Once the legislation was passed, she was the first to benefit from the statute. But Lockwood's saga was not over. In the early 1890s the state of Virginia denied her admission to practice, despite her bar privileges in Washington, D.C., other states, and the U.S. Supreme Court. Lockwood sued Virginia, and her appeal ended up in the Supreme Court in 1894, where the judges sided with the state.[10]

Assumptions about women's proper role further shaped their opportunities within professions. The medical field again provides an illustrative example. The nineteenth-century middle-class belief in women's moral superiority and their emotional and physical fitness for motherhood and domesticity meant that most people expected women physicians to concentrate their efforts in fields related to motherhood, emotional healing, or public health reform. Hence, many women physicians found employment in insane asylums, as obstetricians or pediatricians, in public health, as faculty in state university medical schools, or as corporate doctors in fields such as insurance, where they usually treated female patients. Even many female physicians themselves claimed that they and other medical women could improve the quality of care and the profession itself by exerting a calming and nurturing influence on male practitioners. The therapeutics of mid-nineteenth-century medicine, which tended to be oriented to the total patient, less specialized, and less scientifically objective, fit well with this feminized image of health care. But by the late nineteenth century, modern approaches to therapeutics, which emphasized specialization and treated the patient as a series of discrete and fragmented problems, fit less well with the arguments made in support of female physicians and with many women themselves who were interested in medical careers.

The notion that women and men were inherently different also led to the belief that they had different educational needs. Some believed that expecting women to train in the same way as men would harm women physiologically as well as intellectually. Studies done in the late nineteenth century of the first generation of women educated in coeducational institutions demonstrated that women were not harmed by the experience. But coeducation was difficult for women for other reasons. Between the 1850s and 1890s women physicians normally trained in gender-segregated schools, which offered female role models and a more supportive environment than did coeducational schools. Male students and faculty in coeducational institutions often responded to female students with social ostracism, baiting, and denial of necessary information or resources. The difficulties women faced in therapeutics and education led to the creation of a new woman's profession that built on a long-standing set of domestic skills: nursing. Unlike the colonial or early-nineteenth-century nurse, however, the nursing profession stressed the same type of rigorous training as that required of physicians, with the difference that nurses assumed the care not just of the body—male physicians' territory—but the spirit as well. Nursing emphasized nurturing and psychological skills as well as "helping" physicians by taking over many routine functions such as administering medicines and changing bandages.

The belief in inherent differences between men and women allowed some college-educated women to carve out for themselves "a female dominion" in reform and social work.[11] Extragovernmental institutions evolved by the 1930s to local and federal bureaucracies. The founding of Hull House in Chicago in 1889 by Jane Addams (a graduate of Rockford Female Seminary) began a series of social experiments known as settlement houses. Settlement houses were philanthropic neighborhood-based organizations designed to assist working-class and immigrant women and children through vocational training, job bureaus, child care facilities, communal kitchens, and transitional homes for battered women and children. College-educated women such as Jane Addams, Florence Kelley, Ellen Gates Starr, and others opened and operated settlement houses in several major cities. The settlement movement's essentially philanthropic and reformist base gave women an acceptable way to live a public life, manage complex organizations, have a career, and gain a certain degree of independence from their families; men had other avenues for their ambition, and settlement was essentially a female endeavor. Many women who got their start in settlement, such as Florence Kelley, also were interested in Progressive reform in general. Kelley became executive secretary of the National Consumers' League, a watchdog and advocacy group for consumer protection. Other settlement managers were leaders in the National Women's Trade Union League, which organized women workers and advocated protective labor legislation.

Ultimately such national reform efforts brought professional women, including some Progressives, directly into the federal government. In 1912 former settlement organizers and activists Lillian Wald, Jane Addams, and Florence Kelley culminated several years of lobbying and work within the Republican and Progressive political parties on behalf of child welfare by overseeing the legislation that created the federal Children's Bureau within the Department of Commerce and Labor. The first chief of the bureau, Julia Lathrop, was the first woman chief of any federal bureau. Lathrop, who had made her reputation as an advocate for the rights of the insane, had been a pioneer in the creation of juvenile court systems. The Women's Bureau was also staffed primarily by women who had worked as reformers, social welfare workers, and administrators.

In addition to the creation of governmental bureaucracies, court systems, and settlement houses, the women's reformist impulse found expression in the creation of the Chicago School of Civics and Philanthropy, which later became the School of Social Service Administration. This school began to professionalize social work by standardizing a curriculum and establishing certification guidelines for social workers. The women managers we saw in the early nineteenth century overseeing women's hospitals, running orphanages, or directing charitable organizations were the direct antecedents of the professional social workers who began to graduate from the School of Social Service and other similar programs by 1910.

Curiously, for women clergy the road to professionalization was harder and narrower. Women could have argued for their unique ability to act as clergy because of their nurturing skills, but they did not make great strides as pastors and ministers. The pattern of increased but circumscribed opportunities we have seen developing in law and medicine was true for women clergy as well. It was still possible to found a new church or spiritual organization or act as a lay preacher (e.g., Mary Baker Eddy in the 1880s founded Christian Science), but women's opportunities as church leaders in major organizations shrank after 1860.

The failure to promote women within the pastoral ranks stemmed from several causes. As with other professions, the clergy's close connection to individual denominations, which provided schools and ordination (or certification), meant women would have to be accepted within the ranks rather than, as with social work, invent new ones. There was also the force of the traditional notions of female domesticity we have already encountered. It also came from the process of centralization and standardization typical of the professionalization movement at the turn of the century, to which churches were no more immune than baseball teams. Among the best examples of this process are the Unitarian and Universalist organizations. The liberal religionists of these two denominations historically had been supportive of an enhanced status for women. If women were to make gains among the national denominations, these two organizations would seem likely candidates. And, in 1890, 70 women were ordained as liberal clergy. But very few of those female clergy actually had pastorates and even fewer were paid, full-time ministers. Mary A. Safford and Eleanor E. Gordon, both ordained Unitarian clerics, fought in the 1890s to keep local control over their parish in Sioux City, Iowa, even as the national organization tried to offer advice, centralize finances at the national office, and standardize the liturgy. So long as they were able to run their church like a small business, accepting donations, soliciting local financial support, and dealing with local merchants for supplies, women ministers were able to control the type of spiritual solace and theology their churches offered. The push to centralize on the part of a national organization, as in other areas, meant that it was more difficult for women to maintain their position as clergy.

Probably the best illustration of the strengths and limitations of the female professional model was the advent of domestic science, or home economics, in the 1890s.[12] The home economics movement, spearheaded by women such as Ellen H. Richards, brought the Progressive interest in reform and scientific approaches to social problems together with business values such as efficiency to create a new field of study. Professional home economists trained in one of numerous home economics departments in colleges and universities. These colleges and universities funded separate home economics departments, including laboratory facilities for research in applied science, and awarded female graduate students master's and doctorate degrees in the field. In 1908 home economists created their own national professional organization, the American Home Economics Association. They entered settlement and social welfare work, education, government bureaus, commissions, and extension services. Home economics included studying nutrition and chemistry; advocating child welfare and manual training; devising ways to make cooking, ironing, and cleaning more efficient and easier for the average housewife; promoting informed and socially responsible consumerism; and advocating personal thriftiness. In short, home economics encompassed anything and everything to do with the family, household, and women's sphere.

The principles of home economics, in turn, brought business values such as efficiency, accounting procedures, system, budgeting, and management principles directly into home and family life. Home economics took the private world of the home and family and explicitly connected it to the public sphere of business, government, education, and reform. The result was a major new field for women that created professional opportunities at all institutional levels. It was a field, however, premised on the paradox that woman's place was in the home, even if she had to leave it in order to make it run more smoothly.

The record of women's entrance into professional careers is a checkered one. The existence of new types of jobs and of women's increased access to professional work did not spell long-term change in the definition of women's place. That place in fact was reinforced by the advent of home economics. Initial gains in the professions were offset by eventual loss and the redefinition of certain types of professional work as "women's work." This shift meant a concomitant reduction in status and pay. In 1900, when not quite 1 percent of lawyers and 5 percent of physicians were women, women college graduates began forging entirely new professions in the fields of social work, librarianship, and nursing. These so-called helping professions grew out of women's involvement in teaching, social reform, and medicine. By 1930 they had become feminized professions: 68 percent of social workers, 91 percent of librarians, and 98 percent of nurses were women. None of these fields paid as well as the male professions of law or medicine.

Consumers, Managers, and "Women's Work"

The gendered definitions of work in the new corporate economy did not stop at "women's professions." Women, and men interested in their welfare, attempted to make a case for women's ability to contribute uniquely to other business areas. This contribution was particularly relevant in areas in which women consumers became important, such as retailing, banking, and insurance. In retail sales, women went from 24 percent of all sales workers in 1880 (already an increase over previous years) to 30 percent by 1930. In most retail stores (department, general mercantile, specialty, women's ready-to-wear clothing, dry goods, and general apparel stores) after 1870 women made up a majority of the workforce, with the figure as high as 88 percent in some locales at certain times. Particularly in large department stores, women were not only salesclerks but also managers, buyers, supervisors, and personnel administrators. Women found their way into retail work for several reasons. Employers could justify paying them lower wages because of the belief that women were "covered" by a male wage. Many believed that women were more empathetic and would be better able than men to deal with female customers. Others were convinced that female customers preferred dealing with female clerks. As the numbers of women shoppers increased at the end of the century, retail stores lured them into "palaces of consumption" by offering service with a feminine smile. The customer-clerk relation was fraught with tensions, particularly when overworked clerks were expected to be consistently polite and self-effacing to often officious managers and imperious clients. Nonetheless, the argument that women made better retailing employees than men continued to hold sway.

The gendering of various business positions and of consumer markets provided opportunities for women in several fields. In the early twentieth century, for example, privately owned utility companies sold both energy and household appliances such as gas ranges and electric irons, sometimes under agreements with the appliance manufacturers (such as General Electric). They identified homemakers as their primary market and used female sales agents to persuade these female consumers of the benefits of gas- or electric-powered home appliances in order to boost energy use. To demonstrate the appliances, companies sent out female "home service agents," who had received special training in "domestic science," to cook up recipes on new gas ranges or explain the benefits provided by electric irons. Female consumers and sales agents were thus "agents of diffusion" in the spread of urban energy networks.[13]

The growing number of female consumers of insurance and banking services made employing women agents in these fields seem a good idea. Arguments about women's suitability to deal with other women surfaced in making a case for female insurance executives and agents and led to the formation of women's agencies in the years after 1890. For years women had operated their fathers' or husbands' insurance sales accounts if the men became ill or died. That role was well within the tradition of widows assuming the responsibilities for family support by taking over a family business. This type of inherited agency management continued well into the twentieth century, in part because most insurance agencies remained small, independent businesses. New after 1890, however, was the presence of agencies owned, managed, and staffed by women (sometimes right down to the certifying physician) for the express purpose of appealing to female customers. The Equitable Life Assurance Society, for example, in the 1890s had a woman's agency managed by Florence Shaal, who was an officer in several regional insurance organizations and went on to establish a national reputation in the life insurance industry.

While women's managerial and sales opportunities in the insurance industry began in the 1880s and increased steadily throughout the period under study, banking was slower to develop a female contingent. Maggie Walker was somewhat unusual in this regard. She not only was a bank president—a feat few women could copy—but began her banking career before World War I. As had been the case with previous wars, World War I took men from the labor force and opened up many job and career opportunities to women managers, workers, and executives. Banking in particular saw a sharp rise in the number of women clerks, accountants, and bookkeepers. By 1917, for example, many women found work in the federal reserve banking system as clerks and tellers but also as bookkeepers and cashiers—positions previously dominated by men. The war also opened up executive banking positions to women. Mrs. F. J. Runyon, for example, presided over the First Woman's Bank of Clarksville, Tennessee, between 1919 and 1926, and Virginia D. H. Furman was an official of the Columbia Trust Company in New York City by 1915. In 1919 Furman was put in charge of Columbia's newly inaugurated women's department. By the late 1920s women managers and executives in banking and insurance had formed their own regional professional organizations, such as the West Coast–based Association of Bank Women and the Women's Bankers Association of Texas. Several women bankers formed the nationally based Association of Banking Women in 1921, which instituted its own professional journal, *The Woman Banker*, in 1923.[14] Many of these positions, however, were lost to women during conversion to peacetime after 1918. Banking remained a male-dominated field even at the lowest job levels until World War II brought large-scale, permanent feminization.

Like the insurance companies, banks and trust companies that wanted to attract women customers created "women's departments" after about 1915. Women executives typically oversaw these departments. They designed programs to educate female customers in the use of checking accounts, made loans to women, and supervised female tellers and other staff. These departments often amounted to parallel divisions with separate operating structures. As Elizabeth Barry, a vice president of the United States National Bank in Portland, Oregon, explained it in 1926, "Many women hesitate [to] approach a man bankers [sic] with their problems, for fear of exposing their ignorance, although they will usually tell another woman everything; therefore, only women are employed in these departments—women tellers in both commercial and savings divisions; women in the advertising and publicity departments; in the new business department; foreign exchange; personal service; trust department, etc."[15] However, most of these separate divisions disappeared in the 1930s when financially strapped companies consolidated and restructured departments.

The development of personnel management is a useful case study of the various issues raised by the feminization of certain types of occupations. Personnel management grew out of two distinct streams. One was the movement to rationalize the workplace initiated by Frederick W. Taylor and promulgated under the name *scientific management*. The other was welfare capitalism, or welfare management, which reached its fullest realization in industrial concerns such as the National Cash Register and the Pullman Company in the 1890s. Welfare management emphasized workers rather than the production process. It assumed that workers who were well trained, well adjusted in their personal lives, and carefully matched to compatible jobs would be loyal and productive. Scientific management was based on engineering principles: measurement, the ratio between time and energy expenditure, and integrated factory design. As an engineering specialty, it was mostly closed to women from the beginning.

Among the earliest welfare programs that focused on personnel management was that created by Elizabeth F. Briscoe at the Joseph Bancroft and Sons Company in Delaware in 1902. Briscoe came to personnel from a career as a teacher and school principal, suggesting that the early function of such managers was essentially educational. Early personnel managers were called welfare secretaries or social secretaries and served as liaisons between workers in manufacturing plants or white-collar offices and company executives and managers. Briscoe summed up their duties in this way: "The Social Secretary should have the ability to interpret the position of the employer towards the employee and the employee towards the employer; and she is the exponent of friendly interest of the employer in those employed." Good welfare secretaries needed "tact, patience, good judgment, resourcefulness, firmness, good common sense, enthusiasm, and a sense of humor."[16]

Welfare management grew out of the same streams as Progressive reform and the same underlying assumptions about social relations that gave rise to the settlement movement and social welfare work. Because of its roots in reform and the widespread assumption that women were better "people persons" than men, college-educated women dominated early on in the arm of welfare management that dealt directly with personnel administration. Female personnel administrators hired, interviewed, and offered on-site health and safety education. They also did what we might now call counseling—paying attention to and trying to deal with workers' personal as well as job-related problems. Echoing the ideas of Elizabeth Briscoe, many men and women involved in business believed that women brought intrinsic qualities to the art of dealing with workers: empathy, intuition, tact, patience, and a "motherly interest" in others' welfare. Here, as elsewhere, beliefs about women's essential difference from men opened business doors.

But the argument from difference, as in other cases, also barred further advancement, narrowly defining women's business by their sexuality rather than their competence. Women were not admitted to advanced graduate programs in business schools such as Harvard or Columbia and were not a presence in engineering programs; both were male preserves. Most women's business schools offered certificates in secretarial or lower-level management skills rather than in management theory or advanced training. They assumed that most women interested in business were not ambitious and probably would eventually marry and leave the workforce. Women in personnel management had general college backgrounds, had some experience in welfare work, or, after 1915, could enroll in the new program in research and personnel administration at Bryn Mawr. Whatever their training, female personnel administrators were usually found in white-collar corporations. Metropolitan Life Insurance Company was an early devotee of personnel management, as were large department stores, both seen as appropriate workplaces for young, middle-class white women.

World War I put the final touches on women's personnel work for the next 60 years. As with banking, the war initially provided a boost for women in personnel administration. By 1915 personnel concerns had become a standard aspect of administering large bureaucracies.

The war increased not only the federal bureaucracy but also the female workforce in factories, offices, mail-order companies, public utilities, and banks as men went into war production and the armed services. After the war the number of women employed in white-collar work exploded, and by 1930 fully 96 percent of all stenographers and typists were women. The number of women personnel administrators increased during the war, and their position seemed secure. However, between 1918 and the early 1920s this stability was reduced drastically. The return of men from the war brought pressure to hire them. Men eventually replaced women, who quit or lost their jobs because of the severe economic downturn business suffered right after the war.

As the war and the early 1920s brought massive labor strikes and increased unionization, support waned for the "liberal" approach to workplace relations. Fewer people believed that welfare management was the most effective tool in worker-management relations. A growing interest appeared in a more rationalized personnel administration based not on feminine intuition but on psychological statistics and experiments and a return to Taylor's emphasis on efficiency and cost accounting. To the extent that women had built their position within personnel management on the basis of gender difference, they lost their rationale for inclusion when the prevailing current no longer valued that difference. After 1920 most women in personnel work were office or personnel managers. Personnel administrators, the higher position in the occupational hierarchy, were mostly men.

Business Traditions Undermined

Many of women's older occupations persisted into the twentieth century, but economic growth did not always work to the advantage of traditional women's businesses. Prostitution and the dressmaking and millinery trades are cases in point. The reasons were different, but for both of these customary avenues for female proprietorship the movement to centralize, professionalize, and appeal to broader consumer markets undermined women's entrepreneurial autonomy.

The period between 1880 and 1930 witnessed the recriminalization and segregation of prostitution and its subsequent slide into the hidden world of vice. After 1880 commercialized prostitution experienced much the same sort of business evolution as other industries. As the profits to be gained from the sex trade and other forms of illegal activity increased with urban growth, more and more capital was invested into the busi-

ness. One reformer estimated in 1911 that in Kansas (not even a particularly urbanized state), vice districts represented more than $400,000 in
capital investment. The sex trade in Chicago did about $15 million of
business per year at the turn of the century. In New Orleans's Storyville,
Catholic priests who owned brothel properties raked in their portion of
the business's annual $15 million in profits. At its peak, Storyville had an
estimated 230 "sporting houses" and 2,000 prostitutes.

The growth of the industry led to increased efforts to regulate it.
The reappearance of urban reformers before World War I led to successful efforts to physically segregate various forms of vice to specific
urban districts. Usually these areas were inhabited by or contiguous to
marginalized city dwellers: recent immigrants, the poor, or people of
color. Chinatown in San Francisco, for example, became an important
vice district, as did Storyville, a traditionally black section of New
Orleans. These red-light districts enabled the police to keep tabs on
the underworld and to some extent control behavior through raids
and police harassment. Laws requiring licensing made oversight and
bribery systems easier. Bribery systems favored larger brothel owners and discouraged smaller, independent proprietors, who could not
afford hefty payoffs.

As more capital went into the trade and it became more regulated
and pushed into vice districts, women proprietors were squeezed out.
Although very few women could amass the money necessary to start
or maintain a brothel in expensive urban areas, there were a few spectacular examples to the contrary. Aida Everleigh (1864–1960) and
Minna Everleigh (1866–1948) started the Everleigh Club in Chicago
in 1900. The two sisters employed about 30 "professional" prostitutes.
They hired someone to deal with the day-to-day running of the house,
while they kept the charge accounts for important clients, including
corporate expense accounts. Their brothel had a national reputation
for luxury and excellent "service." In San Francisco African-American
Mary Ellen Pleasant became an important local entrepreneur after
1880, running a boardinghouse that also served as a brothel, restaurant, and gathering place for some of the most powerful men in the
city. At one point Pleasant's considerable fortune allowed her to invest
in local real estate as well as a ranch in Sonoma County. The Everleigh
sisters and Mary Ellen Pleasant were the exceptions and among the
last holdovers of the older tradition of women brothel keepers as the
trade came under the control of male capitalists and pimps. Further, as
with all illegal businesses, brothel keepers did not have the right to

legal protection and were always subject to closure. The Everleighs were shut down by a reform mayor in 1911; legend has it they kept their fortune. Pleasant was stripped of her assets in a series of court battles over property and died virtually penniless, probably in part because her fortune threatened the white establishment.

Increasing numbers of women became permanently involved with the trade as professionals rather than casual sex providers. Municipal authorities concerned about respectability and control hounded the independent operator, the streetwalker. Most women who engaged in prostitution took refuge in brothels or under the "protection" of male pimps (who sometimes beat them if their earnings were poor). Like the farm women who became textile mill operatives in the early nineteenth century, prostitutes became more like wage workers, servicing customers in an establishment that paid for the overhead and kept most of the profits.

Although prostitutes came from all types of backgrounds, the trade increasingly reflected racial and ethnic biases and the economic marginalization of certain groups. In the Southern cotton belt, for example, prostitutes were predominately black and on the West Coast predominantly Asian or Asian-American. However they came into the trade, prostitution continued to reflect the lack of alternative economic opportunities for many women. Surveys taken of New York City prostitutes in the early 1900s document that these women saw prostitution as one among several economic choices. Prostitutes sometimes favorably compared what they did for money with the unpaid sexual services of wives or pointed out that they could make more selling sex than selling soap in a department store. In addition, some prostitutes observed that they preferred the sense of autonomy they had to the subservience of waitressing or typing.

In the millinery and dressmaking trades, new technologies and the separation of production from sales meant the virtual end of proprietorship by 1920. By 1870 the sewing machine and paper patterns made it easier for women who were not artisans to make clothing at home. The use of the sewing machine in a factory setting made it possible to mass-produce standardized clothing, first for men and by the 1890s for women. However, the impact of these technologies in the end mattered less than the new sales methods and relationships brought about by the advent of the department stores and the "democratization of fashion"—the greater availability and increasing simplicity of women's clothing.

Millinery and dressmaking establishments were the province of female artisanal entrepreneurs: highly trained specialists who produced unique and individualized products and sold those products directly to customers. Because of the specialized nature and complicated construction of nineteenth-century women's clothing and hats, dressmakers and milliners usually produced and sold in local markets. Their relations with their wholesale suppliers (who were usually men) tended to be very personalized, which aided women trying to do business in a volatile market such as fashion. Since most clothing and hats were designed expressly for individual female customers, there was little need for elaborate displays of products. Customers acted as walking advertisements. Consequently, most shops were small, sometimes merely a room in a woman's home.

The new business and marketing methods of the late nineteenth century radically changed dressmaking and millinery. The ready-made clothing industry relied on mass production, with its attendant need for large-scale capitalization, a nonspecialized workforce, wide markets, and heavy advertising. Until around 1890, women's clothing and hats remained complex enough that the ready-made industry found its largest market in items such as shawls, cloaks, and "shirt-waists," the uniform-like white blouses worn by female office workers. As women's clothing became looser fitting and simpler in design, however, manufacturers began to produce more types of ready-made clothing and hats. Although small businesses continued to dominate retailing in 1900, wholesaling had begun to adopt many of the same features as other big businesses. These included the loss of personalized relationships between wholesalers and their customers (retailers), the separation of production from retailing, and the creation of regional and national associations to devise and enforce standardized business relations. In the case of millinery, for example, the Millinery Jobbers' Association, formed in 1907, brought together regional suppliers to enforce standardized interest rates, capitalization requirements, and payment schedules for retailers. All of these policies disadvantaged the female small proprietor, who often operated on a tiny margin and needed a great deal of individual flexibility.

In addition, the growth of the ready-made trade favored the development of larger stores, whose economies of scale allowed them to provide customers with many types of goods. Department stores began offering a plethora of items by the 1890s; their triumph over small retailers was nearly complete by 1920. With a few exceptions, department stores separated production from sale. They had ample display space and could offer many types of goods under one roof. The variety and quantity of products available in department stores made them extremely attractive to busy urban shoppers. Department stores absorbed the exclusivity of the female artisanal trades by offering high-priced custom shops within the department store itself. These shops hired skilled dressmakers and milliners, now reduced from proprietors to employees.

Women and Developing New Business

As both prostitution and the millinery and dressmaking trades suggest, traditional ideas about women's work and women's place sometimes fared poorly in a big-business climate. But several developments in business generally afforded new opportunities for women. Particularly in the areas of ethnic businesses, new technologies, and the appearance of a uniquely modern phenomenon—the celebrity—women experienced important new possibilities even as they faced familiar patterns.

Ethnicity operated as both a bar and an opportunity for many women in the business world. Social and economic segregation of ethnic groups had long been a part of American life, but it took on renewed vigor with the end of slavery and the appearance of scientific and racial justifications for ethnic differences. For African-Americans released from slavery, economic viability quickly became a vital issue. Its importance was widely discussed, beginning with the economic demands of politicians and black leaders during Reconstruction. Booker T. Washington's articulation of a philosophy of self-help and segregation as a necessary temporary stage on the way to full assimilation merely framed in new form what many African-Americans had long known. Without meaningful economic autonomy, social and political power and "race uplift"—the improvement of the social and economic status of all American blacks—would be impossible.

Throughout the major cities of the South, where most black Americans lived, local leaders and entrepreneurs began in the 1880s to build an economic infrastructure of African-American businesses—banks, barber shops, restaurants, and insurance companies—that would undergird autonomy. Maggie Lena Walker's St. Luke's Penny Thrift Savings Bank was one of many similar organizations throughout the South. The presence of black consumers, the growth of black businesses, the segregation of occupations that reserved certain types of businesses and jobs to blacks, and the traditional business niches afforded women allowed black businesswomen to operate hairdressing, confectionery, and catering establishments, as well as restaurants, laundries, and taverns. African-American Fannie B. Rosser, for example, started as an assistant bookkeeper at North Carolina Mutual Life, a black insurance company, in 1914. She worked there 32 years in a job that would have been closed to her in a white company, as both an African-American and a woman.[17]

One of the most spectacular success stories of this era was that of Madame C. J. Walker (no relation to the banker), who started a traditional type of women's business—beauty aids—by identifying the particular needs of African-Americans and building on the existing support networks for black businesses. She was among the first women in the United States to become a millionaire through her own efforts. Another child of Reconstruction, Walker (1867–1919) was born to former slaves. Her life began in absolute poverty and was marred by the early death of her parents and physical abuse by her brother-in-law. She was married at 14 and widowed at 16 with a two-year-old daughter to raise. She moved in with relatives in St. Louis, Missouri, and earned a precarious living doing laundry. Then, in 1904, Walker began marketing a hair-care preparation, the recipe for which she claimed to have learned in a dream. Along with her daughter, sister, and nieces, Walker bottled her home remedy, which was designed to meet the unique needs of African-American women, many of whom did not have access to running water and struggled with products designed for a different type of hair. The product found an eager public, and Walker's business expanded quickly, in large part because of her shrewd entrepreneurship.

In 1910 Walker had more than 5,000 African-American women selling on commission her hair preparation and a hot comb she had invented. By 1919 Walker agents numbered 25,000. She founded several beauty schools to teach the Walker hair-care method, developed a real estate complex in Indianapolis, built a personal mansion on the Hudson River, and contributed to numerous educational and philanthropic charities. Illiterate, she hired tutors to teach her reading and writing. Like Maggie Walker, Madame Walker was profoundly interested in the fate of black women and consciously aimed both her products and her self-help message at them. "The girls and women of our race," she observed, "must not be afraid to take hold of business endeavors. . . . I have made it possible for many colored women to abandon the washtub for a more pleasant and profitable occupation."[18] Like many progressive blacks of her day, Walker saw economic development and business entrepreneurship as an avenue to racial uplift. She also believed, like many reformers, in the importance of women's financial autonomy.

Ethnic businesses also embodied many of the contradictions of negotiating ethnicity in a nation that reserved its largest rewards for the assimilated. Madame Walker's hair preparations, for example, generated intense controversy because the tonics and hot combs she sold were designed to straighten and smooth African-American hair, making it appear more like that of whites. Some black newspaper editors and community leaders deplored the use of such products, arguing instead for maintaining the physical markers of ethnic identity. However, the popularity of Walker's products suggests that African-American consumers saw advantages in adopting white standards of beauty and self-presentation, advantages that probably ranged from passing for white to merely striving to emulate the mainstream white ideal. The tensions between assimilation and ethnic assertion could be found in many products that catered to ethnic groups.

Ethnicity also affected whether women went into business at all. Recent immigrants since at least the mid-nineteenth century have consistently found small businesses attractive. These entrepreneurial ventures draw on family and kin networks as well as voluntary associations and mutual aid groups and require less capitalization. The more than 2 million immigrants from southern and eastern Europe between 1870 and 1910 included a large contingent of Jews. Eastern European Jewish culture afforded women—who handled household finances and often participated actively in family businesses—importance as economic actors within the family. Consequently, urban Jewish women were among the most active entrepreneurial women in the United States at the turn of the century. Usually these businesses were small, such as corner groceries. Sometimes they could be spectacular successes. A case in point is Lena Himmelstein Bryant (1879–1951), who came to the United States in 1895 and took work in a lingerie factory until she married. When she found herself a widow with a small child in 1906, she pawned earrings her husband had given her and bought a sewing machine and went back to making lingerie. She was particularly skilled in designing clothing that hid figure flaws, and her attractive creations sold well. Her biggest marketing innovation was to address the ready-made clothing needs of women who were ignored by other companies. She designed and produced clothes that pregnant women could wear on the street, and maternity wear became the basis of the Lane Bryant Company's fortune. After World War I, Bryant began production of a line of clothing for larger women. By 1923 the company had several stores in major cities and an annual sales volume of $5 million. Lena Bryant continued to run the business until her death.

New technologies—particularly the development of film at the turn of the century—radically altered the world of popular entertainment and generally opened important business avenues to women. Moving pictures went from a curiosity at their inception in 1895 to the status of a full-fledged industry by the 1920s. Film has had·a major influence on how we see our world, and women have played a vital role in the development of the film industry. The first film director, and probably the first person to construct a narrative film (the 1896 *La Fe aux Choux*), was French-born Alice Guy Blaché (1875–1968), who came to the United States as a director in 1910. In 1912 she formed the Solax Company, a film company that constructed one of the earliest and best-equipped studios in the world. Solax's films successfully competed in the market until about 1920, by which time it was becoming increasingly difficult for any independent film company to rival the new, and newly powerful, major studios.

Women's entrance into film was a by-product of the general growth of leisure after 1880, the lack of sex stereotyping in what was a new technology, and women's increased literacy. The history of women's involvement in the film industry is in many ways a scenario typical of women's opportunities and limitations in any new industry. In its earliest years, making films was a seat-of-the-pants process. Most films were "written" as they were being filmed, the actors often contributing ideas, direction, and even production money. Since virtually all of the tasks involved in filmmaking were new, there was little previous gender typing with which to contend. Film's antecedent, the theater, traditionally had made room for women. In addition, as Wendy Holliday has argued, the work culture of filmmaking—the set of behaviors and expectations generated within this community of workers—emphasized the sort of individualized, even masculinized, behavior connected with the image of the modern "new woman."[19] These new women, like the settlement house founders, Progressive reformers, and professionals of all types, were committed to their careers and believed in the importance of economic independence for women. Finally, in its earliest years, the industry was financed mostly from internal sources, and investors were willing to take a chance on an unknown director, actor, or writer. This generally more open and unrationalized climate allowed women full participation in the growth of the industry, and women took advantage of these factors.

The most common avenue for women entering the fledgling industry before about 1920 was as screenwriters. Women made up about 50 percent of all screenwriters in the silent era. However, women could be found in every aspect of filmmaking, from props and cameras to acting, producing, and directing. In fact, acting and writing often led to producing and directing. The most famous actress of her day, Mary Pickford (1893–1979) was also the first person to make a million dollars from acting. Her on-screen image as a fragile and helpless orphan was belied by her firm control over her career and her steely business acumen. In her early career, she insisted on and got the same pay scale as comparable male stars. Unable to get the extravagant terms that she wanted from two major production companies in 1919— essentially complete control of the product—she created her own studio with her second husband, Douglas Fairbanks, and Charlie Chaplin. As studio owner, star, executive producer, and director of United Artists, Pickford gave herself the gross proceeds of her films.

The theater also provided women an avenue into filmmaking. Mae West (1893–1980), who went on to become the second-highest-salaried individual in the United States in the mid-1930s (after William Randolph Hearst), started her entertainment career in vaudeville, achieved renown as a Broadway playwright, and entered motion pictures at the relatively late age of 40 in 1933. That year, Paramount Studios asked her to convert her 1928 hit Broadway play, *Diamond Lil,* into her first motion picture, *She Done Him Wrong.* The unique ability of motion pictures to bring fame to a few recognizable faces worked to many stars' advantage, as it did for Mary Pickford and Mae West, among others. To get West and her play in 1933, Paramount had to concede to her absolute creative control over the script, casting, production values, and directorial choices.

The best-known woman director of the early twentieth century started as a typist in 1919 at Famous Players-Lasky and went on to a 24-year career in film. Dorothy Arzner (1900–1979) directed or codirected 21 attributed films and worked as first or second director on countless others. Arzner's career spanned the shake-ups brought to the industry by the advent of talking pictures and job specialization, the creation of the star system, and the corporate mergers that created the major studios after 1920. She survived, in fact, as the only woman director in the major studios by 1930. One film historian has observed that "she was, and remains after her death, the only woman able to build up a coherent body of work *within* the Hollywood system."[20] She is credited with inventing the "boom microphone," which freed actors from having to stay close to a stationary mike. She had a reputation as a star maker, bringing to wide attention actors such as Katherine Hepburn (in the 1933 classic *Christopher Strong*), Ruth Chatterton (in *Anybody's Woman*), Fredric March (in the 1929 film *The Wild Party*), Irene Dunne, and Rosalind Russell. She always attributed her staying power in Hollywood to her ability to bring films in on time and under budget—an efficiency expert in a risky and often decidedly inefficient business.

The film industry underwent profound changes after World War I. Various developments increased the complexity of filmmaking, and the marketing, production, distribution, and exhibition of films became more expensive. As the capitalization needs of production companies increased, it became more difficult for independent companies to compete. Larger production budgets were needed to cover the swelling costs of new technologies. The conversion to multiple-reel films after 1910 and the advent of indoor filming between 1910 and 1920 and sound after 1929 all required larger capital investment. Popular stars demanded heftier salaries, and the sheer numbers of people necessary to the complex production process swelled expenses. All of these costs led production companies to search for capital sources from banks, investment companies, and stockholders. The resulting corporatization of the film industry created a much more conservative investment atmosphere—and sometimes the intrusion of powerful outside investors into artistic decisions. In this environment actors, directors, writers, and editors became more like laborers, and even the most popular stars found themselves bound to salaries and exclusive contracts. These changes in the industry made it less open to women in positions of power, such as producers, directors, and studio heads. Not until the 1980s would women again attain the important institutional presence they had in the earliest years of the film industry.

A uniquely twentieth-century phenomenon—the celebrity—allowed some women with special talents or abilities to achieve not only fame but also a measure of financial independence. The celebrity, in effect, is a person who makes himself or herself into a business by selling an image, persona, or talent. We have already seen the effect of celebrity status on the bargaining ability of some film stars. Some of the most popular and visible celebrities of the early twentieth century were in sports, entertainment, or other challenging arenas such as aviation. Although fame is not a modern invention, the intense public scrutiny and familiarity that fed celebrityhood was made possible by the mass media of the twentieth century: radio, film, and sound recording. It became possible, for the first time in history, for anyone to hear and see individuals performing in their own living rooms or the corner theater.

Probably one of the best-known Americans in the early twentieth century was Amelia Earhart, the aviatrix whose flights across the Atlantic and Pacific Oceans made her a household name. "Earhart the Aviatrix" was the product. In addition, Earhart started and oversaw her own line of casual clothing for women. As was typical of women celebrities who were independent of a film studio or other institution, Earhart was "managed" by her husband. He sought out contacts and funding for her flights, handled publicity, arranged scheduling, and supervised their domestic arrangements. She flew at a time when both flying and women pilots were highly unusual and fascinating. Her widely publicized transoceanic and cross-country flights, as well as her clothing business, brought in enough money to support Earhart, some of her family members, and her husband and to allow her to continue flying.

New recording technologies, celebrityhood, and the amazing appetite of Americans for entertainment made a market for radio, sound recording, and film. These markets in turn fueled the development of mainstream entertainment consumption and a variety of ethnic markets. Good examples of the impact of these new technologies and the increase in dollars spent on nonessentials in a variety of smaller regional markets can be seen in the expansion of Anglo- and Mexican-American ethnic music in the 1920s. In both of these areas, family groups such as the Carter family were typical, although individual stars, such as Lydia Mendoza and Patsy Montana, also became popular. (Montana's 1935 recording of "Cowboy Sweetheart" became the first record by a female vocalist to sell a million copies.) Troupes of entertainers from Mexico traveled throughout the American Southwest, and some of these theatrical groups were operated by women, such as Virginia Fábregas in the 1920s. Film production provided further opportunities for ethnic women. For example, the Mandarin Film Company, which was the only company producing Chinese-language films in the United States at the time, was founded in 1917 and presided over by Marion E. Wong. She also acted in some of the company's films. The early 1920s saw the first female African-American film producer, Maria P. Williams. Her Western Film Producing Company, headquartered in Kansas City, Missouri, produced films for the African-American market.[21]

From the beginning of professional rodeo in 1882 through the 1920s, women competed successfully as stunt riders and skilled cowgirls. In the earliest years, vehicles such as Buffalo Bill Cody's Wild West Show presented women as trick riders and fancy ropers and featured not only Anglo-American but also Mexican, Mexican-American, and Native American women performers. Also in this early period, many women competed directly against men. Some claimed, as did Lucille Mulhall, that women were treated as men's equals in the competitions. After World War I, and particularly after the institution of rodeo in the Madison Square Garden in 1922, rodeo became a popular national sport drawing huge crowds. Professional women rodeo riders got into the business for a variety of reasons, ranging from helping out with family bills because of the death or desertion of male earners to a love for the sport or the competition. The monetary rewards were not enormous but could be better than most women's wages. All of the early rodeo women had some prior experience with horses, and most came from farms and ranches and had grown up "on horseback" as members of ranch or farm families. In addition, daredevil stars such as "Tad" Lucas, Mabel Strikland, and Alice Greenough were outstanding athletes. Lucas was the biggest female rodeo star of the 1920s, winning nearly every major competition in trick riding in both the United States and Europe. She started originally as a bronc rider, but her bravery and outstanding physical abilities led her into trick riding. A particular crowd pleaser was her rendition of the "suicide drag," wherein she leaned out over the back of the horse, held in the saddle only by the stirrups, and dangled just over the flying rear hooves.

Aviators, entertainers, and cowgirls aside, most women continued to inhabit the business world in much more traditional ways, even as the environment in which those traditional forms operated changed, sometimes dramatically. New technologies in farming and agriculture, for example, influenced women's involvement in this type of business.

In many ways women's farming tasks in 1930 were the same as those of 100 or 200 years earlier. They raised poultry, prepared butter, preserved food, sewed, cleaned, and cooked. By 1900, however, agriculture had changed radically. Farming had become oriented almost completely to a mass-production market. Cash crops had also become increasingly specialized. Farmers grew wheat but not rye, celery but not tomatoes. Processing companies interposed themselves between farmers and ranchers and their markets. The railroads transported crops to market, canneries processed them, and chain stores sold them. The nation's farmers and ranchers were almost completely integrated into the national market economy.

The gap between men's and women's experience within the family farming business widened. New machines and other products that could simplify both household tasks and general farm chores such as plowing, reaping, and milking became available. Among these products were washing machines, the telephone, self-feeders for animals, mechanical corn shredders, indoor plumbing and running water, modern cookstoves, and home canning equipment. But whether a farm woman had access to these new items involved a complex set of equations. Farm families made their economic decisions on much the same basis as any other business: where to place resources so that they would generate the most return. Since about the late eighteenth century, generating the most return meant putting financial and human resources back into major cash crops, the province of men, rather than into improvements that would assist or simplify women's contribution to the household economy. Many farm women were faced with continuing to operate their part of the family business in an almost preindustrial environment while men's farming tasks were mechanized and rationalized—in short, modernized. The economic decision-making process that was part of farming as a family business widened the gap between men's and women's work and thus their contribution to the household economy, which further devalued women's labor.

The Commission on Country Life, appointed by President Theodore Roosevelt, reported in 1909 on this and other problems associated with changing rural life. The commission was a rural version of urban Progressivism and had as its goal making rural life more efficient and "scientific." To that end, it urged that everything be done to give women access to more modern facilities and training in home economics via the agricultural extension services of land grant colleges. Without that access, the commissioners feared, women's dissatisfaction would lead to an exodus from the family farm and the continued inefficiency of agricultural business.

The advent of new agricultural technologies and practices had a different impact on women's lives depending on their class and ethnicity and the relative marginality of their landholdings. The white, native-born middle-class women who were the commission's prime audience were, in fact, better able to take advantage of many of the new technologies than other rural women simply by virtue of their economic status. The women of sharecropper families, Exoduster communities (towns founded by ex-slaves) such as Nicodemus in Kansas, and black women on farms elsewhere, generally did not have the financial resources to lavish on self-feeders, gasoline-powered irons, or washing machines. This was especially true in the difficult climatological and geographical conditions of the Plains states.

Other traditional business venues remained for women as well. Women continued to operate family businesses and businesses in typically feminized areas such as catering, confectionery shops, hairdressing, and boardinghouses (table 2). In 1900 85 percent of all boardinghouses were owned and operated by women. About 30 percent of confectioners and 99 percent of dressmakers, seamstresses, and milliners were women. These numbers remained relatively unchanged from 1890. In Wilmington, Delaware, Edith McConnell took over the D. B. Jones catering and confectionery company in 1921 and ran it successfully until about 1957. The complexities of the catering business had increased from a similar type of business 100 years earlier. McConnell was typical of small-business owners in doing most of the work herself, including bookkeeping, dealing with a variety of vendors, hiring waiters and maids for large public functions, and—after the passage of the federal income tax amendment in 1913—paying federal as well as local and state taxes.[22] As was also true historically, running a boardinghouse, making baked goods or liquor for neighborhood sale, and taking in laundry were often the province of widows or female-headed households with few other options.

Women continued, as they had in the past, to move in and out of different occupations and types of business over time, even as they remained economically active throughout most of their adult lives. Helen Schultz (1898–1974), the "Iowa Bus Queen," grew up on a farm and then went to work as a stenographer, however, she wanted to open her own bus company to take advantage of the need for motorized public transportation. She was unable to find a bank willing to lend

TABLE 2

Women as a Percentage of all Proprietors, Selected Businesses,
1890 and 1900

Business Proprietors	1890	1900
Dressmakers	99.7	99.4
Milliners	99.4	98.0
Seamstresses[a]	97.3	96.8
Corset makers	88.8	89.8
Laundresses[b]	87.2	86.9
Boardinghouse keepers	73.5	83.4
Restaurant keepers	12.5	14.3
Photographers	11.0	13.3
Retail merchants	3.8	4.3
Hucksters or peddlers	3.8	3.8
Saloon keepers	3.2	2.5
Wholesale merchants	0.6	0.6

Source: Information based on table XLIV, Bureau of the Census, *Special Reports: Occupations at the 12th Census* (Washington, D.C.: U.S. Government Printing Office, 1904), cxxv–cxxvii. The compilation includes only those types of businesses likely to be proprietorships in this period. Undoubtedly some women were sole proprietors in other areas (such as printing, bookbinding, pottery, etc.), but the census did not distinguish between proprietorship and employment by others.

[a]Some seamstresses no doubt worked for dressmakers rather than operating as sole proprietors.

[b]Some laundresses were likely employed in commercial laundries. However, in this period many would have been independent operators, probably most of them African-American.

money to a woman for such purposes, but she found a private source of capital in a Minnesota contractor for whom she had worked. She ran the company from 1922, survived through some difficult times, and finally sold out to another transportation company in 1930. She invested the proceeds in a tire agency and automobile service station.

The female economy of barter for goods and services also remained in full force, particularly in areas where resources were slim

or where traditional notions of community interaction supported
barter arrangements. Among Hispanic women in the Southwest, for
example, where men often traveled many miles looking for work and
were gone for weeks or even months at a time, women pooled
resources, trading homemade cheese for homemade soap or flour.
Women raised cash crops such as chili peppers and goats or wove
blankets for sale. Trading clearly had social as well as economic functions: prepared food was rarely ever sold but frequently traded, and
unprocessed crops and nonfood items became part of a general market exchange or were sold for cash. Among poor rural whites and
African-Americans, particularly in the South but elsewhere as well,
women continued to trade midwifery skills (assisting at births and
tending the new mothers) and nursing the sick for goods and services
or, sometimes, cash. Although regular physicians had gained control
of the birthing process for most middle- and upper-class women,
working-class and poor women continued to rely on the services of
experienced but not necessarily school-trained local midwives well
into the twentieth century.

Conclusion

The bright prospects that seemed attainable in 1880 seemed less possible 50 years later. New types of businesses and technologies, as in
motion pictures, provided new opportunities for women but also followed the familiar process of narrowed opportunities as industries
matured, requiring more capital, adopting professional management,
and addressing larger markets. Although early in this period women's
access to professional training in areas such as medicine and the law
increased, by the 1920s those opportunities had shrunk, and instead a
series of "women's professions" had developed in social work, librarianship, teaching, and nursing. These professions were less well paid
than related professions for men. Patterns of gender segregation first
noticeable in the early nineteenth century continued on into the twentieth, even as new jobs appeared in various white-collar industries.

Some of the largest gains ever in wage work for young, single
women came between 1880 and 1930. These years witnessed women's
virtual takeover of positions as stenographers, typists, and secretaries.
But the growing number of women workers brought attention to old
problems. Although World War I had less impact than the Civil War on
the numbers of women working for wages, it revealed one of the

biggest difficulties facing women workers: The war brought relatively few new women workers into the labor force but witnessed large numbers of women leaving "women's work" to take jobs vacated by men during the war. Nearly half a million women shifted from waitressing to heavy machinery and from typing to accounting. The explanation was wages. Women who became streetcar conductors, for example, could increase their earnings as much as 30 percent over typical female employment. Debates over women's status throughout the period continued to question women's right to equal opportunities with men. These debates revealed deep schisms among Americans about women's role as economic and political citizens.

Race and ethnicity continued to divide women's experiences. On the one hand, ethnic business could be a protected haven for women's opportunities, as Lena Bryant's and Maggie Lena Walker's dealings suggest. Producing a product for a specialized market, such as African-American hair care, made more than one woman a millionaire. Some of these entrepreneurs put money and opportunities back into their communities, helping other women like themselves to become independent agents. On the other hand, ethnicity could shape possibilities in less positive ways as well. Race and class devalued women's labor, and most women of color worked as domestics or in other marginal occupations. Ethnic businesses often straddled complex tensions among the assertion of ethnic identity and assimilation to mainstream culture. Race increasingly led to the physical segregation of people of color after 1880. White racism stripped black Americans of the vote and other citizenship rights, despite the passage of amendments to the U.S. Constitution.

Some fabulous success stories came out of the years between 1880 and 1930. There is no question that this 50-year period witnessed more profound growth in women's waged labor than any previous time. What is equally important, however, is the fact that traditional models of women's business role continued to hold such force for so many. Women developed a managerial role for themselves, but it was a role justified and shaped by domesticity. During the depression in the 1930s, women's business and professional opportunities would shrink even further as the economy contracted and state and federal agencies stepped in to regulate business in a variety of ways.

Chapter Five

Crisis Management: Women and Business at Midcentury, 1930–1963

*Often a firm which believes it offers every opportunity for women main-
tains discriminations ... [such as] the manufacturing firm, which
reported that all openings in the higher-level jobs are posted and anyone
can apply but no woman ever had, might ask itself whether its hiring
practices do not exclude the promotional type of woman right from the
start. In many manufacturing firms women are hired only for the dead-
end jobs, and the possibility of using women in some of the jobs requiring higher qualifications has never been explored.*

—*Federal Women's Bureau Report on Women in
Higher-Level Positions, 1950*

Esther Mentzer (b. 1908?), the youngest child of Hungarian immigrants, was born in Queens, New York. She grew up in an apartment
above the family's hardware store, where she remembers her uncle
John Schotz, a chemist, mixing skin potions in an improvised laboratory behind the store. She became an enthusiastic creator herself, trying out on her high school classmates various creams and lotions she
had concocted. She attributed her later business success to those
early backyard chemistry experiments. "[Uncle John] captured my
imagination as no one else ever had," she recalled in her autobiography. "It was a precious velvety cream ... that magically made you
sweetly scented, made your face feel like spun silk. ... Maybe I'm glo-

rifying the memories, but I believe today that I recognized in my Uncle John my true path."[1]

The story of how Esther Mentzer, self-identified Jewish-Catholic working-class girl, became Estée Lauder, friend of princesses, movie stars, and socialites; the epitome of female elegance; *and* a "tycoon" in the cutthroat world of the cosmetics industry, is very much a story of women's business entrepreneurship. By the 1930s cosmetics was the 10th largest industry in the United States. Estée Lauder (the corporation) became the nation's leading cosmetics company through a combination of shrewd positioning in niche markets, taking advantage of women's increasing importance as consumers, and promotion of a particular image of female elegance, privilege, and femininity. Lauder engaged in a typical female business, beauty products. She employed a traditional business form, the family partnership, in an age of corporate giants. But make no mistake, Lauder was very much a modern business entrepreneur and a classic self-made (and self-named) woman. She ruthlessly used industrial espionage against her major rival, Charles Revson, and his company, Revlon. She engaged in aggressive and exclusive sales techniques, inventing or taking advantage of consumer needs with such products as Youth Dew and Clinique. She immersed herself completely in all of the details of her business empire for more than 30 years and was a consummate executive. She understood the relationship between her product and the larger economy, and she expanded the company overseas on the leading edge of American intrusion into European markets in the 1950s. Not incidentally, she claimed acquaintance with both Democratic and Republican presidents and was photographed with every First Lady since Lady Bird Johnson.

Men who went into the industry in the twentieth century did so through pharmaceutical training, an avenue closed to women. Instead, Lauder's business followed the same path most other women's businesses have taken since the nineteenth century: She began making the product in her home. She and her husband, Joseph, cooked up facial creams in the kitchen, bottled them, and sold them locally to a beauty parlor. The parlor's owner asked Lauder to provide products for an exclusive salon she was opening on the Upper East Side of Manhattan. Lauder moved from there to demonstrations at luxury resort hotels during the summers and then directly into selling at bridge parties and other gatherings given by wealthy and well-connected New York socialites. She and Joe incorporated in 1946 but continued as a two-person cottage industry. Typical of many depression-era businesses, and of women's businesses generally, Lauder's kitchen shop produced a small quantity of a niche product and sold to a specific clientele.

That small-scale venture changed thanks to a brilliant marketing ploy Lauder introduced in the late 1940s to take advantage of the postwar boom in consumption, particularly for luxury products. Unlike most other cosmetic products, such as Max Factor, Revlon, and Helena Rubenstein (another story of female entrepreneurship), which targeted drugstore clientele, Lauder decided to give large department stores an exclusive claim to her creams and lotions. First introduced into Saks Fifth Avenue, and by the 1950s Neiman Marcus, Marshall Field's, I. Magnin, and Bonwit Teller, Lauder's cosmetics company benefited from the air of exclusivity surrounding department stores, and the growth of consumption. She pioneered in marketing promotions as well. With each purchase of a Lauder product, customers received a free gift of another. She trained in-store saleswomen and expected them to be models of grooming and elegance, "walking advertisements" for the product. She revolutionized the fragrance industry with the introduction of the relatively inexpensive, Youth Dew. In the early 1960s she instituted a marketing campaign with specific female models who were identified as the "Estée Lauder Woman," another technique later adopted by her competitors.

Women's Status and Long-Term Change

Lauder's combination of savvy business sense, appeal to female consumers, and emphasis on traditional female products and markets were hallmarks of women's business involvement during the social and economic swings of the mid-twentieth century. Women in business held their own through this period but did not radically change their traditional roles. The sheer numbers of working women, and of female entrepreneurs and managers, grew throughout midcentury. The types of businesses in which they were involved, however, in general remained in feminized areas.

Depression, World War II, and the cold war contributed to an environment that reinforced conservative stereotypes of womanhood and regrounded women's economic contribution within the family claim during the mid-twentieth century. These events did not end women's involvement in business, as Lauder and other businesswomen make clear. In fact, between 1944 and 1950, the number of female-owned businesses grew from 650,000 to almost a million. Lauder began her business enterprise on the eve of international economic depression. But economic and political crises affected wages and salaries, opportunities, and the rhetoric surrounding working women and businesswomen. As women during World War II took over male positions in industry, they earned more proportionally than women ever had in the United States. However, conservative attitudes shared by government, business, unions, and many women themselves undermined the potential for radical change in women's access to employment and business opportunities. As with banking during World War I, the desire to conserve tradition was evident in the justification for women's entry into male-defined fields such as welding during World War II: their advent was temporary, "for the duration" of the wartime emergency. Many women themselves, even as they enjoyed a level of earning power undreamed of in peacetime, fully expected to hand their positions over to men once veterans returned.

The postwar reconversion, in turn, emphasized women's familial role both in the attitudes of courts and lawmakers toward women's place and in business advertising's emphasis on consumption, female domesticity, and even business involvement. Popular magazines celebrated crowded hospital maternity wards—where, in one woman's words, "everyone, and her sister, was having a baby"—as the nation welcomed its largest generation ever, nicknamed the baby boom.[2] After nearly 20 years of depression and war, which often made family formation and maintenance impossible, perhaps the emphasis on women's domestic nature so emblematic of the 1950s is understandable. The national security needs of the cold war years emphasized female domesticity. In a world in which economic battles had replaced military ones, women's role as consumers became paramount. By 1963, on the eve of the transformative social and economic changes of the late twentieth century, women's roles in business as consumers, workers, managers, entrepreneurs, and professionals seemed firmly rooted in their image as domestic helpmates. As Estée Lauder's life suggests, however, within that traditional image remained a great deal of elbow room.

We can find evidence of this paradox in two fundamental areas. First, women's legal status remained relatively unchanged from earlier periods, despite shifting legal contexts. Insofar as the law was concerned, modern women were pretty much like their nineteenth-century great-grandmothers. Second, however, long-term demographic changes in women's reproductive rates and labor force participation suggested the adaptability and flexibility of gender roles in times of crisis, such as the disruptions of midcentury economic depression, war, and postwar recovery.

Always important, the economic and legal situations for women in the twentieth century have been the best barometers of women's status and the best windows into their business opportunities. Between 1930 and 1963 women's legal status remained closer to nineteenth-century ideals than to those of the present. The passage of the Nineteenth Amendment to the Constitution in 1920, which gave most women the vote, left unchanged many other aspects of women's legal status. It also made even more obvious the inequitable limitations of women's economic situation. In fact, the economic and social upheavals of the mid-twentieth century reinforced the long-standing conservatism of gender roles for women. The economic devastation of the depression of the 1920s and 1930s, the mobilization and emergencies of World War II, and the postwar efforts to return to "normal" in the face of the cold war all created an unsettled economic and social environment. For many, the stability of race and gender relations became a priority.

In these troubled times, the emphasis on women's traditional role was an attempt to preserve the status quo in the face of disaster. These efforts are evident in many ways; three examples will suffice here. Reflecting the notion that women should be protected from night work, importunate men, and disreputable environments, the U.S. Supreme Court in 1948 affirmed a lower court ruling that women did not have the right to serve as bartenders unless they were related to the male tavern owner. Presumably, the wives or daughters of male business owners were of the same class as their male relatives, were "protected" by male family members, and as a men's "property" were not the Supreme Court's to command. The Court reaffirmed this decision again in 1970. Further, women's status as citizens remained fuzzy. Despite the community property tradition of states such as California and New Mexico, the early twentieth century found women in these states legally prohibited from writing wills. The New Mexico law, passed in 1907 and modeled on California's family law, made a woman's husband her automatic and sole heir on her death. California changed its law in 1923; New Mexico's remained in force until the 1970s. As late as 1962, some women in the United States were denied equal status with men for jury duty, with 21 states still prohibiting women from jury service in lower-level courts on the same terms as men. This denial of equality existed despite the fact that the Civil Rights Act of 1957 gave women full rights to serve on federal juries and the Supreme Court decision in *Brown* v. *Board of Education* (1954) recognized the presence of social and political discrimination. Finally, until China became a U.S. ally in World War II, Chinese immigrants were prohibited from becoming citizens. The U.S. Supreme Court in 1922 denied citizenship status to Japanese immigrants.[3] The right to vote in federal elections, in other words, did not ensure that other rights of citizenship or an improved legal status would follow.

Justifications by the Supreme Court, federal lawmakers, and many regular citizens for treating women differently from men grew out of the long-standing belief in women's need for special protections. As we saw in chapter 4, the court system and legislation in the early twentieth century built on precedent in defining women by their relative weakness to men, their biological "destiny" to reproduce, and the presumption that women were less interested in their own economic development than in that of their male relatives. Far from an imposed idea, the notion that women were family members first and individuals second was shared by many feminists, business and labor leaders, and social reformers. This tendency to see women in terms of the family claim, which we have seen throughout our history, was if anything intensified in the profound social and economic crises of the midcentury.

At the same time that women's status as dependents of men was reaffirmed by the courts, long-term demographic trends suggested reality was evolving in another direction. Over the long term, beginning in the early nineteenth century and continuing to the present, the overall rate of childbirth has been decreasing. The so-called fertility rate—the number of babies born per 1,000 women in the population—has declined overall between 1800 and the present. For example, in 1840 the fertility rate for urban women was about 700 births per 1,000 women; the rural rate was approximately 1,200 births per 1,000 women (with an overall mean of 950). By 1960 the overall rate was 118 and by 1990 about 67. In addition, as the comprehensive birth rate went down, it also went down in terms of individual women. In 1800 the average number of births for women of childbearing age was 7 or 8 (with greater numbers among rural women and women of color). By the 1960s that number was 2 to 2.5 and by 1990 about 1.5 to 2. Thus, even as the overall population grew, individual women had fewer child care responsibilities.

Combined with several other factors, the falling birth rate led to two other important long-term twentieth-century trends (table 3). The first was the increasing percentage of women in the labor force. In 1890 women over the age of 16 made up only 15 percent of the labor force; by 1940 that figure had risen to nearly 26 percent of all workers, by 1960 34 percent, and by 1980 45 percent. The percentage of women over age 16 who joined the labor force also increased in this period, from 19 percent in 1890 to 33 percent in 1945 to 58 percent in 1990. During this same period, men's labor force participation rate decreased, from 88 percent in 1945 to 76.1 percent in 1990. Demographers predicted that by the year 2000 the percentage of women in the labor force will increase to 63 percent, while men's participation will remain constant at about 76 percent.

The second important long-term demographic shift has been the growing number of married women in the workforce. Until World War II, by far the largest group of women wage workers were single, white, never-married young women. Up to the 1930s, they (like Estée Lauder) were also likely to be the daughters of recent immigrants. The proportion of married women (with a spouse present) in the labor force increased from 5 percent in 1890 to 26 percent during World War II. Despite a small decrease to about 21 percent by 1947, this segment has continued its climb (to 60 percent in 1990). But racial differences existed between wage workers. Black women had always made up a disproportionate part of the female labor force, for example, and continued to do so during the general growth in the numbers of female workers (table 3). Black women tended to work for wages throughout their lives, regardless of whether male breadwinners were present. White women entered the labor force in their early 20s but left it during their child-raising years or while a husband was present. White women more often than women of color had the luxury of raising their children at home. In 1950 married black women made up about 33 percent of the labor force, as opposed to 25 percent of married women in the general population. In this period, black women and women of color in general tended to be clustered in specific jobs, such as domestic household laborers, or segregated in ethnic communities. The general growth in clerical work that continued after 1930, for example, had little impact on most women of color.

The typical female worker in 1900 was a young, white, single woman, often the child of immigrant parents. The odds were good she was doing some sort of clerical or sales work. The typical female worker in 1950 was married, in her 40s, and could have come from either the middle or working class. She probably still would be doing clerical or service work. The typical black or Hispanic female worker throughout this period was married, between the ages of 20 and 60, and engaged in domestic labor. In fact, by the late 1960s, the majority of women worked for wages at least part of their lives.

Paradoxically, these trends have existed alongside the notion that

TABLE 3

Percentage of Women in the Wage Labor Force, 1890–1999

	1890	1940	1960	1980	1999
Women as percentage of wage labor force[a]	15	26	34	45	46.3
Percentage of women over age 16 employed					
Total	19	33	38	43	60
White	16	31	36	51	59.6
Nonwhite	40	46	43	51	57.5
Percentage of married women in the labor force					
Total	5	26	31	57	61.5
White	3	31	30	NA	60
Nonwhite	23	46	41	NA	65

Source: Adapted from Claudia Goldin, *Understanding the Gender Gap: An Economic History of American Women* (New York: Oxford University Press, 1990), chapter 3: table 6-1, Paula Ries and Anne J. Stone, eds., *The American Woman, 1992–93: A Status Report* (New York: W. W. Norton, 1992), 308; Department of Commerce, Bureau of the Census, "Table 669, Employed Civilians by Occupation, Sex, Race, and Hispanic Origin: 1983 and 1999" and "Table 653, Employment Status of Women by Marital Status and Presence and Age of Children: 1970 to 1999," *Statistical Abstract of the U.S.: 2000* (Washington, D.C.: U.S. Government Printing Office, 2000), pp. 416, 409; Council of Economic Advisors, *Economic Report of the President, Transmitted to Congress February 2000*, p. 352; and Figure 4-1, "Women in the Labor Force, 1948–1998," Cynthia B. Costello and Anne J. Stone, eds., *The American Woman, 2001–2002: Getting to the Top* (New York: W. W. Norton, 2001), p. 227.

Note: Percentages are rounded off to the nearest whole number.

[a]Figures are for all full-time workers in all economic sectors.

women are not really workers at all. Throughout the mid-twentieth century we find that expectations surrounding the family claim have continued to shape the context of white women's business experiences—as workers, entrepreneurs, professionals, or managers. The notion that women were "covered" by a male breadwinner long outlived its foundation in the common law. It encouraged the perception that women did not *need* to work and thus only worked to pay for extras or personal luxuries—for pin money.

Even women who entered paid employment or business ventures out of necessity were tarred with the same brush. Women consistently earned less than men, for example. The median annual wage income for full-time white and nonwhite civilian men in 1963 was about $7,000 and $4,400, respectively. For white and nonwhite women, median incomes were around $4,100 and $2,700, respectively. Men's annual incomes were higher than women's no matter what the field, position, or job as late as the early 1960s. Throughout the twentieth century, women have earned an average of 66 cents for every dollar earned by a man (table 1). In some ways more disheartening, although both men's and women's earning power increases as they age (and presumably become more experienced), at the same time the gap widens between them. This discrepancy results because young men and women begin at about the same salary level, but over the course of a lifetime men receive more consistent and higher rewards for their skills. Women in their 50s who have been full-time workers most of their adult lives still earn about the same amount as a woman of 25.

More than shifts in the fertility rate encouraged these long-term trends. (In fact, the causal relation between changing decisions about how many children to bear and whether or not to work outside of the home is ambiguous; both probably worked in tandem.) First, the general growth of business made more jobs available, so more workers were needed over the long term. Second, some women took advantage of the expansion of higher education to receive a more extensive and better educational background, thus making them more desirable as workers. Third, women in general were becoming more economically dependent on themselves. Depression and war brought women into the workforce in larger numbers than ever before out of necessity as well as choice. That factor coupled with the swelling divorce rate during the first 60 years of the twentieth century meant that women were increasingly on their own. And they were on their own in a job market that was sex typed and paid women less whether they were in "women's jobs," such as clerical, or female professionals in education, law, or medicine. Fourth, the gender stereotyping of jobs in some ways worked to women's advantage in the sense that the greatest expansion in the economy came in the service sector; consequently, job growth came in areas that, although they paid less, had already been culturally assigned to women: clerical, sales, and personal service (e.g., food preparation, waitressing, and domestic labor). The mid-twentieth century, in other words, witnessed the continuation of long-term expansion of women's share of various business areas, although still not on equal terms with men.

Women and Business Developments

In addition to these factors, several general trends in business development were important to women's opportunities. First, governmental regulation of business, begun in the Progressive period, was strengthened and extended during the federal and state governments' legislative response to the depression, war, and postwar recovery. Government, in fact, became the single largest factor in the economy. The overall effect of governmental regulation between 1928 and the early 1960s was twofold. First, the size of governments grew to the point that by the mid-1960s, local, state, and federal bureaucracies employed 12.5 percent of the workforce. Second, government regulation supported the growth of big business, although both the Hoover and Roosevelt administrations encouraged numerous legislative programs for small businesses and family farms. Declining prices after World War I hit the farm economy early and hard. During Herbert Hoover's presidency Congress created the Federal Farm Board, designed to pump money into efforts to make farming more "efficient." It also shored up large businesses with loans provided by the Reconstruction Finance Corporation. The relative decline of small businesses in relation to large ones that occurred between 1921 and 1971, however, was not halted by the efforts of the Small Business Administration, created in 1953. The mobilization of war further strengthened large firms, brought the economy out of depression, and cemented close relations between the federal government and big business. The postwar need for reconstruction in Europe and the expanding world markets of the 1950s built on federal policies that encouraged the beginnings of globalization of the U.S. economy. All of these factors nourished the general growth of a consumer economy and stimulated spending for workforce skill development, especially for managers and professionals.

The spate of federal regulation engaged women's interests in two ways. In the first case, state and federal legislation addressed issues concerning women's business involvement. Protective labor legislation for women remained in force at midcentury. This issue extended the debate begun in the nineteenth century over the relative advantages and disadvantages of either working for equality with a male standard or treating women as a special category. Within the women's movement this debate was visible after 1913 in the split between Alice Paul's militantly egalitarian National Woman's Party (NWP) and the loose coalitions of labor and feminist leaders—including those involved in the National Federation of Business and Professional Women's Clubs (BPW) and the federal Women's Bureau—who sought the extension to male workers of protective labor legislation. This debate also surfaced in the American Federation of Labor and Congress of Industrial Organizations' (AFL-CIO's) movement during the depression for a family wage, by which the powerful union organization meant a man's wage. Throughout midcentury unions and government emphasized keeping male wages high. The managerial approaches taken to the use of women's labor even during World War II, when there was a severe shortage of employable men, reflected these discussions. In industries as varied as automotive and electrical, women were segregated into jobs defined as "female" during the war. Union supporters defended their right to wages comparable to those of men for the same work on the grounds that if women's presence in those jobs was allowed to depress wages it would adversely affect returning male veterans.

In the second case, feminist groups united to push for women's equality with men in regard to credit wages. However, the NWP, BPW, and Women's Bureau came together over the issue of equal pay for different reasons. Those reasons grew out of their dissimilar assumptions about the nature of women's role in business and labor. They also demonstrate that even though there were fundamental disagreements on women's nature and economic role, the organizations agreed about how best to achieve the same goal. The notion of equal pay for equal work had been around since the late nineteenth century, and the NWP, BPW, and Women's Bureau had been publicly discussing the issue since the 1920s. The BPW believed in women's right to equality as female workers and businesswomen. However, it also espoused the view that the gender segregation of jobs benefited women by providing them a guaranteed space for their talents and energies. The Women's Bureau was more conservative, generally seeing women's business role as supportive of men's and emphasizing women's basic status as wife and mother. Both of these groups, for different reasons, wanted to maintain the gender segregation of the labor force. To undermine that view would challenge an assured position for women within the business world and encroach on men's territorial rights to male-defined arenas. At the same time, the two groups supported the notion that to keep wages up for both men and women, women's wages for the same or similar work should equal those of men. The NWP's position was simpler. For Alice Paul and her supporters, women engaged in the same or similar labor as men should receive the same wages, no matter what the field, as a basic individual right.

Despite their underlying disagreements over woman's nature, the coalition was able to focus on shared goals. Its support for equal pay led to the passage of equal pay bills in several states after 1919. World War II made the issue even more pressing, because women performed successfully in men's jobs during the conflict. Between 1943 and 1955, 16 states added equal pay laws to their books. A federal law was introduced to Congress in 1945 and reintroduced periodically throughout the 1950s. Equal pay was linked in public debates with Keynesian arguments about strengthening the economy by increasing the value of production and consumption. Women wage earners could nourish the economy by earning good wages and spending them on their families. President Eisenhower supported the idea of equal pay in his 1956 state of the union address.

In the Kennedy administration, Vice President Lyndon Johnson and Esther Peterson, director of the Women's Bureau, convinced the president to create the Commission on the Status of Women in 1961. This group focused on, among other things, the issue of equal pay. The end result was the passage of a federal law in 1963. Unfortunately, by that time the debate had veered firmly away from the NWP's argument that equal pay was an individual right. The rationales of the BPW and Women's Bureau were less threatening in the long run than the specter of women acting as individuals in their own right, demanding "men's jobs" as well as their pay. Congressional supporters presented the equal pay act as a way to protect gender segregation and male jobs and solidify women's position as helpmates to the family and the nation. The equal pay act ironically remained embedded in the notion of fundamental differences between men and women.

The second way in which government regulation had an impact on women's business involvement took the opposite tack: legislation and government policy often ignored women's needs altogether. In particular, the plethora of "alphabet agencies" created as part of Franklin Roosevelt's New Deal often did not address issues of concern to women in business. The Small Business Administration, for example, did not recognize women's need for capital and the importance of their particular gendered niche to their economic survival. Government agencies ignored such things as beauty parlors and boardinghouses in their loan policies. Most New Deal legislation designed to aid businesses and protect workers—such as the National Industrial Recovery Act (1933), the Social Security Act (1935), and the Fair Labor Standards Act (1938)—exempted categories of workers most likely to include women of color: domestic servants and agricultural laborers. Some agencies, on the other hand, developed an excellent record of incorporating women's concerns and women themselves into their policies and approaches. Both Franklin D. Roosevelt and his secretary of agriculture, Henry A. Wallace, for example, opened channels of communication with rural women not only to make them a part of the planning process for farm aid but also to enlist their help in legitimizing New Deal policies.

The third general aspect of business development of relevance to women's experience was the shift from a producer- and product-driven to a consumer- and services-oriented society. Obviously, industrial and manufacturing firms continued to create products—and still do. At the same time, however, service-sector "products" such as life insurance, banking services, nondurable consumer goods, and personal services took on new economic importance. Consumerism rose to a position of importance in the guiding economic theory of the post-war United States, promulgated in John Maynard Keynes's emphasis on full employment and spending on consumer goods. Women's importance as consumers continued to increase as the economy grew through midcentury. The internationalization of the American economy, and its rapid growth in the service sector throughout midcentury, made finding customers for all of those products essential. Women were workers with money to spend, business owners with markets to satisfy, and housewives with family budgets to manage. Advertising campaigns aimed at female consumers through radio, magazines, and, after World War II, television hawked durable consumer goods, clothing, domestic products, and personal items. For example, American automobile manufacturers recognized both the purchasing power of individual women and their persuasive role in family financial decisions. They addressed women consumers specifically in advertising designed to appeal to perceived female requirements for safety and ease of operation. The appearance of daytime soap operas on the radio in the 1930s and television in the 1950s constructed a connection between entertainment, women whose workdays were spent in household labor, and products that promised to lighten that labor load. By the early 1960s the top 10 advertisers on television were primarily companies with products aimed at female consumers: Procter & Gamble, General Foods, and General Mills among them.

The increased buying power of women led as well to new educational opportunities and professional niches for women in management and product development. Women not only *were* consumers, in other words, they also *studied* consumers. Helen Resor, of the husband-and-wife advertising partnership that owned the powerful James Walter Thompson agency after 1917, made her mark as an advertiser by supplying, in her words, "the feminine point of view."[4] Her clients included Yuban coffee and Lux detergent—both household products. Recognizing the importance of female consumers to its sales figures, in 1929 Corning Glass Works in Corning, New York, hired Lucy M. Maltby, a college-educated home economist, to oversee its new customer service orientation. By studying the needs and desires of consumers, corporate advisers such as Maltby promised more sales through product development designed to fit what those consumers wanted. Women such as Resor and Maltby became professionals because of the persistent belief that women, even trained scientists, understood female customers better than men did.

Beginning in the late nineteenth century, the tendency to professionalize management had created new opportunities to engage in corporate work for college-trained women such as Maltby. She was one of a new generation of women with graduate training in fields related to so-called women's professions such as social welfare work and home economics. Between 1930 and 1950 women college graduates more often worked for at least a portion of their young adult lives. By the early 1960s, in fact, college-educated women were more likely than women with only a high school education to be gainfully employed: 60 percent as opposed to 40 percent. And although the percentage of women in college dropped slightly overall between 1930 and 1960, the absolute number of women attending college rose throughout the middle of the century.

The final major trend in business development affecting women was the decentralization of managerial structures. As corporations grew in size and became more complex in their product offerings, opportunities increased for women at midlevel management positions in areas such as personnel. Although never in a majority, and certainly underpaid and underutilized in relation to men, women managers in a variety of fields made inroads into business, particularly during World War II. At the beginning of the war, probably less than 10 percent of midlevel managers were female, and most of them were owners and operators of their own small businesses rather than corporate employees.

A variety of factors kept women out of management. Over the course of the early twentieth century, most large corporations sought more professional managers. *Professional* increasingly meant not only the need for a college degree specifically oriented to business skills such as accounting also but a lifelong, uninterrupted commitment to corporate work. For most women, both were impossible. Not only did management schools exclude women, but in some cases governmental and corporate policy prevented married women from working. "In the 1930s, 84 percent of the nation's insurance companies, 65 percent of the banks, and 63 percent of public utilities had restrictive rules preventing married women from holding *any* jobs," historian D'Ann Campbell has observed.[5] Senior managers often believed (perhaps rightly, if unfairly, given historical trends) that the entrance of women into all areas of management would undermine both prestige and salaries in the field. However, women did become managers. Especially welcoming to women were areas designated by their job functions or image as "female," either because of the traits needed for the job (such as the empathy demanded of personnel work) or because the job entailed dealing with female consumers (such as purchasing for department stores). By the end of World War II, in fact, about half of all department store buyers were women.

The Impact of Depression, War, and Recovery

These broad changes in business generally were part of the midcentury triptych of depression, war, and recovery. The depression of the 1930s was a disaster for most American businesses.[6] Between 1929 and 1932 alone, more than 100,000 U.S. businesses failed and industrial production plummeted. Especially hard hit were the sort of small-

and medium-sized firms women most often ran. The number of bank failures provoked state governors and ultimately the federal government to temporarily close banks to slow down withdrawals by panicked customers. The gross national product (GNP) fell from a high of $104.4 billion in 1929 to $74.2 billion in 1933. The depression also was a human tragedy of enormous proportions. After an unemployment rate of only 3.2 percent in 1929, by 1933 more than a quarter of the workforce was unemployed, and the unemployment rate remained at a high 17.2 percent as late as 1939. Business failures devastated both owners and those they employed. Total personal income went from $84.4 billion in 1929 to $47.2 billion in 1933. People turned to the federal government as their best hope and elected a Democrat to the presidency in 1932 for the first time since 1916. They also returned a Democratic majority to Congress, making clear their dissatisfaction with the limited Republican response to the emergency.

Efforts to maintain the family's claim on women appeared almost immediately on many fronts. Seeking to shore up male breadwinners and secure jobs for them, many advocated keeping married women out of the workforce. Asked in a 1936 Gallup Poll if married women should work if their husbands were employed, 82 percent said no. Letters to politicians, business leaders, and newspapers put pressure on businesses to fire married women. Private citizen Earl Leiby, from Akron, Ohio, wrote to President Roosevelt in 1933, voicing the sentiments of many: "Homes are being wrecked daily due to the fact that married women are permitted to work in factories and offices. . . . You and we all know that the place for a wife and mother is at home, her palace. . . . These same women's husbands would naturally be paid a higher salary, inasmuch as male employees demand a higher salary than females."[7] When states passed laws barring them from teaching, married women were forced to quit. In 1933 the National Economy Act stipulated that only one partner in a marriage could take home a federal salary. Since men generally earned more, it made sense for husbands to be the "partner" who remained on the job.

None of these efforts worked completely. In fact, the number of married women workers increased 15 percent during the depression. Many people were desperate and earned money however they could. Women worked to replace or supplement the wages of unemployed, underemployed, or underpaid spouses or to support themselves and their children or other dependents as men migrated, looking for work. Many of the jobs that disappeared during the 1930s were in areas of

so-called men's work in manufacturing and heavy industry, while
white-collar, light industry, and service jobs—women's work—
remained steady or increased. Women of color found domestic work
more available by the mid-1930s. Two million women worked as
domestics in 1940—20 percent of the female labor force—more than
half of them African-American. But domestic work paid poorly. Two-
fifths of the black women on unemployment relief in 1935 were primary breadwinners and heads of households. For all of these reasons,
married women remained an important group of workers during the
1930s.

The depression affected women's participation in business and
their business opportunities in many other ways and in fact reinforced
women's economic importance. At the same time that the federal government focused on the economic needs of agriculture through such
legislation as the Agricultural Adjustment Act, state-sponsored agricultural extension continued and expanded the country life movement's emphasis on women as the economic and emotional center of
farm life. Farm women knew that to be true. They increased their
efforts to contribute to the family economy through bartering, food
preservation, recycling and repairing clothing, and using butter-and-
egg money to pay taxes or purchase farm equipment involved in crop
production. Some sold magazines, furniture polish, and Avon products.

The need for cash during the depression increased the dependence
of some on market relations. The women of Ácoma Pueblo, west of
Albuquerque, New Mexico, had been contributing to the pueblo's economic life for centuries, particularly by making and trading pottery.
The drought and crop failures of the 1930s made it increasingly difficult for these Indians (and many others) to subsist independently of
the market. Consequently, Ácoma women plunged deeper into the
mainstream economy. In addition to more direct dealings with the federal government through a variety of crop and development programs,
Ácoma women expanded their production of domestic crafts, particularly pottery, during the 1930s. They fine-tuned their product to meet
customer demand and developed new patterns, techniques, and products such as candlesticks and ashtrays that appealed to Anglos. By the
mid-1930s, more than a third of Ácoma women were making pottery
for market.[8]

Ethnic cultures encouraged women's business participation in
breadwinner roles in a variety of ways, and economic depression and

war drew on these contributions to face the emergency. As the daughter of Eastern European immigrants and with her Jewish background, Estée Lauder's business involvement is typical of many ethnic women in the twentieth century. Jewish culture not only allowed women to engage in business but also encouraged their entrepreneurship and afforded them control of family finances. For example, Jewish women's employment outside of the house, as wage workers or in family businesses, was fairly common in many urban areas, such as New York City and Kansas City, Missouri, by World War II.

The business experience of Fanny Goldberg Stahl (1887–1961) provides an excellent example of many of these issues.[9] Stahl used entrepreneurship to support her female-headed household, building on ethnic economic attitudes as well as niche markets. Stahl migrated from Poland to the United States in 1914 with two of her four children (and pregnant with a fifth). Her husband, preferring life in Poland, never rejoined her. The need to support her dependents made Stahl economically active in a variety of ways from the time she migrated. She plucked chickens, nursed newborn babies, cooked in a restaurant, and operated a boardinghouse. In the late 1920s she moved into entrepreneurship, first with a restaurant, then a candy store, and finally a delicatessen. The depression apparently contributed to the loss of these business ventures, and after moving to Brighton Beach in the mid-1930s Stahl began selling homemade challah and knishes from a basket she carried to the beach. The basket led to a beachfront kiosk and just before the war to a store at the corner of Brighton Beach and Coney Island Avenues. She continued to operate Stahl's Knishes until her death in 1961. The business provided employment, at one time or another, for all of her children (and eventually their spouses). It was sold, and the new owners continued to produce knishes, kugel, plaetzls, and other delicacies—from Stahl's original recipes—that were sold throughout Manhattan. The waves of Jewish migration to America, the support for female entrepreneurship in Jewish culture, the existence of ethnic communities such as Brighton Beach, and ultimately the expansion of the market for ethnic foods all "fed" into Fanny Stahl's ability to succeed.

Women of color, who were hard hit by the economic devastation in predominately agricultural areas, also found that ethnic patterns provided survival strategies. Hispanic women in the Southwest became more economically important to their families and communities as Hispanic men migrated almost constantly looking for work. As job opportunities shrank and wages decreased, the labor of African-American women became even more critical to survival. Taking in laundry and boarders, doing domestic work, and sharing resources among kin and neighbors remained important strategies for economic survival among many ethnic groups. Particularly among Native Americans, African-Americans, Jews, and Hispanics, the depression strengthened long traditions of community activism and cooperation as individuals and families relied on barter and sharing resources to get by.

The economic strategies of Fannie B. Rosser (1867–1968) and Virginia Cabell Randolph (ca. 1879) are illustrative.[10] Rosser worked as a bookkeeper at the North Carolina Mutual Life Insurance Company for years, from 1914 until 1946. In addition, she owned several rental properties, some of them in Durham and others in her hometown of Lynchburg, Virginia. The Lynchburg properties, at least, seem to have been somewhat marginal and constantly in need of repair. Randolph, who lived in Lynchburg, was Rosser's lifelong friend and business partner in the rentals. Rosser depended on Randolph to keep the houses in repair, solicit renters, buy furniture and other items, collect rents, and keep Rosser apprised of what was going on. Randolph, who was a teacher during the first part of the century, did many of the repairs herself: carpentry, brick masonry, paperhanging, plastering, and painting were all within her expertise. A self-described "Jane of all trades," she also bought and sold used furniture and other items for Rosser's rentals as well as for herself. Rosser provided the capital by continuing to earn a decent salary, saving, and loaning out small sums of money to friends at interest. Randolph provided the construction skills, labor, and a knowledge of barter networks to maintain the properties. It was hard to tell where friendship left off and business began.

Some white women took advantage of their political clout as newly enfranchised citizens to try to influence federal and local business policy developments. Virginia E. Jenckes of Indiana was a widow who had inherited sole ownership of the family's 1,000-acre farm and continued to manage it herself. She was so frustrated by low prices and the government's approach to the farm crisis in the late 1920s that she created a local improvement association to deal with floodplain policy and then got herself elected as a Democrat to Congress in 1932. The federal Women's Bureau in the Department of Labor continued throughout the depression to gather and publish information on the conditions of women's labor in a variety of industries. It also pushed for improved wages, working conditions, and opportunities for women in several business fields. President Roosevelt, at the urging of his wife, Eleanor, recruited 28 women to deal with issues related to women. This "women's network" included highly visible and politicized social welfare professionals, such as Mary "Molly" Dewson, who became director of the Women's Division of the Democratic National Committee, and Frances Perkins, who was secretary of labor (the first female cabinet member). These administrators oversaw the reform of working conditions for women and urged governmental oversight on issues such as poverty. Mary McCloud Bethune, appointed to head Negro Affairs at the National Youth Administration, had been a teacher and started her own vocational school, Cookman College, in Florida. She brought her concerns about education for African-Americans into federal policy discussions. These reformers, professionals, and private citizens, acting from both within and outside of government, played a central role in shaping the New Deal and, ultimately, the so-called welfare state.

Other women took less formal avenues to push for change, writing passionate letters to their governmental representatives, volunteering, and joining organizations of business women such as the national BPW.[11] Denied the vote because of race, African-American and Hispanic women formed voluntary organizations, boycotted, or joined in other organizational efforts. In Harlem members of the Young Women's Christian Association led pickets and consumer boycotts of white-owned stores, while others protested discriminatory hiring policies among major department stores in New York City. Jewish women participated in the Hebrew Ladies' Relief Society. Between 1930 and the late 1940s Hispanic and Jewish women cannery workers in Los Angeles led a successful movement to unionize the industry around issues such as hours, safety, and wages. To ensure people would have food and fuel, in 1931 urban and rural women organized an enormous consumer barter network in Seattle. They oversaw an exchange of fruits and vegetables from agricultural eastern Washington for timber and fish from the western part of the state. Women established other similar large-scale barter networks in other states.

The depression was not ended by federal policy pronouncements or legislation but by the mobilization for war. From the late 1930s, as the Allies began purchasing supplies from the United States, American business swiftly recovered. With the advent of war against Japan late in 1941, thousands of men traded their tools for uniforms, swelling the ranks of the armed forces and depleting the ranks of the civilian labor force. Women stepped in to fill the gap for the duration of the war. As with all wars, the shortage of men meant widely expanded business opportunities for women. Business and government welcomed and even recruited them. Wall Street sought out women experienced in higher education, hospital administration, and welfare work to replace male corporate executives called to run government agencies. Banks took on so many women as managers, bookkeepers, and tellers that the industry, which had persisted as a male bastion, became permanently feminized. The media touted women as superlative war workers, as "heroes" of the homefront forces. Some argued that training women to replace men would even provide a permanent reserve labor force, one that could be called on in any future crises.

For many women, the war brought a new awareness of opportunities. Rose Stolowy of Kansas City, Missouri, took advantage of the climate of support for women outside of the home and borrowed money from the bank to open a shop. She was so successful that she brought another woman in as a partner. Other women took advantage of openings in manufacturing and war industries, where they worked in men's jobs for men's wages. Rosie the Riveter became the emblem of women working to further the war effort, and many took jobs for patriotic reasons. Just as many, however, worked for the money. At shipyards and companies such as Lockheed, women welded, riveted, and made ammunition. For the first time in U.S. history, women were formally and officially enlisted in the armed services, not only in sex-typed jobs such as nursing and clerical work but also as auto mechanics and airplane pilots. More than 4,000 black women served in the Women's Army Corps, many of them as officers. Advisory committees and directors were drawn from the ranks of female college presidents, executives, and members of philanthropic boards.

For first-and second-generation Japanese-Americans (Issei and Nisei), the war brought personal and economic devastation. Thousands were uprooted from their homes and businesses and transported to internment camps. On the eve of World War II, Issei owned or leased major agricultural holdings throughout the West and in Hawaii. In 1940 they farmed vegetables on thousands of acres, growing 95 percent of the celery and snap beans produced in California, as well as strawberries, onions, peas, and other fruits and vegetables. Most of these farms were family affairs, with husbands and wives working long hours to develop their fields and market the crops. Women, as was often the case, had a double day: housework and child care along with fieldwork. "I got up at 4:30 A.M. and after preparing breakfast I went to the fields," recalled Yoshiko Ueda. "I went with my husband to do jobs such as picking potatoes and sacking onions. . . . Coming back from the fields, the first thing I had to do was start the fire [to cook dinner]." Kimiko Ono started at 6:30 in the morning preparing breakfast for the family. While her husband took produce to market, she watered and cared for the greenhouse plants, taking their children with her (perhaps to pick bugs off the tender leaves). She and her husband worked in the evenings, and after putting the children to bed she sorted and boxed tomatoes for the next day's market, sometimes not finishing until after midnight.[12]

Federal and army policy dictating internment of all so-called enemy aliens meant that those carefully tended farms and greenhouses were confiscated, sold, and in most cases never recovered by their owners. In Hawaii, very few Issei and their families were interned, probably partly because they were such a large portion of the population and isolated on the islands. To intern them would have severely disrupted the island economy. In California and Washington, on the other hand, local business leaders and Anglo farmers enthusiastically supported internment and confiscation. Many of them owned Issei farms by the war's end.

For some women, business opportunities improved in a variety of areas, not all of them strictly war related. Beauty shops did not get war contracts, but their owners' wages rose nevertheless. Women who could work in factories for good money were not interested in earning less cutting hair. Even the wages of domestic servants doubled because of the difficulty of filling such positions. The demand for food meant that farm and ranch women maintained their importance to family businesses, sometimes taking over management of farms and ranches during the absence of the men at war. One of the most important results of the war for gay and lesbian Americans was the development of gay and lesbian businesses and business communities in major cities. These businesses would provide job and investment opportunities in the postwar 1950s. However, the war devastated small businesses in general, closing many down. Despite the efforts of the Small Business Administration and the enormous growth in some wartime industries, small businesses were hit particularly hard. Especially in markets for clothing, some durable goods such as washing machines and automobiles, and other key products, materials for manufacture were in short supply. In their niche market providing specific services and goods to female consumers, such as garment shops, many women's businesses suffered.

The effects of wartime mobilization spilled over into increased educational opportunities for women in male-dominated professions. As in so many other areas, the shortage of men meant training, hiring, or promotion for women. Harvard Medical School first admitted women in 1944, and more hospitals began taking female interns. Large corporations began hiring women chemists and other scientists, such as Stephanie Kwolek, who became a research chemist at Du Pont in 1946.[13] Female lawyers, teachers, and accountants found positions in local, state, and federal governments and consumer and social services. The private sector hired women in banking and as factory supervisors or matrons dealing with the new influx of women workers in manufacturing. War even provided some unusual federal managerial positions, such as that held by Mabel Thomas. Thomas ran the huge Maluhia Club, one of the army's two recreational facilities on Waikiki in Hawaii. Responsible for finding entertainers, arranging dances, dealing with the army command and sometimes aggressive patrons, Thomas managed as many as 10,000 club visitors a day.

The economic boon of wartime was particularly important to the sex trade industry, which geared up to serve congregations of men often far from home with little to occupy their time while they waited to be shipped out to combat. Honolulu's Hotel Street is an excellent example of the ongoing importance of this often hidden part of the economy. As was true throughout the states and U.S. territories, by 1940 prostitution was illegal in Hawaii. Nonetheless it had existed happily for years, segregated, as also was common, in areas populated by people of color, the poor, or marginalized groups, such as men in military service. During the war, women from the mainland replaced the indigenous madams and prostitutes on the islands. Economic opportunity drew them to Hawaii from Chicago and San Francisco just as it drew Southerners to Detroit and Midwesterners to San Diego for war industry jobs.

Prostitutes' working lives were usually short, riddled with drug and alcohol abuse; venereal disease; and harassment by police, madams, and sometimes customers. In Hawaii, where women typically serviced 100 men a day, about 20 days a month during the war, the working conditions were particularly debilitating. However, for women who could stand the pace, the rewards were enormous: up to $30,000 to $40,000 a year when a well-paid woman in a regular job could expect to earn

$2,000. Even with the fixed expenses of tips to maids, percentages to madams, laundry, board, and medical examinations (and, for some, opium and morphine), prostitutes could make enough to retire from the trade. Madams could clear more than $150,000 a year. In 1943 one madam voluntarily paid taxes on a $383,000 income. Best estimates are that Hotel Street brothels took in more than $10 million every year between 1941 and 1945.

Far from a fringe industry, the sex trade was fully integrated into the island economy. The revenues from prostitution essentially replaced those from tourism, which was suspended for the duration of the war. Respectable mainstream merchants loaned start-up money for brothels, and the police department took its cut of the proceeds. The military supported the growth of prostitution on the theory that it would keep the soldiers, sailors, and marines happy, out of trouble, and "manly" (a euphemism for concern about homosexual activity). Military authorities tried only to regulate the medical side, in an effort to curb the incidence of venereal disease that accompanied the sped-up pace of the business. The sex trade ensured that the thousands of military dollars that flowed into Hawaii during the war would be recirculated within the local economy. Women who worked as maids in the brothels (who were usually Chinese, Hawaiian, Portuguese, Filipina, Japanese, or of mixed racial ancestry) made more money than they ever had in their lives. Local street vendors, many of them Asian-American women since Hotel Street was in Chinatown, sold food, souvenirs, and other goods to the servicemen waiting in line (sometimes for as long as two hours) for their turn. Saloons, tattoo parlors, restaurants, and barber shops all took their cut of the largesse. Wealthy madams invested in local real estate, restaurants, stores, and commercial property. The boom times ended only when the governor ordered the houses closed in 1944. The military quietly acquiesced, perhaps in part because the advent of penicillin made less imperative the need for regulation for military purposes and by then the war appeared close to its end.

Although Hawaii is a particularly extravagant example of the impact of war on vice-related businesses, it is representative of the effect of the military presence on a local economy. Near every town where a military base was located, prostitution, gambling, and liquor were the order of the day, the revenues lining the pockets of local merchants—and often city officials. For the duration of the war, the sex and vice trades blossomed even as they remained physically segregated in red-

light districts. The postwar reaction returned these trades once more
to invisibility and fringe status. The end of the war did not, however,
mean the end of prostitution and its related vice businesses. Nevada,
in fact, became the national postwar vice center in the neon glow of
Las Vegas's casinos.

The war made particularly vivid a long-term dilemma and problem
for working mothers: what to do about child care and household
responsibilities. Women who worked or ran businesses outside of the
home have always been under the pressures of the "double day":
when paid labor is done, domestic labor remains. The war made conditions particularly bad. For example, relying on kin or stable neighborhoods to find a pool of child care providers became more difficult
as women and men migrated for war work. After putting in a six-day
work week, some women found they had little time left to do the laundry, cleaning, and shopping. Since most businesses closed early in the
evening, women often did not get off work in time to buy groceries—
when there was anything worth buying. Rationing of various staples,
such as sugar and flour, made routine cooking more difficult. The federal government seemed insensitive to these issues, spending several
years "studying" the problem and finally near the end of the war instituting a program for child care. Since the facilities were few and far
between, open short hours, and staffed by inexperienced people, most
women could not or would not take advantage of them.

These problems were especially acute during the war but were not
unique to it. In 1954 one working mother observed, "Working denies
me the privilege of being a good housewife and, shall we say, a more
patient mother."[14] In 1960, for the first time, a national conference
addressed the issue of child care for working mothers, and the
Department of Labor's Women's Bureau published a major study of
the subject in 1953, spurred in part by the remobilization that
occurred during the Korean War. The long-term trend in married
women's labor has meant the increasing need to address the problem
of the double day.[15]

The ultimate impact of the war on women's business opportunities
and experiences was mixed. On the one hand, it surely accelerated the
long-term trend toward women's paid employment, and many women
came away with a new sense of their own capabilities. Some business
and civic leaders continued to argue for maintaining women in business as a reserve army and even strengthening their ability to be self-
supporting and to contribute to the national economy. The outbreak of

hostilities in Korea in 1950 reinforced these arguments. In New York the governor created a Women's Council, within the Department of Commerce, whose task was to aid women displaced by returning veterans to set up small businesses. This approach would not only reestablish the thousands of small businesses lost during the war but also allow women to continue to contribute to the economy of the state. National magazines, such as *Reader's Digest*, praised the program, urging other states to follow New York's lead.

On the other hand, if anything, World War II and the Korean conflict strengthened many people's desire for domesticity. The New York Woman's Council, for example, sought its goals by advocating home-based entrepreneurship: producing food and knit goods or running a gift shop. A 1945 Gallup Poll found that only 16 percent of men and 20 percent of women believed that married women should work outside of the home. In the automobile industry, women went from 25 percent of the workforce in 1945 to 9.5 percent in 1946. The National Woman's Party renewed its lobbying efforts for an equal rights amendment, hoping World War II would do for the ERA what World War I had done for suffrage. The Senate approved the amendment in 1946, but it was defeated in the House. As we have seen, even the passage of a federal equal pay act was shrouded in rhetoric about women workers who would consume more goods and be more content in their gender-defined place if they had higher wages.

It was also true, however, that the majority of women themselves wanted domesticity. Recent discussions about career women in their late 30s sometimes focus on their sense that they are running out of time to start a family. The biological clock that signals the end of childbearing years seems a contemporary problem. But what now seems a phenomenon for affluent career women affected an entire generation between the two world wars. Young women born between 1915 and 1925 came of age in depression and war. Many believed they would never have the chance at a family of their own. War's end brought peace and prosperity but also new insecurities with the specter of nuclear weapons and the cold war. Helen Fritchie (b. 1918) is a representative example.[16] She was among the oldest of eight children in a Southern farm family. From the time she was 10, in 1928, she worked summers for wages in a candy factory, did telephone solicitation, and provided occasional care for a homebound polio victim. The wages went to family maintenance. During the rest of the year she helped on the farm, planting, hoeing, picking vegetables, and watching out for her younger brothers and sisters. After high school she worked in a professional laundry and as a clerk in an automobile parts store. She proudly became an auto mechanic and driver in the Women's Army Corps in 1943. But she wanted nothing more than to settle down in 1946 with her new husband and raise children. After her marriage, she worked for a couple of years so they could save enough money for a down payment on a house. The down payment, her retreat from wage labor, and the first baby came in the same year. After surviving the depression and the war, Helen Fritchie welcomed the chance for domesticity.

The prosperity of the early 1950s meant staying home was possible for many, mostly white, women. By the early 1960s the nation had experienced economic boom times that raised the standard of living for more people than ever before. In 1940 33 percent of Americans lived in poverty. By 1960 21 percent did so, and the number kept going down. In the years after the war, consumer spending went up 60 percent, most of that on household furnishings, appliances, recreation, and automobiles. Home ownership also rose, from about 45 percent of Americans in 1945 to 62 percent in 1960. The Serviceman's Readjustment Act of 1944 (the GI Bill of Rights) made college a possibility for an entire generation. Veterans (3 percent of whom were women) swelled the nation's college classrooms to bursting by 1950. The return to the status quo and domesticity after the war did not shut women out of business—quite the contrary. Although research on women's postwar business history is just beginning, the evidence so far suggests a vital, if somewhat traditional, role for women in business after the war.

Information about female entrepreneurs and women in business generally before the 1980s is notoriously difficult to find. That makes the activities of the BPW especially useful. By 1954 the BPW had almost 3,000 affiliated local clubs located in small towns and big cities all across the country. Those numbers continued to grow throughout the 1960s. The mother organization added a new dimension, acting as a consultant to the United Nations on international women's issues such as family and property law, political rights, and educational and business opportunities. In 1957 and 1958 it lobbied Congress on a variety of issues related to women, including enlisting support for federal employment opportunities commensurate with those of men, a federal equal pay law, "uniform retirement age and benefit provisions for men and women under the Social Security Act," and "removal of and prevention of discrimination on the basis of age, sex, or marital status in both government and industry."[17] This was a fairly sweeping agenda for change in national law and policy. The BPW, in other words, remained an important political and economic organization at the grass-roots, national, and international levels. Businesswomen were clearly organized and aware of their political and economic importance, and the BPW was their premier organization.

In 1952 the BPW surveyed its 160,000 members. Eleven percent (17,561) responded to a series of questions designed to elicit information on wages, investments, demographics, political activism, and a range of other subjects related to businesswomen. Although a statistically small and clearly self-selected sample, the survey used federal census categories that enabled the compilers to make comparisons with national figures.[18] The general outlines of the survey also dovetailed with one conducted in 1950 by the Women's Bureau of the Department of Labor. The results of the BPW questionnaire reveal the outlines of women's business experience at midcentury. The federal census of 1950 classified about half of the women in the labor force as business and professional women: 64.4 percent were in clerical or sales positions, 23.2 percent were in professional and semiprofessional positions, and 9.4 percent were "proprietors, managers, or officials of business." BPW respondents were weighted more heavily in the professional or semiprofessional category (38.6 percent) but were fairly representative of the other two categories. Survey respondents also tended to be older than the general female labor population (61 versus 27 percent were over the age of 45) and more likely than the general female labor force to be never married, widowed, or divorced (67 percent as opposed to 45 percent). They also were better educated. But some patterns coincided with national ones. Women with more education, living in large cities, employed in government service or education, or self-employed as business owners (if single) earned more than other women in comparable positions. Although slightly skewed to an older and perhaps more activist population of women in business, the survey suggests some general trends for businesswomen.

Respondents to the survey overwhelmingly worked to support themselves or dependents, whether they were engaged as professionals, clerical workers, or entrepreneurs. Women who earned between $4,000 and $10,000 per year (in the middle of the range), whether single, married, or widowed, contributed the most to their families' incomes. Like male breadwinners, many also found satisfaction in their work beyond their earnings. The largest number of respondents clustered as secretaries, stenographers, typists, teachers, nurses, and social workers. However, there were also a substantial number of proprietors, managers, and "officials" in real estate, food service, government, beauty shops, mortuaries, finance (banking, insurance, and stockbrokering), publishing, bookkeeping, and sales. Federal census returns registered an increase in the number of nonagricultural "proprietors, managers, and officials" between 1940 and 1950. After hovering around 1.5 percent of all workers in this group in 1910, by 1940 the figure reached 3.5 percent. Then World War II caused a tremendous spurt to about 13 percent. By 1950 women made up about 15 percent of all people in these categories.

According to a Women's Bureau survey in 1950 of several types of concerns in four U.S. cities, management saw very different reasons for the difficulties women faced in achieving promotion into management or advancement once in the managerial ranks. When asked "What factors deter the advancement of women in your type of business?" the majority of those in department stores cited family responsibilities. In insurance it was a close race between "traditional attitudes of management" and "lack of permanency." In banking the main reason given was management's attitudes. In manufacturing a lack of business or technical knowledge, management's attitudes, and a perceived lack of interest in advancement on women's part topped the list. When it came to factors that encouraged women's advancement, three stood out in managers' minds. They cited the number of women employed in an industry, a female customer base, and the vague "suitability of women for this type of business."[19] Women workers and managers in these industries, when asked the same questions, gave essentially the same answers. Business wisdom in the early 1950s, in other words, reflected the long-standing profile of women's development in management. An emphasis on sex-typed jobs and clientele, the development of feminized managerial slots, and the perception that the claims of family and domesticity shaped women's paid work all continued to govern women's managerial role.

Information in the BPW survey on female entrepreneurs, always the most difficult to find, revealed that the two largest categories of business ownership were nonspecified retail (32.5 percent) and personal service establishments (11.2 percent) (table 4). Real estate; insurance, finance, and educational institutions (taken together) made up an additional 20.8 percent. Most of these businesses (45 percent) employed fewer than five people, and 66 percent employed between 1 and 24 people. The largest percentage of women in all categories (single, married, widowed, divorced, and separated) reported incomes from their businesses of between $2,000 and $5,000, with most of those in personal service establishments (57 percent) earning less than $3,000. In general, single women (never married, divorced, widowed, or separated) who owned their own businesses earned more than married women, but married women more often than single women owned their own businesses. This difference may stem, in

TABLE 4

Woman-Owned Businesses, by Type and Percentage
of Total Respondents to 1954 BPW Survey

Type of Business	Percentage
Retail businesses (otherwise unspecified)	32.5
Personal service	11.2
Real estate, insurance, or finance	10.7
Educational institutions	10.1
Hotels or restaurants	5.7
Sales organizations	5.3
Printing, publishing, advertising, editorial, radio, or the like	3.8
Manufacturing or construction	3.3
Farm or nursery	3.0
Professional or semiprofessional (otherwise unspecified)	3.0
Medical practice or organization	2.5
Legal practice or organization	2.0
Interior decorating, photographic studio, or art studio	1.8
Wholesale business (otherwise unspecified)	1.7
Accounting or statistical organization	1.7
Transportation or public utility	0.9
Dressmaking or millinery establishment	0.5
Library	0.3

Source: Adapted from appendix table 21, Babette Kass and Rose C. Feld, *The Economic Strength of Business and Professional Women* (New York: National Federation of Business and Professional Women's Clubs, 1954), 115.

part, from the fact that many of the married women who responded lived in smaller communities with correspondingly smaller businesses in terms of inventory, capital, and market. The clustering of women's businesses in these areas and the incidence of income and family status affirm that long-standing patterns of female entrepreneurship still held sway in the mid-twentieth century.

Elva M. Chandler (1900–1990) is an instructive example of someone whose career spanned the years between 1930 and the early 1960s and who fits the profile of the businesswoman visible in the BPW survey.[20] Chandler attended Goldey College in Wilmington, Delaware, a business school for secretaries and bookkeepers, sometime in the mid to late 1920s. Her first major job, as a secretary with the Pigments Department of Du Pont Chemical Company in the early 1930s, involved her in international correspondence, tariff issues, and federal regulations. By the late 1930s she was working for the Delaware Trust Company in Wilmington. Chandler was active in national and local organizations, including the Wilmington BPW and the American Institute of Banking.

But such involvements did not exhaust her business activities. Chandler's waged work coexisted with entrepreneurship. From at least the 1950s, when she would have been in her 50s, Elva owned and managed a series of local businesses. Between about 1956 and 1969 she owned a general store in Mount Cuba, Delaware, that sold gasoline, automobile supplies, and food items such as ice cream, milk, and baked goods. Tax records indicate that she employed at least one person to run the store. She also had an apparently short-lived gift shop in Wilmington. In addition, she belonged to a local stock investment club and, according to property tax records, owned at least five lots, some with rental houses, in the Wilmington area. She may, in fact, have been somewhat overextended. When she turned 65, Delaware Trust exercised mandatory retirement. Chandler did not welcome being forced out and asked, unsuccessfully, to be considered for part-time work in the company. Despite an annual income of more than $9,000 in 1974 (a respectable sum for the time), she was billed for delinquent taxes on her rental properties in 1970; some of the taxes dated back to the mid-1950s. She had suffered from unspecified economic troubles in those years, which clearly left her struggling well into the early 1970s. Nonetheless, by the mid-1970s she was driving a one-year-old automobile, had paid her taxes, and appeared to have recovered financially. Her rental properties and the general store had kept her afloat.

Chandler clearly was an ambitious businesswoman, not confining her economic activities to earning a corporate salary. She invested her salary in stocks and real estate, actively pursuing involvement in professional organizations that continued even after her official "retirement." As a lifelong single woman, she had control over her own business decisions. She also had to rely on herself for her material well-being. Chandler was well enough connected locally that when another woman started up a business in 1982, the Woman's Center at the University of Delaware referred her to Chandler for help in publicizing the shop among the local businesswomen's community.

Women, Business, and Long-Term Trends

Women's work in the corporate world remained closely connected to traditional women's roles of helpmate, mother, caregiver, and domestic manager. By the 1950s women's relationship to corporations was threefold. First, as clerical workers women continued to dominate the lower echelons of business: in 1968 women filled 68 percent of all clerical positions, the only occupational category in which women predominated. Second, some women continued as managers or professionals, especially in "women's professions" such as social work, some areas of banking, and other clerical industries (such as personnel) that were sex-typed as female. Third, as wives of corporate executives, whose increasing importance was emphasized in films, novels, and advertising throughout the period, women provided unpaid labor and cultivated social networks crucial to promotions. First studied by William H. Whyte Jr. in the 1950s, the role of wives of corporate executives and managers constituted what one sociologist termed "the two-person single career," much like that expected in the military.[21]

The postwar return to traditional feminine images and expectations of women had a detrimental impact on women's participation in some professions, particularly medicine and academia. In 1929 women made up 12 percent of all medical school graduates. By 1955 that figure had dropped to only 5 percent—less than in the first year of World War II. Women's representation on college and university faculties went from an all-time high of 27.7 percent in 1940 to 22 percent by 1960. However, here again, although the percentage of women in relation to the total number of professionals decreased quite precipitously, the absolute number of women who completed undergraduate and graduate degrees increased, even as the female student population became more ethnically and racially diverse.

Women continued to use older economic forms, such as barter. Particularly in rural areas and among the poor, trading goods and services remained a viable economic activity. But many services traditionally provided by the family or through exchange networks began to slip into the marketplace during this period. Child care is a useful example. During World War II many women with children traded child care duties with other women or relied on family members to care for the children so that the mothers could work. The mobility of the wartime population meant that family members often were no longer available to provide this service. The government responded, somewhat feebly, by offering some day-care facilities. By and large, however, they were either too inaccessible to be useful or women rejected them in principle, preferring their own arrangements. Neighborhood networks traded child care tasks, and some women operated localized, informal day-care services. Since the early 1970s, with the growth of married women's labor force participation, child care has been commodified and subject to licensing requirements like any other business. It has become yet another female-dominated business niche. It remains difficult, however, for many women in part-time or underpaid jobs to afford commercial day care. The problem of the double day persists as well.

As the BPW survey and census reports suggest, women continued as small-scale entrepreneurs. They owned beauty shops, grocery and clothing stores, catering and decorating businesses, or boarding-houses or simply took in laundry or worked as domestics in private homes. The continuing overall decline in small-business funding and markets made this traditional form of female entrepreneurship more difficult to negotiate. The ongoing gendered segregation of small business, as with employment opportunities, meant certain types of businesses remained essentially reserved for women. Women also continued as members of family or spousal partnerships. Betty Leavitt, of Kansas City, Missouri, kept the books and did the advertising for her family's business. Other women worked behind the counter in neighborhood mom-and-pop stores. Victorine and Samuel Homsey built up a large and successful architectural firm in Delaware that took on jobs ranging from private homes to office buildings and schools. In 1956 they produced the winning design for the new American embassy building in Tehran, a daunting project involving reams of red tape, federal forms, and international contracting. Victorine did the books and the interior decorating; Samuel did the architecture. Like many women in business, Victorine was a member of professional and voluntary organizations, in her case the National Trust and Advisory Board for the American Historical Building Survey. Women also engaged in speculative business ventures, not always successfully. Guyencourt Nurseries, Inc., in existence from 1929 to 1939, incorporated to experiment with a growing method for hybrid rhododendrons. Mary Phelps, chair of the board of directors, contributed funds and took stock in the company as collateral. The principals hoped, in vain as it turned out, to capitalize on the market for rare plants.[22]

An important shift in women's participation in farming and ranching came during World War II. In fact, the years during and after the war probably represented the most profound transformation in family farming and ranching since the invention of the steel plow. The federal census of 1920 documented the end of rural dominance in the United States. In that year, for the first time, more than half of the population lived in urban areas. But farming and ranching remained vital family businesses despite the encroachments of agribusiness.

Two things in particular affected women's economic role on family farms. First, changing technologies (such as the rural electrification movement of the 1930s and 1940s) had an impact. Tractors became an increasingly important piece of farm equipment after 1930, as farm families purchased these machines to make large-scale field labor easier and more efficient. Although clearly designed to aid in the production of cash crops, and thus focused on the male half of the farm family economy, tractors encouraged important changes for women as well. Sociologists of rural life estimate that before the introduction of tractors, 25 percent of the expenditures for hired farm labor (which in some areas accounted for as much as 79 percent of all farm workers) came "in kind" directly from women's work: caring for hired hands' clothing (washing, sewing, and mending), cooking meals, and cleaning quarters. The other 75 percent of expenditures were cash wages. By reducing the need for hired labor, tractors reduced women's in-kind labor caring for hired hands, even as they encouraged farm families to use more of women's labor in the field. In addition, many women used the tractor engine and belt to run a variety of other machinery—for grinding and shelling corn or pumping water. Tractors shifted women's economic contribution to the family economy.

Second, the swings in agricultural markets—from the good markets after World War I through the depression of the late 1920s and 1930s and then the boom years of World War II—contributed to a shrinking farm population. As technologies replaced hired hands, women were more often called upon to fill in as field workers. Large-scale corporate farming and particularly the consolidation of the egg and poultry industry took over markets from this traditional women's area. Mass-produced goods became less expensive. Canned and fresh vegetables grown by giant corporations replaced women's labor in truck and vegetable gardens. During the years immediately after the war when farm prices once again began to drop and the pressures of large-scale corporate farming marginalized family farms and ranches, farm women began to search outside of the farm itself for wage work. Joining the many married women in the labor force of the late 1940s and 1950s, farm women's economic contribution to the family partnership shifted from in-kind labor to the provision of supplemental wages. The result was that farm and ranch women increasingly began to resemble their urban sisters. They commuted to work for wages to supplement the family income rather than contributing labor and skills directly to the family enterprise.

The growth of consumption after World War II also meant the growth in leisure activities for most Americans. Women were figures in the developing leisure industry and helped open up these areas to female and male entrepreneurs. Georgie White Clark, first drawn to the natural beauty of the Grand Canyon area in the early 1940s when she rode the Colorado River through the gorge in a life preserver, started a river rafting company in the early 1950s that was still running the rapids in 1990. Other areas of leisure consumption with long-term importance to career-minded women were professional sports and entertainment, which continued to afford opportunities.

In sports women such as golfer Mildred "Babe" Didrikson Zaharias (1914–56) and figure-skater (and actor) Sonja Henie (1912–69) successfully marketed themselves as professional athletes. Between 1930 and the 1950s Didrikson parlayed her exceptional athletic talents— she won three track and field medals at the 1932 Los Angeles Olympics—into a career as a professional golfer. Semiprofessional women's baseball appeared in the late 1930s, with teams such as Chicago's Rockola Chicks attracting large crowds. In 1942 chewing-gum magnate Philip K. Wrigley started the All-American Girls Baseball League. Operating between 1942 and 1954, at its peak the league had teams in 10 cities and more than a million fans. Althea Gibson (b.

1927), a self-described "Harlem street rebel," began her professional tennis career in the early 1940s and became the first African-American international competitor in professional tennis. She won the national championship in both singles and doubles at Forest Hills in 1957 and went on to win at Wimbledon in both events the following year. Because professional tennis did not yet provide a hefty income, Gibson retired at the age of 30 to pursue careers in acting, singing, and, in the mid-1960s, professional golfing.

Women in sports faced many of the same problems as women in other types of business ventures. In addition, professional female athletes had to "prove" their femininity by marrying and wearing nail polish, curls, and dresses. Gibson's professional career was stymied for years by racist attitudes that prevented her from playing in professional matches. None of these sports paid big dividends in the early years. Nonetheless, athletes such as Didrikson and Gibson paved the way for a generation of exceptional sportswomen including Billy Jean King and Martina Navratilova. In fact, it was King who, in 1970, became the first professional woman tennis player to earn more than $100,000 a year. (No surprise, the top male winner that year, Rod Laver, took in almost three times that much while winning only a third as many tournaments.)

In entertainment the powerful women stars of the 1920s who had used the star system, their popularity, and the existence of competing companies to gain leverage for scripts, parts, or productions gave way in the 1930s to increasing industry centralization and consolidation because of the introduction of sound technology (see chapter 4). During the 1940s some powerful female stars of the 1930s such as Joan Crawford retained their leverage. But not until the appearance of Lucille Ball in her own television productions of the 1950s would women again operate as entrepreneurs in Hollywood. Ball was able to control and produce her own television shows because the medium in the 1950s was where movies were in the 1920s. As an infant industry with new technologies and markets, there were no set rules for organization and no body of individuals already employed.

However, a surprising number of women remained as producers, scriptwriters, and film editors into the 1950s. Screenwriters Isobel Lennart (1915–71) and Betty Comden (1919) were among the better known. Lennart's most popular work in this period included *Please Don't Eat the Daisies* (1960) and *The Sundowners* (1960), although her first film was produced in 1942 and she worked steadily between that

year and 1968. Comden shared screen credits with her writing partner, Adolph Green, between 1947 and 1964, including such films as
Singin' in the Rain (1952) and *Auntie Mame* (1958). Comden also
wrote scripts and lyrics for the theater and that new medium, television. The real survivor, however, was humorist, screenwriter, and playwright Anita Loos (1893–1981). Loos wrote her first motion picture in
1912 and her last in 1942, and she continued to write and edit plays
into the 1970s. Her screen credits include such diverse films as D. W.
Griffith's *Intolerance* (1916) and *Gentlemen Prefer Blondes*, adapted
from her 1928 play. Other women made a place for themselves in the
managerial aspect of the industry. Virginia Van Upp (1902–70) became
executive producer for Columbia Pictures in 1945, the only woman to
hold such a position until 1975, when Marcia Nasatir became vice
president of production at United Artists.[23] Van Upp, who began her
industry career as a child actress just before World War I, became a
writer, actors' agent, and producer. She worked continuously for 30
years, with a short break to give birth to her daughter. Van Upp's production and authorial résumé included a fair number of female characters who were businesswomen or politicians or possessed a self-aware
and independent sexuality.

As we have seen with prostitution since the late nineteenth century,
women sometimes have provided services that society defined as illegal even as the market for those services kept demand high. Although
not in the same business category as prostitution, we can see this pattern at work among abortion providers, for whom this period also
brought important changes. The usual image of the back-alley abortionist before the legalization of abortion in 1973 is of a dirty, untrained
opportunist, or perhaps an alcoholic physician down on his luck who
carelessly butchered young women for profit. This type of abortionist
no doubt existed, and illegal abortions certainly were dangerous.
However, some abortionists ran antiseptic clinics under the watchful
eye of pragmatic law enforcement officials and physicians who realized that since women *would* seek abortions, someone who provided
them safely at a reasonable price was better than the alternative.
Although women had surrendered most of their duties as midwives to
male physicians by the early twentieth century, many still trained or
apprenticed as nurse midwives. Some learned and specialized in the
abortion trade. Throughout the United States, clinics providing illegal
abortions on demand flourished in the years before World War II. One
of the best-known abortion providers was a woman who earned her

fame during the years after the war when local communities clamped down on illegal providers. Ruth Barnett's clinic in Portland, Oregon, offered safe, efficient, and affordable abortion services for 50 years.

Between 1918 and 1968 Barnett estimated that she performed more than 40,000 abortions, never losing a client. She charged what she thought a person could pay and treated incest and rape victims and inexperienced teenagers with the same professional expertise. At the peak of her practice, Barnett was one of the wealthiest women in Portland. The queen of the city's demimonde, she entertained in her home underworld figures such as pimps, gamblers, and madams but also politicians, police officials, and newspapermen. However, by the mid-1950s, such clinics had begun to close down under pressure from the medical establishment, which had been scalded in the press for its collusion with abortionists. Local communities also became concerned with cleaning up all kinds of so-called vice in the conservative backlash after the liberalities of wartime. After a highly publicized trial, Barnett "retired" in 1953. Given the market demand, however, she continued to perform abortions, in her home rather than in a clinic, and in a shadowed world of secrets, passwords, and nighttime darkness, into the mid-1960s.

Ethnicity and racism continued to circumscribe opportunities for some Americans. As small-scale agriculture increasingly gave way to large-scale agribusiness, the needs of American agriculture for labor and the output of small farms shrank. The end of the sharecropping system by the late 1940s turned black tenant farmers into hired hands. Black women continued to work as field laborers in Southern agriculture until the mid-1950s, when the mechanical cotton picker and other new technologies rendered even this type of work nearly obsolete. Increasingly concentrated in cities by the early 1960s, black women found traditional work as domestics disappearing and few jobs opening up to take their place. Some continued to take in laundry or opened small neighborhood shops. But increasing numbers of black female-headed households slipped into poverty, existing on the fringes of the vaunted prosperity and feverish consumption of the 1950s and 1960s.

Black organizations at the local and national level, such as the National Association for the Advancement of Colored People (NAACP) and the Congress of Racial Equality, used consumer boycotts to protest segregation, refusing to ride city buses or patronize white stores. Black women who were professional beauticians and beauty shop owners used their identity as entrepreneurs to support race issues in their communities. Black-owned businesses, such as North Carolina Mutual Life Insurance Company in Durham, North Carolina, continued to provide jobs and financing for businesses within black communities in places such as Kansas City, Detroit, and Chicago.

Similar patterns held for other ethnic groups. For Asian-Americans integration also remained elusive, even as local communities provided job opportunities for their own. One Nisei high school student in California observed in the 1940s that "After I graduate, what can I do here? No American firm will employ me. All I can hope to become here is a bookkeeper in one of the little Japanese dry goods stores in the Little Tokyo section of Los Angeles, or else be a stenographer to the Japanese lawyer here."[24] As this quote suggests, ethnic segregation created both ambivalence and opportunity, depending on one's perspective. Dorothy C. Gee started out as a bank teller and in 1932 became manager of the Chinatown branch of Bank of America in San Francisco. The percentage of Hispanic women in clerical and sales positions increased from 13.6 percent in 1930 to 23.7 percent in 1950. In African-American banks, women were more likely than men to be bookkeepers by the 1930s; all positions in white banks remained male dominated until World War II. Employment in, or the creation of, ethnic businesses, in other words, remained an option so long as ethnic and racial segregation were in force.

Conclusion

The years of the mid-twentieth century essentially marked time for women in business, riding out the storms of economic and diplomatic collapse while witnessing incremental change in the number of women workers, managers, and entrepreneurs. World War II sped up some transitions already in process in 1900, such as the increase in married women workers, but it did not revolutionize women's economic role. Throughout midcentury, women such as Estée Lauder and Fanny Stahl found business opportunities in sex-typed industries and positions and built successful ventures on kitchen recipes or by asserting a public place for domesticity through careers in the helping professions or home economics. Others sought economic viability as domestics, laundresses, and boardinghouse owners. None of these efforts marked radical departures from the situation of the previous 100 years.

But in the crises of war and economic depression, holding one's own may have been as crucial as breaking new ground. By the 1950s popular discussions, the business community, and the federal government had all publicly recognized the economic and social importance of businesswomen. The next 30 years would build on these long-term trends, reinforcing some aspects of women's business involvement but also supporting what appeared to be stunning new departures from the status quo.

Chapter Six

Difference at Work: The Renewal of the Businesswoman, 1963–2000

Executive women have to thread the eye of the needle. You have to be feminine but not too feminine. Aggressive but not too aggressive. High on initiative but still a team player. Men can have quirks that women can't have.
                              —Dee Soder, Executive Consultant, 1995

"Hanging our own names on the door was the moment of truth," [said] the mother of a three-year-old girl and an infant daughter.
                              —On Women as Venture Capitalists, 1996

Open almost any newspaper or pick up any magazine addressed to a business audience in the 1990s and you will find an article dealing with women in business. The general message they convey is that women's business involvement is an unprecedented development. Articles focus on either women as employees, managers, entrepreneurs, or chief executive officers (CEOs) or general issues relating to women in the business world, including salaries and wages, opportunities, and gender stereotyping. Some detail the global scope of women's business involvement and its financial impact on international trade, business practices, and corporate earnings.[1] Popular magazines such as *Working Mother* and *Working Woman* appeal to an audience of businesswomen. World Wide Web pages about women in business cover directories of female-owned businesses, networks, and organizations. In fact, there has been an explosion of local and national organizations, foundations, and research groups focused on businesswomen, such as the National Foundation for Women Business Owners (NFWBO), the National Association for Female Executives, and the National Association of Working Women (9 to 5). Beyond the popular press, scholars in business and women's history are increasingly interested in questions surrounding women's business role. In other words, women in business has been among the hottest topics of the 1990s. Given the history outlined in previous chapters, perhaps this sudden interest should not be surprising. But what appeared on the surface to be a revolution, on closer inspection seems more like a revival.

Take Dawn Steel (1946–97), who in 1986 became the first woman to head a major Hollywood movie studio, Columbia Pictures. Steel had impeccable credentials, having been a prominent film producer for Paramount Studios. She was widely admired by other producers, as well as by other women in the business. Former screenwriter Nora Ephron credited Steel for encouraging her to become a director, and many actors found her a supportive and skillful producer. Several of her spectacularly successful film projects at Paramount (among them *Flashdance, Top Gun*, and *Fatal Attraction*) brought her to the attention of Columbia executives.

But accusations and dissatisfactions also dogged her career. Some colleagues described her as a "witch," "famous for her big hair and short temper," impossible to work for, a superior who verbally abused secretaries, and an executive who "set back the cause for women in [the film] business. She was everything men wanted to believe that women who have power become." Called "The Queen of Mean" and "Hell on Heels," Steel made so many enemies in Hollywood that when she was pushed out of Columbia in 1991 the sound of rejoicing was rumored to have been heard for miles. "I was angry about this whole notion of trying to be a man," she observed in 1993. "I was exhausted from it. The hostility was extraordinary. It became a sort of feeding frenzy about 'how much we can hate Dawn Steel.' All of those people who hated me had never met me! They hated me on *spec!*"

Steel's management style had its limitations, and she acknowledged that she sometimes misdirected her anger. However, "there were times when people fucked up and I got angry. Period. I had to turn a company around. I had a job to do. If you weren't competent, you were gone." In an industry known for its backbiting, volatility, and intensity, Steel's behavior was little different from that of countless male CEOs, producers, and studio chairmen. The difference was that Steel was a woman approaching a male-defined job in the way a man might have done. Although there were shortcomings in Steel's managerial behavior, what is instructive is that her detractors chose to focus their ire on things that identified her as a woman: her clothing and shoes, her hairstyle, and the notion of women as emotionally out of control. As one supporter within the industry commented, "This is basic Hollywood sexism. She gets a bum rap because she had a terrible temper. Well, all these people bluff their way in on nerve and temperament."[2]

Steel's case recalls one of the continuing paradoxes we have seen in the history of women and business. Admitted as a peer with men into male-defined positions, particularly after 1880, women found that expectations about their difference were as important as their skills. This perspective became even more clear after 1963 as women like Steel increasingly made inroads into the workforce and into areas previously seen as the province of men. To be sure, not all of these changes led to the sorts of personal antagonism Steel experienced. But as women increased their representation in the professions, as managers and executives, entrepreneurs, and workers, debates over women's place in business grew more urgent and politically charged.

One major reason for the intense and sometimes bitter debates after 1963 resulted because there were simply more women in business. Continuing the long-term trend first seen in the late nineteenth century, women as managers, entrepreneurs, professionals, and workers had become a powerful economic force by the 1990s. Census reports and surveys chart the increasing presence of women and minorities as master of business administration (MBA) degree recipients, managers, and entrepreneurs of small businesses. For example, between 1985 and 2000, women earned 31 percent of all MBAs, up from an all-time high of only about 6 percent in 1977. Women went from making up 5.0 percent of all wage and salary executives, administrators, and managers in 1974 to 12.4 percent in 1994. As table 5 shows, women's share of the legal, medical, and dental professions increased between 1900 and 2000, and most of that growth came after 1975. Census figures document the continuation of the long-term trend in the expansion of the female labor force and in the percentage of married women working outside of the family home (table 3, p. 135).

In the entrepreneurial arena, between 1972 and 2000 the percent-

TABLE 5

Percentage of Women in Selected Professions

Profession	1900	1980	1999
Attorneys	0.9	12	28.8
Dentists	2.7	10	16.5
Physicians	5.6	20	24.5

Source: Adapted from table XLIV, Bureau of the Census, *Special Reports: Occupations at the 12th Census* (Washington, D.C.: U.S. Government Printing Office, 1904), cxxv–cxxvii; table 2–4, Cynthia Costello and Barbara Krimgold, eds., *The American Woman, 1996–97: Where We Stand, Women and Work* (New York, W. W. Norton, 1996), 279; and Department of Commerce, Bureau of the Census, "Table 669, Employed Civilians by Occupation, Sex, Race, and Hispanic Origin 1983 and 1999," *Statistical Abstract of the U.S.: 2000* (Washington, D.C.: U.S. Government Printing Office, 2000), p. 416.

TABLE 6

Women-Owned Firms as a Percentage of All Businesses by Industry, 1972, 1982, and 1994[a]

Industry	1972	1982	1994
Construction	1.5	5.7	10.8
Manufacturing	1.8	15.8	6.1
Transportation, public utilities	1.6	8.1	3.5
Wholesale and retail trade	6.5	26.6	30.0
Finance, insurance, real estate	2.8	15.5	8.6
Services	6.8	29.7	36.8
Other	12.2	17.2	4.2
Total, all industries	4.6	23.9	34.0

[a]Adapted from U.S. Department of Commerce, Bureau of the Census, *Women-Owned Businesses, 1972*, May 1980, Table A; Cynthia M. Taeuber, ed., *Statistical Handbook on Women in America*, 1985, Table B5–15, p. 140; and National Foundation for Women Business Owners, *Women-Owned Businesses: Breaking the Boundaries, The Progress and Achievement of Women-Owned Enterprises*, Table 4 (The Organization, 1995), p. 43.

age of all U.S. firms owned by women increased from 4.6 to 34 percent (table 6). By 1994 there were 7.7 million women-owned businesses, employing 15.5 million people, with revenues of nearly $1.4 trillion, and women owned 72 percent of all service and retail firms. Further, women-owned business was an economically dynamic development; it was the fastest-growing entrepreneurial segment, with revenues growing twice as fast as those of all U.S. companies. The employment growth rate among women-owned firms exceeded the national average between 1991 and 1994: 11.6 percent compared with the national employment rate of 5.3 percent. Women-owned firms employed

TABLE 7

Percentage of Women Employed in Managerial, Executive, and Professional Positions

Occupation	1900	1974	1986	1996
Total managerial, executive, administrative and professional	10.9	17.6	11.9	30.3
White			12.4	31.5
Black			16.7	22.8
Hispanic origin			13.7	17.4
Executive, administrative, and managerial	2.2	5.0	9.3	13.3
White			9.8	13.9
Black			5.9	9.6
Hispanic origin			8.3	8.9
Professional specialty	19.6	12.6	14.4	17.1
White			14.9	17.6
Black			10.8	13.1
Hispanic origin				8.9

Source: Compiled from table XLIV, Bureau of the Census, *Special Reports: Occupations at the 12th Census* (Washington, D.C.: U.S. Government Printing Office, 1904), cxxv-cxxvii; figure 13, Sara E. Rix, ed., *The American Woman, 1987–88: A Report in Depth* (New York: W. W. Norton, 1987), 308–9; table 17, Sara Rix, ed., *The American Woman, 1988–89: A Status Report* (New York: W. W. Norton, 1988), 381; and tables 4–13 and 4–14, Cynthia Costello and Barbara Krimgold, eds., *The American Woman, 1996–97: Where We Stand, Women and Work* (New York: W. W. Norton, 1996), 58–59.

approximately 35 percent more people in the United States than worked around the world in Fortune 500 companies in 1994.

The transitions between the mid-1960s and the 1990s are measurable and dramatic. More difficult to determine, however, is whether this was a point on a long-term upward trend or a peak in a long series of ups and downs. For example, if historical estimates are correct about the colonial period that about half of all urban retailers were women, then 72 percent seems a less radical departure. Further, women's share of the professions was smaller in 1994 than in 1900, 16.3 as opposed to 19.6 percent, although their share of some professional areas increased substantially (table 7). We need a good deal more research on the history of women in business, especially in the nineteenth century, if we are to put the late twentieth century into its proper context. We can outline events and weigh the paradoxical meanings of recent changes in women's business roles; what is less clear is just how revolutionary the years after 1963 have been.

Legal Status, Demographic Change, and Debates over Woman's Place

Writing in 1991 the historian Joan Hoff observed that "the legal status of women in the United States changed more rapidly in the last twenty-five years than in the previous two hundred."[3] These legal changes were among several sources for women's advancement in business after 1963. Some legal change came from governmental actions. Between 1963 and the mid-1990s federal and state laws and judicial decisions increasingly supported the notion that women were entitled to the same rights and opportunities as men. The passage of the federal Equal Pay Act in 1963 (see chapter 5) was followed closely by Title VII of the 1964 federal Civil Rights Act, which included the word *sex* as a nondiscriminatory social category. Title VII created the Equal Employment Opportunity Commission (EEOC), which led in turn to President Lyndon Johnson's formation of the Office of Contract Compliance to ensure that the federal government would not only avoid discriminating against those listed in the bill but also take "affirmative action" to expand the opportunities available to minority workers. Women were specified in Executive Order No. 11246, issued June 9, 1970, by then-Secretary of Labor George P. Schultz.[4] Many federal and state laws and U.S. Supreme Court decisions between the 1960s and mid-1990s supported women's efforts to achieve parity as workers, managers, executives, professionals, and entrepreneurs. The passage of the Equal Credit Opportunity Act (1974, revised in 1977) gave women for the first time access to business credit in their own names, but problems with some provisions led to further changes in the 1980s. The House Select Committee on Small Business issued a report on women business entrepreneurs in 1988 that anticipated women would own 50 percent of small businesses by 2000, thus making gender discrimination in business and commercial credit a crucial issue for American business development.

These changes in the legal system came as a result of massive social revolutions over the civil rights and status of racial and ethnic minorities and women. The African-American movement for civil rights was followed by similar efforts by Hispanic Americans and Native Americans. White middle-class women raised issues surrounding woman's place in the context of the so-called women's liberation movement of the late 1960s and 1970s. These coalitions in particular brought forward the issue of diversity in the American population and pointed to the ways social categories such as race and gender led to inequities in economic opportunities, access to basic citizenship rights, and attitudes (such as racism, sexism, and ageism) that denigrated a person's value because of seemingly inherent differences.

Women found parallels to the civil rights movement in discrimination based on sex. The roots of the women's liberation movement of the 1970s were various. Some women experienced direct discrimination in the political organizations fighting for black rights or against the war in Vietnam. Others became dissatisfied with the promises of suburban motherhood. Still others were energized by personal experiences of discrimination in the workplace or their homes and turned to the language of civil rights. The second wave of the mainstream liberal women's movement officially surfaced with the formation of the National Organization for Women (NOW) in 1966.[5] NOW was born out of frustrations over the EEOC's failure to enforce the clause in Title VII dealing with sex discrimination in the workplace.

Another source for women's advances in business lay in increased educational opportunities and the fact that more women were spending more time in high school, college, university, and trade school. The percentage of black, white, and Hispanic girls graduating from high school went up after 1970, and the populations of colleges and universities became more diverse as the numbers of enrolled women and minorities grew. Between 1960 and 1990 women came to outnumber men as recipients of associate's, bachelor's, and master's degrees. In 1974, women earned only 12.8 percent of all undergraduate business degrees; in 1996, they accounted for 48.6 percent of the total. Older women sought access to higher education as well. In 1970 only about 16 percent of female college students were over age 30, but that percentage had risen to nearly 34 percent by 1990 (where it stayed throughout the 1990s). As the percentage of women in professional degree programs increased, women entered more prestigious schools such as Harvard and Stanford. Overall the numbers of women graduates of the top 20 law schools in the country grew an average of 20 percent. (Between the mid-1980s and the early 1990s women in all racial categories experienced a slight drop-off in college enrollments, but enrollment for all groups remained at historic highs in 2000.)

The results of a proactive federal approach, widespread movements for social change regarding the status of minorities and women, and increasing levels of education appear in some senses to have been spectacular. Despite these stunning successes, however, affirmative action policies and private-sector efforts at structural change found racial and gender inequities to be stubbornly resistant. Although women college graduates had invaded nonfeminized fields such as the biological sciences in some numbers by 1990 (51 percent of all degrees in this field went to women that year), in the late 1990s women remained dominant in traditionally female-defined fields such as health care (84 percent of degrees), education (78 percent), English (68 percent), and the arts (61 percent). Black professional women clustered in female-defined areas such as teaching, nursing, and social work. Further, women remained children's primary caregivers, and married working women with small children faced continuing problems with child care. Whether through choice or necessity, the number of married women with children under 6 years of age working outside of the home grew exponentially, from 19 percent in 1972 to 63 percent in 1996. Most of these women shunned commercial child care because they found it inadequate, too expensive, inaccessible, or unavailable. In 1993 70 percent of all working mothers with young children chose their own or another's home to meet their child care needs. Only about 18 percent of working mothers used commercial child care facilities.

More critically, since it affects all women, white men consistently earned more than any other group, and a gap remained in the ratio of women's to men's earnings (table 1). Since the early nineteenth century, the differences in men's and women's wages have shrunk; however, rather than a steady progression, major leaps came in the period between 1815 and 1850 (with the onset of the industrial revolution) and again in the 1980s (with the impact of affirmative action, equal pay laws, and the women's movement). Women's earnings remain proportionately less than men's in all categories; as late as 1996, the figure was 76 cents on the dollar. Racial differences in the earnings ratio between men and women have also been seen. In 1995 white women working full-time earned 72.3 percent of the amount earned by white men, and the story for other women was worse. Full-time black women workers earned 62.8 percent and Hispanic women workers 53.2 percent of white men's salaries. Black and Hispanic women earned about 85 percent of what black and Hispanic men earned.

Earnings also show gender differentials according to the type of position. These differences are due to a variety of factors (table 8), including, for example, whether unions are present and the degree of feminization in a job field. Figures for 1998, the most recent available at the time of this writing, show that female bookkeepers and accounting and auditing clerks earned 88 percent of men's wages for the same jobs. However, this is a feminized job category (about 90 percent female), which keeps men's wages low. In the most prestigious and

TABLE 8

Employed Women by Occupation and Race, and Female-to-Male Earnings Ratio by Occupation, 1998 (numbers in thousands)[a]

Occupation	*White*	Percentage *Black*	*Hispanic*	Ratio of Women's to Men's *Earnings*
Total number, in thousands	50,327	7,685	5,273	76.3
Managerial and professional	32.6	23.2	17.3	72.4
Executive & administrative	14.6	10.1	8.1	68.4
Professional specialty	18.1	13.0	9.2	76.2
Technical, sales and administrative support	41.1	39.1	37.4	69.1
Technicians & related support	3.8	3.5	2.7	72.9
Sales Occupations	13.4	11.4	12.6	59.8

TABLE 8 *(continued)*

Occupation	White	Percentage Black	Hispanic	Ratio of Women's to Men's Earnings
Administrative support, including clerical	24.0	24.2	22.1	80.7
Service occupations	16.3	25.0	26.7	76.1
Private household	1.3	1.5	4.7	NA
Protective service	0.6	1.7	0.6	78.5
Other service	14.4	21.9	21.4	90.8
Precision production, craft & repair	1.9	2.0	3.0	69.5
Mechanics and repairers	NA	NA	NA	86.6
Construction trades	NA	NA	NA	74.9
Precision production occupations	NA	NA	NA	64.2
Operators, fabricators, & laborers	6.8	10.4	13.7	71.7
Machine operators, assemblers & Inspectors	4.3	7.0	10.1	69.5
Transportation & material moving	0.8	1.4	0.8	71.9
Handlers, equipment cleaners, helpers, and laborers	1.6	2.0	2.8	85.9
Farming, forestry, & fishing	1.2	0.3	1.9	88.6
Total percentage	**100.0**	**100.0**	**100.0**	

[a]Adapted from Tables 4-12 and 5-5, Cynthia Costello and Anne J. Stone, eds., *The American Woman 2001–2002: Getting to the Top* (New York: W. W. Norton, 2001), pp. 246, 272. Data was not available for Native Americans and Asian/Pacific Islanders.

male-defined professions, in contrast, the earnings gap was much higher: 76.9 among lawyers and 58.2 among physicians. In both these cases, men tended to concentrate in the higher-paid specialties, such as corporate law and neurosurgery, while women clustered in less well-paid areas, such as public defense or general practice medicine.

Female executives have consistently made less than male executives with the same training, education, and experience.

The growth in women's small-business ownership between 1977 and 1987 came largely in traditionally female-dominated fields: service (38.2 percent); finance, insurance, and real estate (35.6 percent); and wholesale and retail trade (32.9 percent). The boards of directors of Fortune 500 industrial and service corporations in 1999 remained predominately white and male (88 percent). Women were represented on corporate boards of directors at a ratio of less than 1:8 and women of color 1:17. As of 2000, more than 85 percent of Fortune 500 companies have no women among their five highest-earning officers, and only 1.3 percent of those companies have corporate officers who are women of color. A male investment professional's median salary in 1999 was $155,000, 21 percent more ($26,750) than the median salary of female investment professionals.

As previous chapters made clear, some of these problems were the result of historical gender segregation that goes back to the early nineteenth century. Others reflected the relatively late start women (and minorities) had in some areas of management because of institutional segregation. Women were first admitted to the Harvard-Radcliffe program in business administration only in 1959, for example. Even then they had to be willing to earn their degrees from Radcliffe, sit in the back of the Harvard classes, and take their examinations on the Radcliffe grounds. Not until 1963 did women receive full citizenship rights at Harvard and thus access to the prestigious Harvard MBA, which feeds executive talent into some of the richest, most powerful, and most politically connected companies in the country.

Much like earlier concerns about women's suffrage, the failure of states to ratify the Equal Rights Amendment (ERA) by the 1982 deadline was due to a backlash among conservatives over women's public role and fears that gender equality would undermine the patriarchal family. The failure of the ERA was a severe setback for the long-term liberal goal of male and female equality. Efforts to cover the bases of the ERA through piecemeal legislation were also relatively unsuccessful. Senators introduced an omnibus Economic Equity Act (EEA) to Congress in 1981, and it has been kept alive in various forms since. Only portions of this package had been passed by 1997. One successful provision, the Retirement Equity Act, equalized the ways pension plans dealt with women's often interrupted working cycles. Other provisions regarding employer-sponsored child care and citizenship rights for female legal immigrants had not become law as of this writing.

When the word *sex* was added to Title VII, most people did not believe sex discrimination was a real problem in the workplace. However, sex discrimination suits were among the largest group of early cases brought to the EEOC for litigation and settlement. Despite the willingness of women to utilize Title VII, the EEOC's record has been poor in this area. White males, fearful for their jobs and pay status, successfully charged reverse discrimination in many affirmative action cases. Until the early 1970s the EEOC was unable to bring suit in court on behalf of complainants, and women and women's groups had to press the agency to devote time to sex discrimination issues. The Pay Equity Act worked to obtain some equality in wages but primarily for well educated women in traditionally male dominated professions: medicine, law, banking, and accounting. Most women workers, who were in white- or blue-collar work that remained sex segregated, received no benefit from the act. Finally, the record of the U.S. Supreme Court on sex discrimination cases has been a checkered one. In *Johnson* v. *Transportation Agency of Santa Clara County* (1987) the court argued that it was reasonable to use sex as well as race as one of several factors to justify promotions. During the first Bush administration, however, when the impact of new appointments to the Court came most clearly to the fore, majority opinions tended to argue that the equal protection clause of the Fourteenth Amendment prohibited affirmative action plans, a setback from evolving precedents in discrimination cases.

Other legal and demographic changes reveal similar structural problems in the context of long-term change. As the figures on married women in the labor force suggest, American households increasingly came to rely on two incomes after the early 1960s. Women's contribution to that income, however, tended to be less than men's. In part this discrepancy resulted because men often earn more than women employed in the same field. In some cases the difference was because women entered and left the labor force more often depending on a family's needs for home-based care for children or ill or elderly family members. An interrupted work cycle has been typical of women's contribution to the household since the advent of wage labor. Further, women contributed less income because they, more often than men, were part-time workers. In 1996 26.3 percent of all women as opposed to 11 percent of all men employed were working part-time.

Black women are more likely than white women to involuntarily work part-time as opposed to full-time. The number of women holding more than one job also increased substantially after 1970, although men were still more likely to "moonlight." Many of the jobs available to ethnic minorities are in seasonal or heavily cyclical industries, which means a certain amount of underemployment. Patricia Zavella found, for example, that Hispanic women who worked in the fruit canning industries in California had virtually no full-time, dependable jobs available to them. Rather, they and their families had to make complex adjustments to intermittent labor that was nonetheless vital to family security.[6]

In general, the American economy and businesses became more reliant on part-time jobs during the 1980s. In both small and big businesses, rising production costs and shrinking domestic markets meant the replacement of full-time with part-time positions, and the movement of jobs to other countries. Since women made up the largest proportion of the part-time workforce, that shift provided them with more opportunities. But part-time positions carry few or no benifits such as health insurance and retirement plans. They also tend to be much less secure than full-time work.

The rising divorce rate in the 1970s, changes in divorce law, and the lack of recognition of the economic value of housework led by the late 1970s to a phenomenon dubbed the "feminization of poverty." These changes had a direct impact on the nature of women's economic status and business role. Between 1970 and 1995 the percentage of husband-wife households in the United States shrank from 86 to 77. The all-time high of 3.5 divorces per 1,000 marriages in 1970 reached 5.2 per 1,000 by 1980, before falling slightly, to 4.4 by 1996. Another way to look at this change is to note that by 1980 one divorce occurred for every two marriages per year. This growth in the divorce rate is attributable to a complex set of forces, including new definitions of the family and sexuality after the early 1960s. It was made easier, however, by the introduction of no-fault divorce in all but two states between 1970 and 1981. No-fault divorce did not treat marriage as a contract in which an injured party had a right to "damages," as had been the case since the nineteenth century reform of divorce statutes, and essentially ignored the economic dimensions of marriage in American society.

The historian Joan Hoff called no-fault divorce "an almost perfect example of what happens when the legislatures and courts grant false equality to women."[7] In most states, divorced women had no clearly defined right to their husbands' property or earnings. Divorce courts did not recognize the economic value of housework in either community or common law states. Divorced women often ended up the sole providers and caregivers for children, with rusty or few job skills, no health or medical benefits, no credit rating (since all credit transactions would have been in a husband's name), and no Social Security benefits (which do not accrue unless wages or salaries are involved). In very few cases did divorce courts grant women equity in community or family property commensurate with the value of their unpaid household labor during the years of the marriage, which in the mid-1980s was valued at more than $45,000 per year.

Historical popular conceptions to the contrary, the feminization of poverty in the 1970s was not caused by unwed mothers on welfare. It was created by well-meaning courts and legislatures that treated one partner in a marriage exactly like the other despite the legal and economic differences between them. By 1976 one-third of all American female-headed families were living in poverty, while only 1 out of 18 husband-wife families were poor. According to one expert, "the average divorced woman and the minor children in their households experience a 73 percent decline in their standard of living in the first year of divorce. Their former husbands, in contrast, experience a 42 percent rise in their standard of living."[8] The increasing instance of female-headed households (18 percent of all households by 1994) made the problems of the double day and the need for reasonable child care increasingly urgent. Workers distracted by these kinds of problems were absent from the job more often or had difficulty balancing various demands, which became increasingly problematic workplace issues that businesses found difficult to ignore.

For women who work for wages and salaries, and their employers, a paramount question since the 1960s has been the nature of women's place in relation to male workers. Several issues sparked intense debates among feminists of differing philosophical persuasions, business leaders and employers, workers, legislators, and the courts. In fact, as was true in the early twentieth century, deciding what to do about women in the workplace has been among the hottest political agendas of the late twentieth century. The issues raised by the demographic shifts in working women are too numerous to cover in detail here, and history has yet to sort out which ones will prove to be most revealing and influential. But we can observe the impact of the large-scale changes previously discussed by focusing on three main areas that were lightning rods for debate over women's business role after 1963. They suggest the dimensions of the problems and possibilities facing women and business in the twenty-first century.

First, several workplace issues shaped an often bitter debate over women's role in the labor force. We can group together a series of these debates that surround women's workplace status. Discussions about comparable worth, protective legislation (including pregnancy "disabilities" and maternity or parental leave), sexual harassment, and workplace sex segregation are windows into the ongoing debate over the degree to which women should be treated as different from or the same as men. Second, female entrepreneurs arguably were the most potent economic force in small business after 1980. However, the role gender differences played in how they approached business is imperfectly understood. Finally, women's increasing access to managerial positions challenged traditional notions of that aspect of business much as the introduction of women clerical workers did for white-collar work in the late nineteenth century. The resulting focus on the meaning of gender in the workplace illuminates ongoing social tensions over men's and women's work.

Divisive Workplace Issues: Money, Motherhood, Sex, and Power

Comparable worth is a good example of the difficulties attendant on treating a majority as a disadvantaged population. The workforce in 1997 was as gender segregated as it had been a hundred years previously, and the question of the value of women's work in relation to men's remained as critical as ever. Historically, this debate has recognized that while distinct jobs might be assigned to men and women, the real issue is skill. Those concerned about *wage justice, pay equity, or comparable worth*, as the issue has been termed, have argued that questions of skill underlie wage differentials between men and women. Because skills associated with women's jobs historically have been defined as less valuable than those of men's, the argument runs, parity in pay can be achieved only by arriving at definitions of female skills that make them comparable with those of male workers. The comparable worth position did not advocate doing away with a sex-segregated labor force or attempt to alter the underlying conditions that created wage discrepancies. It takes as a given, in a sense, the fact of inequity and proposes creating some equivalences among the different sorts of work done by men and women.

The original equal pay bill, reintroduced into Congress in 1963, contained wording specifically addressing the issue of comparability. It stated that women should receive wages equal to those of men "for work of comparable character on jobs the performance of which requires comparable skills." The difficulty of defining what "comparable" skills were, as well as the reluctance of lawmakers to intrude in what some believed should be a free market relationship, led to changes in the bill. The wording of the Equal Pay Act as passed in 1963 simply advocated equal pay for equal work without attempting to define the terms. Agitation for clarification of comparability was renewed in the 1980s and received some support. The state governments of Minnesota and Washington created and implemented extensive and detailed guidelines for pay equity in state employment, and their programs met with some success. Many other states introduced or passed some aspects of comparable worth legislation. Some labor unions and the Democratic party went on record in favor of the principle.

But in general the courts, legislatures, and business people looked askance at comparable worth. Throughout most of the cases heard in the 1980s, for example, the U.S. Supreme Court avoided implementing comparable worth strategies. Its concern seemed to be that taxpayers and corporations would foot too high a bill in retroactive payments involving pay equity suits. Others feared it would cost millions to implement the enforced elevation of women's wages and salaries. Comparable worth studies tended to advocate raising the wages and salaries of women in more cases than those of men since women's work was so consistently undervalued. However, comparable worth could also create upward adjustments in men's wages since it focused on the value of skills rather than entrenched hierarchies or social attitudes toward particular types of work. Comparable worth would have had no direct discernible impact on the sex segregation of jobs or on male dominance in the most lucrative sectors of the economy. It would not upset the job structure, in other words. Finally, some young professional women attacked comparable worth on the principle that by elevating wages and salaries in so-called women's professions, women would be discouraged from taking positions in male-defined areas of the labor force. Thus, sex segregation would continue to be a problem. On the one hand, to the extent that comparable worth solutions sought to bypass solving the underlying problems of sex segregation, such critics were correct. On the other hand, comparable worth strategies addressed the resulting phenomenon of wage differentials and could provide effective if not substantive equity.

The wage gap between men and women was also the result of differences in the earnings of married women and unmarried women or single men. When wage differentials created by sex segregation are removed, the single largest factor creating inequity in men's and women's earnings has historically been a woman's marital status. In terms of wages, marriage has disadvantaged women. The working status of married women therefore has been one key to placing men's and women's earnings on a more equitable footing. The issues of pregnancy "disability" laws and maternity or parental leave clearly focus the debates over married women's difference.

As we have seen, discussions about pregnant women in the workplace go back to the Progressive period and the passage of protective labor legislation. Much of the early legislation limited hours or provided special working conditions for women on the general theory that they needed special treatment because they were *potential* mothers. Recent debates about the issue of protection have focused on pregnancy itself as a category eligible for disability insurance. Many health insurance plans in the 1970s eliminated pregnancy from coverage as one of several "temporary disabilities." In the U.S. Supreme Court case *General Electric Co.* v. *Gilbert* (1976), the company's plan specifically covered, as temporary disabilities, "sports injuries, attempted suicides, venereal disease, elective cosmetic surgery, . . . prostate disease, circumcision, hair transplants, and vasectomies." Pregnancy was not included. In arguing its case, attorneys for the plaintiff called attention to Title VII of the Civil Rights Act of 1964, particularly the section that spelled out "pregnancy, miscarriage, abortion, childbirth, and recovery therefrom" as job-related temporary disabilities subject to health insurance coverage. But in support of the company's position the justices asserted that no discrimination had occurred based on sex. Since nonpregnant "persons" could be both female and male, and since the category in question was a condition and not a person, they claimed pregnancy was reasonably excluded.[9]

Dissatisfied over the status of pregnancy in the workplace, women's groups lobbied Congress for passage of the Pregnancy Discrimination Act, which went into effect in 1980. This act did not address the Court's evasion of the status of pregnant "persons," but merely made it illegal to treat pregnancy differently from any other temporary disability. In the years after 1980, however, many states passed legislation protecting (i.e., favoring) pregnant women in the workplace. This debate failed to take seriously that women do not get pregnant by themselves and that men have reproductive health issues that affect fertility such as levels of lead or radiation in the environment. Rather than focusing the discussion on fertility, which is an issue of concern to both men and women and at the root of concern about pregnancy, some women's groups, the courts, and the legislatures historically have seen the question as a women's issue. True, men and women do not have the same stake in fertility. But while pregnancy is a transient condition for women, parenthood is neither gender specific nor temporary. Given the persistent definition of women as primary child care providers, pregnancy, fertility, and their status in the workplace have been critical to women as both individuals and employees.

Debates over the suitability of pregnancy's status as a temporary disability led in the 1980s to calls by some women's advocates and legislators for laws dealing with *parental* leave. Whatever else attention to pregnancy accomplished, it brought the ancient dilemma of the double day and women's prescribed social role as caretaker into the open. As we have seen, child care has always been a problem for women, whether as producers in the eighteenth-century household or as workers in the nineteenth-century factory or twentieth-century office. Both women and legislators have raised the problem of child care for working women persistently since World War II. In the 1980s Congress once again focused public attention on the issue. Not surprisingly, the debates were framed as working women's issues rather than as a question of parental or family responsibilities. Not only have women traditionally been the primary caregivers for children and husbands, but many families have also assumed they will leave the workforce to care for elderly parents or other family members disabled by illness or accident. For very different reasons, in the late 1980s both conservative and liberal quarters began to push to make it easier for fathers to assume some responsibilities for family care. Whether encouraging so-called family values or striving for gender equity in both domestic and public life, these efforts to frame the discussion of the double day in terms of parental or family concerns rather than women's responsibilities for the most part were unsuccessful.

Like many issues dealing with women and work, parental or family leave and child care became political footballs in the 1980s and 1990s. A child care bill introduced into Congress in 1989 proved so divisive in terms of funding and the role of the federal government in private decisions that the legislators decided to put off voting on it. A Democratic-controlled Congress in 1990 passed a family leave bill that would have required firms with more than 50 employees to provide up to three months of unpaid leave for workers with family illness or new babies. President Bush promptly vetoed it. By the time the Family and Medical Leave Act finally passed and became law under President Clinton in 1993, many large companies had already voluntarily initiated family leave policies. They believed that although such policies might cost the company some short-term revenues, in the long term they would save dollars because the workforce would be more stable and loyal to the company.

For their part, in response to the act, small-business owners drew gloomy portraits of fiscal doom. A spokeswoman for 9 to 5, the National Association of Working Women, reported that, after the bill passed, the organization's Long Island office received more than 20 telephone calls, "from women, all pregnant, all recently fired by employers who got them out of the way before the law took effect." These fears reflected attitudes toward working women rather than the reality of the law's impact. As of the 1990 census, the act affected 66 percent of all workers but only 4 percent of all companies. Most workers in the early 1990s were employed in firms with more than 50 employees (the cutoff point mandated by the law), but 96 percent of firms in the United States employed fewer than 50 people and thus were exempt.[10]

A recent but far-reaching issue regarding women in the workplace has been the development of attitudes and laws surrounding sexual harassment. Women in various workplaces have long been subject to supervisors or bosses asking for or demanding sexual favors in return for job perquisites. From the textile mill girls of Lowell and the shirtwaist makers of early-twentieth-century New York City to domestic servants in all times and places, women have faced sexual intimidation by employers. What earlier generations saw as a "normal" part of male sexuality or working-class women's personal shame has been redefined. But *sexual harassment* is not just a new term for an old problem. The new parameters of this debate also represented a sea change in thinking on the root of the issue and how to deal with it. Legislation and debate over this issue in the 1980s and 1990s grew initially out of concern about generalized categories of violence against women such as spousal abuse and rape. The feminist critique of this type of violence pointed to the underlying power inequities to which rape and abuse give form. Constituting these as crimes of violence rather than sexual crimes has shifted the way the legal system deals with the issues. A growing body of law and court decisions has successfully constructed such violence as a violation of women's civil rights.

The evolving law on sexual harassment has been premised on the same approach, emphasizing that such harassment is not about sex but about power. One legal scholar defines sexual harassment as the "unwanted imposition of sexual requirements in the context of a relationship of unequal power."[11] Sexual harassment grows out of the unequal workplace status of men and women. Since the issue is power rather than sex, harassment can happen to anyone in a subordinate position and can be perpetrated by anyone in a supervisory position. However, given the fact that jobs have historically been sex segregated and that women have predominated in lower-paying, lower-status positions, most sexual harassment in the contemporary workplace is committed by men against women.

There are no reliable statistics on the extent of sexual harassment in the workplace, in part because reporting is sketchy and in part because disagreement remains over its exact nature. However, this form of discrimination seems to have been more prevalent in blue-collar and military workplaces than in white-collar jobs. Whatever the type of job, surveys and other statistical reporting in the early 1990s suggested that between 35 and 45 percent of women who worked outside of the home had encountered or would experience some form of sexual harassment at some point in their working lives. If not direct targets themselves, most women knew someone else who had been sexually harassed.

Title VII recognized sexual harassment as an actionable category of discrimination, and guidelines for the EEOC published in 1980 defined such discrimination as any behavior that "unreasonably [interfered] with an individual's work performance or [created] an intimidating or hostile or offensive environment . . . [including] unwelcome sexual advances, requests for sexual favors, and other verbal or physical conduct of a sexual nature."[12] The landmark U.S. Supreme Court case on sexual harassment is *Meritor Savings Bank* v. *Vinson* (1986), which for the first time formally recognized workplace sexual harassment as a problem for which there was a legal remedy. In this case a female bank employee had been forced to have sexual relations with her supervisor for several years to maintain her job. In its unanimous decision, the Court found in favor of the employee, charging that such behavior in the workplace violated the sexual discrimination statutes of Title VII of the 1964 Civil Rights Act.

However, the depth and nature of the problem of sexual harassment in general has remained misunderstood and a subject of fierce and sometimes vitriolic debate. The *Meritor* case focused on blatant, repeated harassment. Even so, the justices ruled that it was permissible to introduce "provocative" behavior on the part of the employee as a mitigating circumstance. This type of evidence is no longer allowed in rape cases, in which the plaintiff is assumed not to be on trial along with the defendant. Surveys suggest that men and women have profoundly different attitudes toward the issue of sexuality in the workplace. In one questionnaire collected in 1986, men more often than women stated their belief that "sexual relations foster better communication between the workers involved," that "some sexual intimacy among coworkers can create a more harmonious work environment," and that "when two workers cultivate a relationship that eventually leads to marriage, it enhances their creativity as a unit and helps their company's bottom line." In the same survey, more women than men believed that management should do more to discourage "sexual propositions toward coworkers," that supervisors and other employees who made unwanted sexual advances should be reprimanded, and that it was inappropriate for a worker to be romantically or sexually involved with a supervisor.[13]

The complex and angry response to Anita Hill's accusations of sexual harassment by Clarence Thomas made clear that this issue triggered tensions, misunderstandings, and revelations of discriminatory attitudes toward race as well as gender. Whatever the ultimate legacy of the 1991 Senatorial hearings on Justice Thomas's Supreme Court nomination, several events followed immediately on its heels. Taken together, they suggest that Hill's testimony and the widespread outrage among both men and women over the way the hearings were conducted led to public indignation over the issue of harassment. There was an immediate increase in the number of sexual harassment complaints in the EEOC, which Thomas had at one time headed. The Congressional Ethics Committee investigated and charged several senators with sexual harassment. One, Robert Packwood (a Republican from Oregon), was forced to resign. The U.S. Navy had to deal with an instance of large-scale sexual harassment in the revelations surrounding its Tailhook Convention, and in 1996 widespread problems surfaced in the U.S. Army.

As these examples suggest, the discussion of women's business role has persistently focused not only on the differences between men and women but also on the notion that those differences are unequally valued. As we have seen, this is not a recent development. Women's role in business became a visible and troublesome issue when they began to work for wages in the early-nineteenth-century mills and to enter the all-male office in the 1870s. It has remained an issue ever since. Two broad areas of business experience provide useful windows into the continuing problems created by gender inequity. Changes in women's access to entrepreneurship and trends in management make excellent case studies of the ongoing dilemmas in the debate over women's business roles.

Female Proprietors and CEOs

In the period after about 1970 federal agencies, national organizations, and the authors of longitudinal studies began to gather data on female entrepreneurs and women-owned businesses. We have more information on this category of businesswoman for the years after 1970 than for any other period in the past. It clearly points to the increased importance of proprietorship to both women and the local, regional, national, and even international economies. In addition, female CEOs, often of companies they themselves started or inherited, have become more visible and influential.

One reason for the intense interest was the observable growth of female sole proprietorships since 1970 discussed previously. Another was the general renewal of interest in the economic viability of small businesses in general. According to the definition used by the Small Business Administration (SBA), firms with fewer than 500 employees constituted 99 percent of all businesses in 1982. Small businesses employed 48 percent of the nonagricultural labor force and accounted for 38 percent of the nation's gross national product. Family farms and firms providing services made up 54 percent of these businesses (27 percent each). Sales and manufacturing constituted the rest, in that order by percentage.

After 1974 small firms became increasingly important economically relative to big businesses. One advantage of small firms is that they provide more flexibility in uncertain markets and are better able to be innovative in response to economic change. Since 1970, small businesses have created more full-time jobs, moved into foreign markets, taken advantage of new technologies such as computers to expand their markets, and spread more evenly across the country than big businesses have. The 1970s and 1980s saw recessions that cut deeply into big business's dependence on world markets.

The general movement away from manufacturing and into services was a movement toward the types of products small firms typically provide. The federal government also encouraged the growth of small business by exempting firms with fewer than 50 employees from meeting various federal standards in things such as affirmative action and toxic waste disposal. In addition, there was a renewal of interest in entrepreneurship as a path to self-employment and autonomy. Since most of women's entrepreneurial energies traditionally have been centered on small firms and on providing services, these developments simultaneously strengthened women's market position and made their entrepreneurship an important part of the overall economic picture.

Because most new businesses are small businesses, and women and men seem to approach the creation and continuance of their entrepreneurial endeavors differently, understanding the role of women entrepreneurs has been crucial to understanding the future of small business in America. Female entrepreneurs have had a specific profile that sets them apart from men, and they have faced special problems in starting and maintaining businesses. We do not have complete figures for female proprietorship in the nineteenth century, but we can make some educated guesses about its general profile. As we saw in chapter 3, many probably operated as husband-wife partnerships. Other women no doubt ran businesses that, given property laws, were in their husbands' or fathers' names. Widows were especially prominent as proprietors. Most female proprietors in the nineteenth century were probably over the age of 30, married or widowed, slightly better educated than most women, and operated their businesses with the assistance of family members. This demographic outline likely closely resembled that of female proprietors in the eighteenth century as well.

Federal census reports after 1960 suggest that surprisingly little has changed in terms of this overall profile. Half of all female entrepreneurs after 1970 were married and between the ages of 35 and 52. Many came from middle-class families in which they were the first-born children. Most did not start their first businesses until they were about 35, had earned a liberal arts degree, and had gotten their children into school. Most had some work experience before starting their own businesses, but a substantial minority (about 12 percent) were students or homemakers. Although the number of widows inheriting family businesses is less than in earlier periods, the number of single women over the age of 30 in business has probably remained somewhat stable. Divorce in the twentieth century functions much as death did in earlier periods to create a population of older, formerly married women, many of whom face economic hardship.

As was true in earlier periods, women's businesses after 1960 tended to cluster in the service sector, although they were represented in all areas. Between 1972 and 1982 female proprietors made inroads into male-dominated businesses such as manufacturing, but by the mid-1990s that proportion had shrunk (table 6). Between 1980 and 1985 alone, the number of women-owned sole proprietorships in the transportation industry increased by almost 125 percent, while their share of companies in mining, construction, and manufacturing increased by more than 116 percent. Between 1991 and 1994 women made impressive gains in the construction, transportation, and communication industries (table 9). Women's firms employing more than 100 people were the fastest-growing segment, with a rate of 18.3 percent compared with 9.1 percent for all women-owned businesses. If we recall Rebecca Lukens's nineteenth-century rolling mill, these recent gains may represent a renewal rather than a revolution. Here again further research on the earlier period may help put these developments in perspective.

Female proprietorships resemble the general business picture in several ways. As of 1994 the age of women-owned businesses was approaching the national average: 35 percent were less than four years old, while the national average was 39 percent. Nationally, 30 percent of all firms in 1994 had been in business for more than 12 years. For female sole proprietorships, the average was 28 percent. Women's firms also approached the national average in terms of creditworthiness, and their failure rate (14.7 percent) was only slightly higher than the national average of 13.7 percent.

Women entrepreneurs continued to face special problems in bringing their businesses to fruition. Two of the most common have been the historical difficulties of accumulating collateral and obtaining credit to start and maintain a business. Victoria Fullerton applied for a

TABLE 9

Percentage Change in Number of Woman-Owned Firms, 1991–94

Industry	Percentage Change
Agriculture	18.3
Mining	5.2
Construction	19.2
Nondurable manufacturing	10.7
Durable manufacturing	17.8
Transportation/communication	19.5
Wholesale trade	17.8
Retail trade	−3.5
Finance, insurance, and real estate	21.3
Business services	18.7
Personal services	−8.6
Other services	28.1

Source: Adapted from the National Foundation for Women Business Owners, *Women-Owned Businesses: Breaking the Boundaries* (Silver Spring, Md.: National Foundation for Women Business Owners, 1995), 11.

loan from her bank in 1994 to fund the expansion of her business, which managed health care for 18,000 people. She never received a formal rejection notice, but when she asked her banker about the loan several months later he simply informed her that she had been denied, without any formal reason.[14] Fullerton was not alone. As of 1997 43 percent of women business owners had no more than $25,000 of available credit from financial institutions, compared to 37 percent of men who owned businesses. Only 27 percent of women regularly sought credit for their businesses from banks, whereas 34 percent of men did.

There are many reasons for women's difficulty obtaining credit. Lending institutions have often been leery of loaning start-up capital to small businesses, particularly in the retail sector. In general, they have been interested in a person's track record in financial dealings and his or her management experience. Many women in business, including entrepreneurs, have not accumulated experience with finances or management or have only limited credit references. Women often have lacked experience with financial planning and have been unfamiliar with lending networks and other resources for self-education. For some women, such as Victoria Fullerton, the experience of dealing with traditional lending institutions is "humiliating."

Taken together, these factors suggest women's ability to capitalize their businesses remains problematic. In the 1980s women's use of bank loans for start-up capital actually declined 8 percent while their use of credit cards increased 12 percent. In 1994 52 percent of female-owned businesses as opposed to 18 percent of all small businesses used credit cards for short-term financing.

As we have seen since the eighteenth century, one way women in business have overcome these and other problems is by forming their own organizations or constructing extensive support networks among other women. A group of Washington, D.C., businesswomen started the NAWBO in 1978 as the first dues-paying organization for female entrepreneurs and proprietors. Its research offshoot, the nonprofit NFWBO, began in 1989 to make a wealth of information available to female small-business owners or those interested in starting their own businesses. These organizations also publicized female entrepreneurship, testified in congressional hearings and fact-finding missions, and worked with major corporate sponsors (such as Wells Fargo Bank, IBM, AT&T, and MetLife) to complete studies of women-owned business.

Networks such as Boston's A Team, a group of women hospital administrators, assisted other women in business advancement. Barbara Gardner Proctor in the 1980s used her prominent advertising agency to promote black business growth by taking on only clientele committed to working for a more secure economic future for black Americans. She used existing networks and governmental opportunities to support the growth of black businesses, becoming a member of the White House Task Force for the Small Business Council in 1979 and the first female member of the African American Cosmopolitan Chamber of Commerce in Chicago. Among the most innovative responses to women's lack of access to credit and capital was the formation, in 1995, of Women Incorporated (WI), a non-profit national membership organization whose mission is to aid female business owners. Within five months of its founding, it had 4,000 members, and as of 2001 had grown to 34,000 members. Modeled after the American Association of Retired Persons (AARP), WI works with The Money Store, Bank One, Bank of America, Chase Manhattan and other banks, over 400 micro-lenders, and several venture capitalists to provide a National Financial Network for its membership to help business women get access to capital and credit. WI has convinced its affiliates to use such non-traditional loan pool criteria as rent receipts (rather than real estate, for example) to demonstrate credit-worthiness. WI provides discounts for members through companies such as Kinko's Copying, Federal Express, IBM, and Northwest Airlines for such things as health insurance, communications technologies and systems, office products and business services, and travel that allow small business owners to take advantage of the economies of scale possible for large corporations.

WI's two founders emerge as proto-typical late twentieth century female entrepreneurs, merging their education, experience and creativity with a business ethic that harks back to women's nineteenth century recognition of the economic basis for women's autonomy. Lindsey Johnson Suddarth has a Harvard MBA, was the head of the Office of Women's Business Ownership at the SBA, and has been an active volunteer for battered women shelters and for Planned Parenthood. Judith Luther Wilder is the former executive director of California American Woman's Economic Development Corporation, and a long-time community activist. The WI advisory board forges strong links between the business and political communities through members such as Sherry Lansing of Paramount Pictures, Jill Barad of Mattell Toys and Betty Ford of the Betty Ford Center.

However, even some organizations designed to deal primarily with new businesses and inexperienced entrepreneurs have had spotty track records when it comes to women. In the past 30 years the SBA has been the single largest source of small-business loans in the United States. Designed specifically to facilitate bank loans of start-up capital to small businesses, the SBA has been charged with paying particular attention to women and minority firms and even developed a separate office for this purpose. Yet it has not been effective in opening women's access to capital and credit. As recently as 1994 the SBA acknowledged that its program of loan guarantees discriminated against women and minorities. Black entrepreneurs in 1993 received only 3 percent of the SBA's loans; Hispanic owners received only 5 percent, and women as a group only 14 percent.

Numerous differences continued to be seen between men's and women's small businesses after 1960, some of which made them resemble nineteenth-century concerns. Women's businesses tended to employ fewer people than men's small businesses, and women more often were sole proprietors. They also tended to work fewer hours at their business enterprises than men did, although the reasons for that probably had more to do with family responsibilities and the double day than a tendency toward underachievement. Men more often used investors, banks, or personal loans for start-up capital, whereas women relied on personal assets, savings, or credit cards. For example, according to an SBA study done in 1988, women were more likely to start their businesses without any borrowed capital. About 70 percent of women as opposed to about 60 percent of men got their funding from sources other than borrowing. All of these data suggest one reason why most women's sole proprietorships had smaller revenues than men's: Many male entrepreneurs had some experience at higher levels of management or in financial or manufacturing establishments. Women more frequently had been midlevel managers, if they had any managerial experience at all, with retail or service-sector firms. Men and women also differed in their use of various forms of personal support. Male entrepreneurs were more likely to have outside sources of information such as lawyers and accountants, whereas women sought advice from family, friends, and business associates. Although men and women both start up their own firms "from scratch" (about 80 percent), as in earlier periods women are more likely than men to inherit a business from a father or husband or receive it as a gift from a relative.

Female entrepreneurship has grown in some nontraditional fields. Kim Polese became the CEO of Marimba in 1996. The founders of Marimba, of whom Polese was one, formed the company to take Java Internet software public. Polese offered a unique combination in the computer industry since her background included familiarity with both the technological and marketing aspects of the business. However, most women-owned and women-chaired businesses remained in the personal service sector, their long-time business niche. The top 50 women-owned or operated businesses in the country in 1996 concentrated in food, personal service, nondurable consumer goods manufacturing, and clothing.[15] Included on the list were such well-known firms as TLC Beatrice (whose chair and CEO, Loida Nicolas Lewis, is the widow of the company's founder), Warnaco Group (Speedo bathing suits, Calvin Klein underwear, and the Wonder Bra), Jockey International, and Tootsie Roll Industries.

To a great extent, gender stereotypes continued to construct the public personas of women owners and CEOs. As with Lydia Pinkham in the nineteenth century, however, it was possible to use those stereo-

types successfully to advance business interests. Columbia Sportswear, the largest outerwear company in the United States, grew an
average of 35 percent every year between 1985 and 1995, and its sales
approached $1 billion in the late 1990s. Gertrude Boyle inherited
Columbia from her husband and continued to operate it. Mother
Boyle, as she became known to her employees and those in the industry, began her tenure by remaining in the background. But in the mid-
1990s, at the age of 70, Boyle began to make use of gender stereotypes
in the company's advertising. She and her son, Timothy, toyed with
her age, gender, and the company's family ownership to sell their
rugged line of sportswear, hunting vests, and hiking boots. In one ad
her grandmotherly face, half glasses perched on her nose, peered out
over Timothy's words: "Durable. Rugged. A little baggy and slightly
faded. That pretty much sums up our new jeans—and my mother,
Columbia Sportswear's chairman." Another ad displayed a photograph of Boyle's size 7[h] pumps, while Timothy observed "someday
I'll have to fill these shoes."[16] The ad campaign was highly successful.

Ethnic and racial differences have also played a role in women's
entrepreneurship. Before the mid-1990s African-American women's
sole proprietorships took in smaller earnings than those of white men
or women or black men. As late as 1987 African-American women
were more likely than white women or other minority women to be in
the agricultural sector. As was true for businesses owned by white
women and black men, more than half of black women's businesses
(60 percent in 1980) were retail establishments. However, these businesses tended more than mainstream sole proprietorships to cluster
disproportionately in industries with slower growth, lower wages, and
fewer technologies. This difference is probably in part a function of
the fact that African-American women had less access to capital than
did other racial or gender groups. In 1987 black women made up 4
percent of all female business owners but 11.5 percent of all African-
American business owners, a substantial minority. In 1972, 90 percent
of minority women's businesses were sole proprietorships, and that
business form accounted for 57 percent of revenues. In a 1996 listing
of the 50 fastest-growing, largest woman-owned companies in the
United States, only four were headed by minority women. Hispanic
and Asian women-owned businesses in 1987 made up 3 percent each
of all female sole proprietorships. Native American firms owned by
women in 1987 were more likely to be in agriculture, manufacturing,
and construction than in typical women-owned areas.

Minority women as entrepreneurs or heads of their own firms have also seen some genuine successes. Some of the most spectacular changes in women-owned businesses have come in this sector. In 1980 nearly 17 firms owned by African-American women had receipts of more than $1 million. Federal census materials for 1996 show major increases in the number of minority women-owned firms, including substantial growth in nontraditional sectors such as construction and wholesale trade. Women of color owned 13 percent (1 in 8) of all women-owned firms in 1996. Minority women's firms employed nearly 1.7 million people and produced sales of more than $184 billion. The largest firm with a minority owner in 1996 was TLC Beatrice, of which Loida Nicolas Lewis was chair and CEO of 51 percent of the operating assets. The company was, not incidentally, the largest black-owned corporation in the United States at the time of its founder's death in 1994. When Lewis, who is a Filipina, inherited the company from her husband, Reginald Lewis, in 1994 it was worth $1.7 billion. Sales in 1996 totaled $2.1 billion, and the company had an international workforce of 4,500.

One of the largest African-American firms by the mid-1990s was Oprah Winfrey's Harpo Entertainment Group, which she founded and continues to head. Harpo Productions was not only a success for an African-American woman but also a major power in the television industry in general. Harpo was a wholly owned firm with sales revenues in 1994 of nearly $150 million and about 140 employees. The company produced Oprah Winfrey's syndicated television talk show, which was seen in 65 countries and had nearly a million daily viewers in the United States. The talk show alone grossed about $180 million in 1993 and routinely had a larger audience than all of the three major network morning shows combined. Winfrey was the first African-American and the third woman (after Mary Pickford and Lucille Ball) to own her own studio. In addition to Winfrey's talk show, Harpo Productions made movies and television specials. Harpo was part of a vertically integrated business that had its own syndication arm (King World), book publishing component, and television production studios. As one commentator noted, "[Winfrey] owns the show; she owns the production company; she owns the studio; and . . . she owns a major part of the distributor." Winfrey's control over this conglomerate gave her the ability—rare in the business world—to shape the concerns according to her personal vision.[17]

In addition to her phenomenal business success, Winfrey continued the concern with social and self-help issues demonstrated by such earlier businesswomen as Maggie Lena Walker and Ellen Demorest. She created a supportive and humanistic work environment for her predominately female employees, and her television programs have tended to focus on empowerment issues, spotlighting such topics as child abuse, alcoholism, and family relationships. Winfrey has also pursued a variety of charitable activities, including college scholarships and funding for inner-city schools. She has spoken out against child abuse and for children's rights and proposed a bill to Congress (signed into law by President Clinton in 1993) that established funding for a national database of convicted child abusers.

Female entrepreneurs such as Oprah Winfrey and Gertrude Boyle embodied the positive uses to which gendered approaches to business could be put in the 1990s in large part because of their ability to control their own companies. For the majority of female entrepreneurs, being a woman and a proprietor in the years after 1963 meant operating in an economic, cultural, and even demographic environment in many ways little changed from the nineteenth century. Further research on women's entrepreneurial role in the nearly 300 years before 1963, however, may better focus our picture of female proprietors and corporate officers at the turn of the twentieth century.

Management: A Recent Battleground

In addition to the place of female entrepreneurs and CEOs, a great deal of the public debate about women in business after 1963 has focused on women in management, executive, and professional positions.[18] One reason for this focus has been the visible increase of women in these fields. As table 7 shows, by 1974 the percentage of female managers and professionals (17.6) was at an all-time high. Most of those gains since 1900 had come in the professions. However, women in executive, administrative, and managerial positions saw a 44 percent increase from 1900 to 1974, most of which occurred after 1960. By 1996 women made up 30.3 percent of all managers, executives, administrators, and professionals.

There appeared to be several immediate reasons for these increases. One was the passage of Title VII of the Civil Rights Act of 1964 and its attendant emphasis on affirmative action. Another was the raised expectations created by the women's movement in the 1960s and 1970s. Further, the waning of the baby boom and the growth of business and government in the 1960s and 1970s meant a shortage of skilled managers and professionals. When affirmative action became federal law in 1964, some claimed that women would integrate smoothly into managerial positions once a generation of younger men not bound by older definitions of womanhood became managers and once women had other women as mentors and role models. In the early 1970s a flurry of media attention focused on the legal aspects of Title VII mandates. Efforts to conform to Title VII and Executive Order No. 11246 guidelines were also evident in corporate policy making after 1970. In addition, the shortage of skilled managers, some argued, meant management of necessity would become gender neutral as firms hired the best person for the job. "Let's face it," one corporate manager noted in 1975, "times are changing and we can't afford to ignore the women in our Company if we want the best people." In the words of one business commentator in 1980, managers would become "androgynous," using interpersonal and organizational skills that were not dependent on ideas about male and female behavior.[19]

Although by 1996 women's movement into managerial and executive positions had increased substantially the anticipated wide extension of women's careers into top-level positions and parity had not been delivered. The reasons for this change were evident in affirmative action policy, historical gender segregation, and the persistence of the family claim that defined women by their domestic responsibilities. The increase in the number of women in managerial, executive, and professional positions did not lead automatically to equity between men and women. The differential in salaries and wages discussed earlier remained resistant to change. Affirmative action came under increasing attack by those who believed women were not inherently disadvantaged in the workplace. In addition, although they were entering professional schools and positions in larger numbers, most women seemed to be stuck at the lower levels of the career ladder, held there by the so-called glass ceiling. By the 1980s the debate had reasserted the value of apparent gender distinctions among male and female managers. The discussion of specific job skills focused on how women and men were different and what use companies could make of those differences. One mid-sized energy company in the 1970s, which proposed achieving affirmative action mandates by increasing the number of women in managerial positions, focused on "restructuring the jobs to fit the capabilities of women." In response to a survey of employee opinions about women managers, one person wrote, "Women have better people skills than men—they should stay with personnel-type work."[20] These interrelated phenomena were an aspect of the historical expectations about women's business role.

Affirmative action has often been misunderstood as a movement to achieve *equal* numbers of different categories of individuals. That was never the intent of either Title VII or efforts to deal with the law. Rather, affirmative action sought *parity*: that different groups be represented according to their population in general or within a given field. For example, if in 1987 women earned 15 percent of all MBAs, then the number of women hired for jobs requiring MBAs in 1987 should approach 15 percent of all hires in that field. Achieving parity, however, seemed easier than it turned out to be in practice, in part because parity was often confused with equality and equality with sameness. These three terms do not have interchangeable meanings, but the debate often clouded that fact. Affirmative action strategies in practice emphasized that women could achieve parity only to the extent that they were treated the same as men.

Historically, the job skills expected of managers had been coded as male and based on attributed male traits. As we have seen, within this masculinized world, early-twentieth-century supporters of women managers carved out a specifically female territory. In life insurance, for example, separate women's bureaus employed female agents because industry leaders, and the saleswomen themselves, believed that women could make female customers more receptive to the product. Some female agents argued that selling life insurance was logically suited to women because of their concern for family and children. Further, sales agents and agency managers articulated their company role using gendered terms. Women insurance managers spoke of female "impudence" rather than male "aggressiveness" and emphasized the cooperative rather than the competitive aspects of managing people. These notions used traditional differences among manhood and womanhood to create a culturally legitimate role for women in the male-defined field of insurance.

The definitional battles of the life insurance industry are a model for understanding other arenas in which women moved into formerly male-defined positions. The argument that women could do certain jobs because as women they were different from men has led to expanded opportunities. In part because they argued from difference, certain kinds of managerial jobs such as personnel directors and low-level supervisors of other women workers evolved, by the 1930s, as female positions with female skills as job requisites.

Business organization reinforced these gender differences. Female managerial or supervisory positions evolved as "staff" positions: those that provide support services for the departments that actually produce or sell a product, such as purchasing, personnel, and public relations. These positions lay outside of the promotional hierarchy for the best-paying jobs, were lower in status than line departments (those producing or selling a product), and typically employed a high percentage of women clerical workers and managers. These departments were expenses rather than income generators and often the first areas to feel the crunch in hard times. Women's managerial role by 1960 thus was well defined: supportive, nurturing, lower in status and pay than that of men, composed of skills perceived to be intrinsically female, outside of the promotional track for male management positions, and expendable.

Given this history, most business commentators responded to calls for gender equity by emphasizing gender differences. Mary Wells Lawrence provides a good example. In 1970 Lawrence was probably the highest-paid advertising executive in the country and the founder and CEO of her own firm. At age 42 she was a well-established self-employed woman who made more than $250,000 a year. She was often cited in the business press as an outstanding female executive. Commenting on gender difference she said, "People aren't aware, sometimes, that I'm a girl."[21]

Lawrence claimed that men treated her no differently from men of comparable power. And she asserted at the same time that she had not bartered away her essential female self. The contrast between Lawrence's position and her self-description was a strategy working women had used since at least 1900. Women office workers in the early twentieth century, for example, generally made a distinction between business girls and businesswomen. The former remained female identified while the latter had traded their femininity for the rewards of a career. A 1987 survey of 93 middle-management professionals on attitudes toward "assertive women" found that women managers were "caught in a bind." They had to behave aggressively as managers, yet to do so violated tenets of womanliness. The response of women in this survey was similar to that of women in 1900: they denigrated perceived masculine behavior such as aggression in women. Women in the survey saw aggressive behavior by other women as alienating and "pushy."[22]

Indeed, most popular commentary on female managers after the late 1980s focused on women's sexuality, their family life (motherhood was a frequent theme), or their defiant sense that women had resources men did not. An article on seven successful female executives in *Fortune* magazine in 1996, aptly titled "Women, Sex, and Power," explained that successful female executives "don't play the man's game, literally or figuratively":

They don't act like men or think like them. They never dress in androgynous suits and those homely bow ties. And they don't golf. . . . This new female elite is definitely not your parents' paradigm. Remember when executive women used to be overwhelmingly single and childless? All of [these women] have children. Five are married and two . . . used to be. . . . These women skillfully exploit [their sexuality].[23]

Granted, *Fortune* has generally offered conservative approaches to business. However, the emphasis on women as mothers and on women's sexuality has been increasingly typical of the public discussion of women executives and managers after 1980. While it is almost impossible to find a reference to the children of male managers and executives in newspaper and magazine articles, it is almost impossible *not* to find such references in articles on executive or managerial women in the 1990s.

Gender expectations sometimes led to behavior potentially damaging to corporate profits and stability or to legally actionable behavior. Attitudes toward Bendix Corporate Vice President Mary Cunningham rendered extremely volatile the company's hostile takeover by Martin Marietta in the early 1980s. Many of those at Bendix could not believe that Cunningham's rapid rise and enormous success were the result of her intelligence, hard work, and business competence. Rather, they fell back on gender stereotypes: she had to be sleeping with the boss. Their attitude led to distrust and political infighting and made it almost impossible for the CEO to negotiate during the tense weeks of the takeover. Ann Hopkins, who was repeatedly passed over for promotion to partner in the powerful Price Waterhouse accounting firm, sued the firm for sex discrimination. Her attorneys argued that she was held back due to sexual stereotyping. The Supreme Court agreed and found in her favor in the landmark *Price Waterhouse* v. *Hopkins* (1989). The case established that sex role stereotyping was a legitimate grounds for suit. Partners in the firm had used very different, sexually coded language to describe the same behavior: some referred to her courage and independence, and others described her as abrasive and arrogant. One partner told her that if she wanted a promotion, she should "walk more femininely, wear make-up, have her hair styled, and wear jewelry."[24]

The phenomena of the glass ceiling and the mommy track were another result of the gender coding of management. By the early 1980s business commentators and researchers on women's business position blamed women's failure to advance in business on the glass ceiling. Women in management could see the top reaches of the job hierarchy, but they were kept from those heights by a combination of attitudes about women's capabilities, their rarity, and the demands of their domestic lives that prevented them from devoting all of their energies to the job. Even women who had no children and mothers who chose to work outside of the home were subject to the glass ceiling. Since the common assumption was that careers in management played second banana to women's "real" job of raising children, all women would have difficulty making it to the top.

A 1989 article in the *Harvard Business Review* proposed a controversial expedient to the glass ceiling. Its author, Felice Schwartz, was an expert on career women and the president of a research group that focused on businesswomen. Like many who were concerned about the glass ceiling, Schwartz believed that it was the family claim that kept women back. She proposed a Solomonic solution: Divide the career tracks of women into two categories, one for "serious" women committed to their work and another for women who were more interested in their family. Committed career women could climb as high as their talents and ambitions took them. Family-minded women could maintain a niche at the middle-management level and be given incentives to remain there in the form of family leave, flexible scheduling, and part-time work. Schwartz even argued that these managerial mothers might make better middle managers since they would be less interested in promotion, happier in the work they were doing, and thus, presumably, more likely to stay.

Quickly dubbed a mommy track by the media, this notion of a division of labor made obvious the discrepancy between ideas about female domesticity and women's paid work, a discrepancy as old as women's labor force participation. Discussions about women in management have recognized difference in part because women workers have concerns, needs, and expectations in the workplace that seem to set them apart from men. But these differences were caused to some degree by the gendered structure of the job market itself, not women making individual choices. Women who gave up management or executive positions to spend time with children often sacrificed job mobility. Of the first substantial group of women to go into management during the 1970s, many who left the labor force to raise children found that in order to return they had to start over. For example, Jacqueline Engel Irwin left a prestigious job as marketing director at a major international lending institution in 1980 because she wanted to spend time raising her young children. During that time she continued to run her own consulting firm. When she reentered the managerial job market in 1988, however, she had to take a position for which she was overqualified and work her way up all over again. Corporations and even smaller firms typically did not recognize the time women were out of the corporate job market as time spent learning or maintaining business skills.

Further, issues such as child care and the all-consuming demands of managerial work are not inherently gender related. What Schwartz simplistically posited as two types of women was in reality a complex equation that stretched across gender lines and career trajectories. Like the debates surrounding pregnancy disability, the mommy track failed to recognize that men might also have interests in family that could be encouraged if career expectations for men were more elastic. Despite the fact that surveys of male managers in the 1970s and 1980s revealed that men listed these areas of their work as problems, business commentators often presented them as specifically female concerns. As we have seen with the parental leave issue, "parent" in business parlance usually meant "mother." (It speaks volumes that there is no popular magazine available entitled *Working Father*.)

The tensions of corporate work, not all of them gender related, led to a disproportionate loss of women managers in the early 1980s. In 1986 *Fortune* magazine noted with alarm that women managers were "bailing out" of the corporate workforce. Of the approximately 8,000 MBAs in its sample who received degrees in 1976, *Fortune* found that "the same percentage of women as men—69%—went to work for large corporations or professional firms." Ten years later, however, 30 percent of the women as opposed to 21 percent of the men "reported they were self-employed, unemployed," or working part-time. MBA graduates of Pace University between 1976 and 1980 showed an even greater disparity: 21 percent of the women compared with only 1 percent of the men were not working full time in 1987. Sample interviews with former women corporate managers found that their reasons for leaving included lack of corporate sensitivity to family needs, lower salaries despite equal training, the pressures of "token" status as women, "organizational rigidity," and "lack of autonomy."[25] Only some of these complaints were related to differences between men and women. The rest were systematic: they were the complaints of workers who wanted more control over their work.

Management's tendency to see problems as personal rather than systematic aggravated the influence of gender difference. Some evidence suggests that corporate efforts at meeting affirmative action goals began with the assumption that it was people and not the workplace that needed changing. For example, at one mid-sized business with home offices in the East, initial responses to affirmative action decrees in the 1970s relied on

training employees to think of where they want to go; identifying for employees what talents and skills are needed to be in the professional and management levels; changing attitudes on job mobility, risk taking, getting more education, and opportunities for advancement; training of managers in career counseling; [and] upgrading those women with the desire and potential for advancement.

The company's human resources managers, charged with identifying the source of job inequities, looked first to the personal beliefs of employees: "Managers (men) are biased. . . . Female employees lack confidence and the required skills." The question of women's ability to do the job sometimes was so ingrained that obviously invidious distinctions went unexamined. One male manager in a 1975 corporate survey of attitudes toward women as potential managerial material observed that when he interviewed men and women for a position, only the men had "potential." When asked how he judged potential, he responded, "It's hard to describe. I guess it's a gut feel."[26]

Some argued for women's right to equal status in the workplace by pointing to the ways work skills enhanced women's domestic domain. *Working Woman* magazine in 1987 argued that managerial training could translate into successful domestic skills. Generating goals, lists of tasks and responsibilities for family members, and complex scheduling could all be implemented to achieve a domestic life that not only did not interfere with paid work but in fact reinforced workplace skills. Some of these articles generated some fairly stringent conditions: a "manageable" husband and children, paid domestic help, live-in nannies who made Mary Poppins look like an amateur, and a salary large enough to smooth over any inadequacies in the requirements. Women could make good wives and mothers, in other words, *because* they were well-trained managerial workers. This argument is especially revealing when we recall one of the original rationales for women's appropriateness for office work in the late nineteenth century: their domestic training suited them for office work. Women could keep a tidy office because they knew how to keep a tidy home. Women were used to dealing with children, and therefore capricious male bosses would be easy to handle.[27]

In other words, notions of women's difference from men were used to both support and negate their managerial abilities. Although this difference could open up opportunities for women—and historically had done so—it also tied those opportunities to the apron strings of the family claim. In addition, the argument from difference had another dangerous tendency: It sometimes conflated learned skills and cultural womanhood or manhood with biological destiny. Claims that women had a "naturally" or "inherently" different management style than men confused social with biological gender. Many even suggested that this style was, in another recapitulation of early-twentieth-century arguments, superior to the masculine approach. *Newsweek* magazine in 1986 acknowledged that men's and women's different socialization led to different behaviors but slipped into concepts such as *intuition* and words such as *natural* and *inherent* to describe women's managerial skills. As one male manager observed, "I've changed a lot of my attitudes about women since I've seen them succeed—they usually do a better job than the men." Another commented, drawing on notions of women's job skills that can be traced back at least 100 years, "Women don't learn as fast as men. They're better at detail work."[28]

The focus on gender difference to explain workplace relations, combined with the increasing visibility of women in management positions, encouraged a shift of emphasis in managerial job skills in the 1980s. This shift can help explain the growth in the percentage of female managers after about 1986, which came hard on the heels of a general reevaluation of American management principles due to the successes of the Japanese economy in the early 1980s. As it happened, the management role defined as the root of Japanese triumphs overlapped neatly with the traditional definition of women's management strengths. Commentators argued that *all* managers should be cooperative, communally oriented, sensitive to other workers, and nurturing: woman's historically derived management role. By the mid-1980s business commentators asserted that the ideal manager was either a woman or a man who acted like a woman. As *Newsweek* magazine put it in 1986, "The very qualities that men had traditionally denigrated as feminine weaknesses—sympathy, sensitivity, a lack of the killer instinct—may often be advantages when it comes to getting the best out of people."[29]

Commentators pushed the argument from difference to its perhaps logical conclusion, claiming that it was up to women to make men feel comfortable in the office. Onto the shoulders of the 1980s version of the nurturing female manager fell the responsibility for learning something about sports so she could talk to men or using "light, appropriate humor" to smooth over tensions. This approach stood in sharp contrast to the tenor of discussion in the 1970s, which stressed that men should adjust to women's presence in management. As one author caustically put it, "Does this sound familiar—women having to be caretakers, even in the executive suite? Haven't we come any further than that?"[30]

By the late 1980s most women managers were in midlevel positions, a fact that reflected their recent entry into male management tracks. The argument from difference may keep them there, as it has in the past, if it continues to focus on and thus reinforce traditional gender images. Or it may change the overall expectations of managerial behavior, creating a feminized corporation, mommy tracks, and an exodus of men from management. Or it may lead to redefining job titles to maintain the continuum of unequal status, pay, and entitlements. Historically, as we have seen, all of these responses have occurred in similar situations.

The entertainment industry provides a useful example in this regard. Since the late 1920s the industry has been visibly and structurally dominated by men: actors, executives, producers, directors, musicians, and singers. In the 1990s it maintained international scope and influence and generated huge revenues. Entertainment's cultural status as a shaper of the consumer market, and its links to the international communications industry, gave the media industry enormous power and significance. All of this helps to explain why Dawn Steel's experience was so revealing. She came face to face with many of the problems that confronted women in business from the 1960s through the 1990s (and into the twenty-first century): sexual harassment, the

glass ceiling, and failed expectations shaped her experience as a corporate executive.

It is possible that Steel's difficulties were partly the product of
being a pioneer. The rising talents of a generation of young women
have invaded many aspects of the entertainment industry, as producers, musicians, singers, actors, radio personalities, and film
directors. By the mid-1990s women's ability to produce a range of
movie types was widely accepted, and all of the major studios and
some independent companies had women well represented in the
upper echelons. Women were executive producers in 21.5 percent
of the top 100 films made in 1999, and producers in 27 percent.
Twenty-four percent of the top-rated television shows in the 1998–99
season had female executive producers, and 31 percent had women
as producers. Among the most successful women in television is
Marcy Carsey, co-founder and partner in Carsey-Werner-Mand-
abach. The company became the first independent studio to have
the three top programs of a season (1988–89 with *The Cosby Show,
Roseanne,* and *A Different World*). The company also has produced
Grace Under Fire and *3rd Rock from the Sun,* won the Emmy, the
People's Choice Award, The Golden Globe, The NAACP Image
Award, the Humanitas Prize, The Peabody, and others which recog-
nize both the principals' talents and their desire to produce respon-
sible television. With her partners Tom Werner and Caryn
Mandabach, Oprah Winfrey, and Nickelodeon executive Geraldine
Laybourne, Carsey created Oxygen, a multimedia company
directed at women. Like Lindsay Johnson Suddarth and Judith
Luther Wilder of Women Incorporated, and Oprah Winfrey, Marcy
Carsey has used her industry clout to produce opportunities for
other women in broadcasting and for other businesswomen through
the company's philanthropic wing.

Women also entered the executive halls of network and cable television. The Fox television network, fX Cable, the Discovery Channel,
USA Network, and the Paramount Studios film division were all
chaired by women in the mid-1990s. Women musicians made inroads
into the rock music industry, a bastion of machismo and male angst.
Women such as Liz Phair and female groups such as Salt-N-Pepa and
Hole accounted for nearly 40 percent of the industry's talent pool in
the mid-1990s.

Past experience, however, suggests a word of caution. In the
words of two students of professionalization, women often "get a

ticket to ride after the gravy train has left the station."[31] Women film producers in the mid-1990s were paid 20 to 40 percent less than male producers and received smaller discretionary accounts than men for purchasing properties—scripts, novels, and story ideas. As the number of women producers increased, both men and women earned less than men did when they dominated the field. This decline may have been the result of the familiar process of feminization. As women approach numerical dominance in a job category, their status as subordinate workers devalues the position. Or it may work the other way around. Perhaps women entered the field of film production at the same time as it was becoming less important to the entire filmmaking process. Probably, in fact, these two causes were related, as has been the case in similar situations such as teaching, librarianship, and social welfare work. If the film industry is any guide, the future of women in management remained problematic at the turn of the century.

Conclusion

To most supporters of women's right to a public, economic role in the early 1960s it seemed clear that women needed an equal footing with men on male terms. The mainstream liberal feminism of the twentieth century, like that of the nineteenth, sought a white middle-class ideal of social and economic equity that would elevate women to the same footing as men. That clarity did not survive the heady days of the late 1960s and early 1970s.

Absolute parity has not been achieved by the late 1990s. Some of the difficulties of achieving parity in this period have deep political and historical roots, as we have seen, and have raised new versions of tough old public policy questions. Are women the same as men and therefore entitled to similar opportunities? Or are women different fundamentally or culturally and thus in a discrete category from men? Or is this simply a false dichotomy? Can women be treated the same as men economically even though they can never be like men biologically? Is the problem the universality of a male standard rather than any specific differences between men and women? Because women are not a minority but a majority of the population (51 percent in 2000), defining the nature of sex discrimination has challenged the courts as well as those concerned with women's status. The U.S. Supreme Court, for example, has consistently treated sex discrimination according to different standards than race discrimination, holding a narrower definition of the problem for gender than for race.

This period has witnessed some apparently revolutionary changes. The growth in the numbers, strength, and valuation of female sole proprietorships after 1970 has continued to gain momentum in the late 1990s. The percentage of women workers has grown, and opportunities have increased, especially in management, the professions, and the executive suite. Although far from resolved, for the first time in our history public discussions of issues such as sexual harassment and the double day have received wide attention, even as more longstanding debates over inequitable compensation and protective legislation are revived and reframed.

Many other difficult subjects have persisted, unresolved. Affirmative action remains a divisive issue, particularly around the differences of sex, in part because of the difficulty of seeing a majority group as the subject of discrimination. Women's work and entrepreneurial activities continue to be defined by the family claim that has shaped women's business role since the seventeenth century. Whether as managers, workers, or entrepreneurs, women in business have filled feminized niches compensated at a lower rate than male-defined fields. Sex role stereotyping and gender segregation endure.

The beauty tycoon Estée Lauder received numerous awards in the 1970s and 1980s for her business acumen and civic contributions. In recognition of her status as a grande dame of the business world and as an example of the dominant model of executive womanhood at the end of the twentieth century, the National Mother's Day Committee in 1984 named Lauder an "Outstanding Mother of the Year." Barbara Bush, the wife of then–Vice President George Bush, was similarly honored. The mother as manager remains a powerful business image, one manifestation of the continuing strength of the family claim.

Chapter Seven

Conclusion

*I want a small stove to put in the Shop . . . only it must be very small as
the shop is so.*
  —*Letter from Jane Farson to Samuel Coats, November 5, 1773*

*She's 25, petite, pretty, stylish and smart and she has three boyfriends.
She also is a company president.*
  —*On Jane Evans, President, I. Miller, 1970*

*Of course you can have it all, if you want it. And it won't be perfect, but
it won't be perfect anyway, so you might as well do what you want.*
  —*Marcy Carsey, co-owner Carsey-Warner, on working women, 1996*

We read histories for the stories they tell us about ourselves. Those
stories often are tantalizingly incomplete, with partially revealed characters and lost endings. The narratives of women's history are especially difficult to reconstruct because women left relatively few of the
sorts of documents historians use to revive the past. Women have also
often been devalued as historical actors, their experiences relegated to
domestic, "private" life. These difficulties underlie the long silence
that has surrounded the history of women and business.

Once reconstituted, however, women's histories can be transformative, asking us to rewrite familiar stories and see the world in new

211

ways. As the examples included in this book suggest, women's business involvement spans our history. The powerful female corporate executive officer of a late-twentieth-century conglomerate stands on the shoulders of Ojibwa fur traders, market women, butter makers, bankers, and "factory girls." Women's stories are important to the history of business as well as to the history of women. Individual women have contributed as entrepreneurs, workers, managers, and slaves to the historical development of business. Small and large firms, consumer markets, and individual economic actors have all been shaped, at least in part, by social categories such as gender, race, class, and ethnicity. Although there is still a great deal we do not know, we have enough information to begin to evaluate these histories. Several patterns have emerged in this discussion, that, when taken together, suggest that the continuities in women's business roles may be more sturdy than the departures.

First, at least 300 years of business engagement by thousands of women preceded the admittedly furious growth of female entrepreneurship and labor force participation after 1970. Although the specifics of women's business involvement in recent years may be new, the fact of their involvement is not. In some cases slave status or poverty has obscured women's market activities. The long-standing notion that women were "covered" by male relatives—first within the legal notion of coverture and later under the rhetorical flags of the family wage, true womanhood, and domesticity—has kept hidden the enormous number of women engaged in business at any given time in our history. Yet female entrepreneurs have been present in virtually every economic sector from the beginning of written records. Women managed plantations and farms, almshouses, and colleges in the eighteenth and nineteenth centuries and have always been a presence in the retail sector.

Second, the apparently revolutionary nature of the years after 1963, and the interest in business women evidenced by the media, the business community, educators, social scientists, feminists, and government, have strong parallels in the transitions of the early nineteenth century and in the years between 1880 and 1930. These periods were marked by demographic, economic, and technological change, which necessitated redefining women's place in business. The transition to waged labor occasioned by the first industrial revolution undermined the perceived economic significance of women's household work, replacing it with a primarily ideological importance. At the same time, some women moved out of the household and into the fledgling wage labor force or maintained retail establishments catering to the growing consumer economy. The recognition of the impact of these economic changes on women's lives led to the first debates over women's rights in the United States, focusing on such issues as married women's claims to property, the economic value of household labor, and women's access to credit. The late nineteenth century, like the years after 1960, was a time of intense scrutiny, sometimes extravagant claims, mushrooming organizational formation, and national debate over women's role in business. Women's dominance in the clerical industries, for example, stemmed from the growth of business and government in this period, as did debates over protective labor legislation and married women's work. The appearance of feminized professions brought women into business and government and influenced the expansion of corporate management and government after 1900.

It is striking, in fact, how the debates over women's place that charged the atmosphere of the early twentieth century are being repeated as the century draws to a close. Whether women should be protected in the workplace because of their unique biological status as potential mothers remains a thorny issue. Questions about the nature of power and hierarchy in the workplace are often expressed as sexual challenges. Comparable worth keeps alive the issue of gender segregation and the devaluation of women's labor that goes back to the late eighteenth century. And although the relative difference between men's and women's earning power has grown smaller, it took nearly 200 years to gain 47 cents on the dollar. At that rate, it will be another 100 years before equity is achieved, if it ever is.

Third, the development of gender segregation in business and the labor force, which grew out of assumptions about "women's place," defined feminized niches for women in business. On the one hand, such divisions meant women had reserved to them, almost exclusively, certain entrepreneurial and work arenas. Women have tended to monopolize the provision of food and domestic services, establishing concerns in such areas as dining, catering, laundry, dressmaking, retail luxury goods, and lodging. Assumptions about women's skills as nurturers led to the gender typing of certain professions, such as nursing, social work, and librarianship. On the other hand, when the gains to be made in an area have become extremely lucrative, or a field has been regularized and licensed, women have typically been edged out, as in cheese making, dairying, the women's clothing trade, and many of the professions. Because of the historical emphasis on the male wage, women's economic status has remained inferior to men's.

The gender segregation of economic activity has not necessarily meant that women and men engaged in business for different reasons. Women's business access has been important to them in ways similar to men: to provide for themselves and their families, to achieve success, to satisfy ambition. But the notion of women's difference from men, which underlies assigning distinct arenas to the sexes, may have encouraged some women to set ostensibly different goals. Further research may reveal that women more often than men have been interested in the creation of social capital through education and philanthropy or the use of businesses to further civil and political rights.

Fourth, running through the entire history of women and business in America are the effects not just of gender difference but of gender inequity. As we have seen, institutional gender segregation has often been premised historically on the idea that men and women are unequally different. Indeed, the root of many reasons for gender disparities in business experience has to do with the historically persistent position of men and women in the occupational hierarchy and in relation to one another. The personnel director for a major Midwestern real estate investment firm observed in the late 1980s that although the affirmative action decrees of the 1960s and 1970s changed the gender composition of her company's executive sales force, almost no one was entirely comfortable with his or her coworkers of the opposite sex. The men preferred to work with other men, and women managers felt uncomfortable about their role. One result of gender differences has been that women have remained outsiders, even as they have made a place for themselves in the business world.

Within these larger patterns is a great deal of room for individual variation and for future modifications as we learn more about the history of women and business. The stories outlined in this book have merely scratched the surface, and there remains a great deal that we do not know. Until we have more information about women's status in the law, especially their access to forms of property, credit, and family assets at different times, we will not be able to detail what their advantages and limitations have been. For example, what has been the impact of women's businesses on the economic development of urban areas throughout our history? How did women's business successes and failures help to shape various regions and communities? How much property have women owned, and to what purposes have they put it? To what extent did women's efforts in areas such as philan- thropic causes help to accumulate and circulate capital in the nine- teenth-century market economy? What contributions did female consumers, entrepreneurs, and workers make to the market and industrial revolutions? What has been the impact of gender segrega- tion on long-term economic change? Do women persistently approach entrepreneurship differently from men, and, if so, why? Women's entrepreneurship—like men's—probably helped fund polit- ical movements, such as the civil rights struggles of the nineteenth and twentieth centuries, the women's rights and antifeminist move- ments, Progressive reform, or even the Ku Klux Klan. What has been the relation between women's business and political change? What role have women's marginal businesses—such as petty trading or the production and sale of home-prepared food—played in the survival of poor communities or the ability of female immigrants to be upwardly mobile? Understanding more about these issues would enable us to rethink the nature of capital formation; its relation to business devel- opment, and women's part in economic change.

These observations about the history of women's business roles raise important issues related to the questions posed earlier about how power has operated in business. Expectations about gender have historically generated expectations about work skills, appropriate businesses for women, and women's economic position in general. For example, assumptions about manhood and womanhood helped shape the original development of factory labor in shoemaking and textiles, consumer markets, managerial and professional behavior, entrepre- neurial arenas, and expectations for white-collar workers. Thus, although a male manager or sole proprietor may want more freedom to shape his career commitments and chronology, he is not likely to respond positively to something called a mommy track or to seriously consider starting a business in an area defined as "women's work."

Women's business history can teach us the importance of *differ- ences*—among consumers, entrepreneurs, workers, managers, and professionals—stemming from gender, race, ethnicity, and class. It can also illuminate the divergent sources of power and interest involved in business issues. The average corporate stockholder, busi- ness apologists, and many politicians assume that *business* is synony- mous with *capitalism* and *democracy* and that capitalism operates according to those neutral laws of supply and demand first articulated by Adam Smith in the eighteenth century. Critics of this viewpoint, however, from labor leaders to social reformers, have been arguing since the early nineteenth century that no economic system is immune from human behavior and belief. The history of women's business experiences suggests, for example, that gender has always been part of job descriptions, self-perceptions, consumer markets, and business niches. There are no "neutral" or "natural" economic laws that dictate how markets and capitalism operate outside of the scope of human influence. Traditional gender images have persistently deflected discussions about work, investment, and capital formation (to name a few issues) away from systemic organizational or economic issues and onto the relations between men and women. Much of what seems to be intrinsic to people, in other words, actually is socially constructed, just as much of what seems to be socially and economically neutral—markets, credit, and risk-taking behavior—actually is hedged by cultural expectations.

The failure to recognize these consequences of cultural expectations in business levies enormous personal, economic, and social cost on men and women workers, on those who hire them, and on the economy. What happens to women managers and their employers, for example, when preferred styles of management change? How will we ensure that those who wish to work can do so without facing insurmountable systemic problems such as unequal pay and the double day? Can we, as many business commentators asked in the 1970s, afford to squander human resources by failing to recognize structural impediments to ambition, skill, talent, and individual work ethics?

The various histories of "others" were born in the desire to understand the roots of differences and inequities that have seemed to resist change. Inevitably these stories disestablish the status quo because they question the very premises on which "business as usual" are based. Business history, in contrast, like the Whig narrative of progress, was born in the celebration of the status quo, and the image of business history as the champion of laissez-faire lingers on. Even more insidiously, the popular image of business is linked to complex notions of patriotism and conservatism and to political agendas that sometimes deny humanistic concerns. Many Americans seem to believe that the purpose of business is to make a few people millionaires. If we ask, as we legitimately could, what the purpose of business is, a more historically accurate and reasonable answer might be to make people's lives better or to raise the standard of living for as many as possible. As I hope this history of women and business suggests, recovering that narrative can teach us a great deal about the central role business development has played in individual lives. Women engaged in business out of choice and out of necessity. What all of them surely desired, however, was a decent return on their risk, some value for their labors, and, if not always roses, at least bread. In that sense, the history of women and business is as crucial to the story of our past as the narratives of political parties, giant corporations, modern wars, and institutional change.

Notes and References

1. Incorporating Others: The Social Categories of Business History

1. Louis Galambos, "What Makes Us Think We Can Put Business Back into American History?" *Business and Economic History* 2d ser., 20 (1991): 1–11.

2. For definitions of *business,* see, for example, *American Heritage College Dictionary*, 3d ed., s.v. "business," and *Oxford English Dictionary,* 2d ed., s.v. "business" and "professional."

3. Susan Ingalls Lewis, "Beyond Horatio Alger: Breaking through Gendered Assumptions about Business 'Success' in Mid-Nineteenth-Century America," *Business and Economic History* 24 (Fall 1995): 97–105.

4. Ronaleen R. Roha, "How Bartering Saves Cash," *Kiplinger's Personal Finance Magazine* 50 (February 1996): 103–7.

5. Suzanne Lebsock, *The Free Women of Petersburg: Status and Culture in a Southern Town, 1784–1860* (New York: W. W. Norton, 1984).

6. Joan Acker, "Hierarchies, Jobs, Bodies: A Theory of Gendered Organizations," *Gender and Society* 4 (June 1990): 129, 146.

7. Juliet Walker, "Racism, Slavery, and Free Enterprise: Black Entrepreneurship in the United States before the Civil War," *Business History Review* 60 (Autumn 1986): 343–82.

8. Rosalind Rosenberg, *Divided Lives: American Women in the 20th Century* (New York: Hill & Wang, 1992), chapter 1.

9. Claudia Goldin, "The Economic Status of Women in the Early Republic: Quantitative Evidence," *Journal of Interdisciplinary History*

16 (Winter 1986): 375–404, and Patricia Cleary, " 'She Merchants' of Colonial America: Women and Commerce on the Eve of the Revolution" (Ph.D. diss., Northwestern University, 1989).

10. Geoffrey Jones and Mary B. Rose, eds., "Special Issue on Family Capitalism," *Business History* 35 (October 1993).

11. This is a widely acknowledged paradox and one that is central to women's history. A useful summary can be found in William H. Chafe, *The Paradox of Change: American Women in the 20th Century* (New York: Oxford University Press, 1991), 72.

2. Female Economics: Women and Business in Preindustrial America, 1550–1830

1. Gary B. Mills, "Coincoin: An Eighteenth-Century 'Liberated' Woman," *Journal of Southern History* 42 (May 1976): 205–22.

2. *Liberalism* comes from the eighteenth-century social theory that posited the individual as the basic unit of society. John Locke, for example, argued that a society is created when individuals agree to give up some of their rights to form a state (a "social contract") that then governs for the good of everyone. This idea of a social contract gained an economic dimension by the early nineteenth century in the notion of laissez-faire: that individuals were the basic unit of market (or economic) relations and that individual economic choices would be the foundation of market relations. The various terms used to describe the economic transitions of the 1750s to the 1830s spring from different emphases by historians on the causes of the economic changes described here. The terms are not interchangeable and refer to distinct aspects of the overall transition from one set of economic relations to another.

3. Thomas Cochran, in *Business in American Life: A History* (New York: McGraw-Hill, 1972), 9, refers to "the business of colonization," which he interpreted quite literally to mean colonial business endeavors. My sense of the phrase is somewhat broader.

4. I am purposely blurring the distinctions among material, ceremonial, and manufacturing uses of trade goods: for the purposes of exchange, all were items of consumption. See, however, James Axtell, *Beyond 1492: Encounters in Colonial North America* (New York: Oxford University Press, 1992); Calvin Martin, *Keepers of the Game: Indian-Animal Relationships and the Fur Trade* (Berkeley and Los

Angeles: University of California Press, 1978); and Christopher L. Miller and George R. Hamell, "A New Perspective on Indian-White Contact: Cultural Symbols and Colonial Trade," *Journal of American History* 73 (September 1986): 311–28.

5. Matrilineal societies are those in which inheritance, family identification, and family history are traced to the mother. In contrast, a patrilineal society (such as we find in the present-day United States) is one that uses a father's lineage.

6. Quotations from Annette Kolodny, *The Lay of the Land: Metaphor as Experience and History in American Life and Letters* (Chapel Hill: University of North Carolina Press, 1975), 4–5. Emphasis in the original.

7. On the idea of the family claim, see Rosalind Rosenberg, *Divided Lives: American Women in the Twentieth Century* (New York: Hill & Wang, 1992), chapter 1.

8. Among the colonies with chancery courts were New York, Maryland, Virginia, and South Carolina. Among those without chancery, and thus less access to equity rules, were Massachusetts, Pennsylvania, and Connecticut. On the development of equity rules, see Marylynn Salmon, *Women and the Law of Property in Early America* (Chapel Hill: University of North Carolina Press, 1986), 80–87.

9. Mary Beth Norton, "A Cherished Spirit of Independence: The Life of an Eighteenth-Century Boston Businesswoman," in *Women of America: A History*, edited by Carol Berkin and Mary Beth Norton (Boston: Houghton Mifflin, 1979), 50.

10. Efforts to regulate access to entrepreneurial and artisanal areas were typical of preindustrial governments and affected men as often as women.

11. Mary Beth Norton, *Liberty's Daughters: The Revolutionary Experience of American Women* (Boston: Little, Brown, 1980), 144–45.

12. Laurel Thatcher Ulrich, "Martha Ballard and Her Girls: Women's Work in Eighteenth-Century Maine," in *Work and Labor in Early America*, edited by Stephen Innes (Chapel Hill: University of North Carolina Press, 1988), 72. For a more extended treatment of female economic networks, see Ulrich's *A Midwive's Tale: The Life of Martha Ballard, Based on Her Diary, 1785–1812* (New York: Vintage Books, 1991).

13. Quoted in Laurel Thatcher Ulrich, "Housewife and Gadder: Themes of Self-Sufficiency and Community in Eighteenth-Century New England," in *"To Toil the Livelong Day": America's Women at*

Work, 1780–1980, edited by Carol Groneman and Mary Beth Norton (Ithaca, N.Y.: Cornell University Press, 1987), 27.

14. Elisabeth Dexter, *Colonial Women of Affairs: Women in Business and the Professions in America before 1776,* 2d ed. (New York: Houghton Mifflin, 1931), 23, 25. Evidence of "she-merchants'" use of business forms such as power of attorney and direct negotiations with ship captains can be found in the Rose Campbell Papers and a letter in the same repository dated November 5, 1773, from Jane Farson of Wilmington, Delaware, to Samuel Coats of Philadelphia, Hagley Museum and Library, Wilmington, Delaware.

15. Jonathan Chu, "Debt and Taxes: Public Finance and Private Economic Behavior in Postrevolutionary Massachusetts," in *Entrepreneurs: The Boston Business Community, 1700–1850,* edited by Conrad Edick Wright and Katheryn P. Viens (Boston: Northeastern University Press, 1997).

16. Caroline Bird, *Enterprising Women* (New York: W. W. Norton, 1976), 32–35. George Washington was one of Eliza Pinkney's pallbearers.

17. Norton, *Liberty's Daughters,* 143.

18. Claudia Goldin, "The Economic Status of Women in the Early Republic: Quantitative Evidence," *Journal of Interdisciplinary History* 16 (Winter 1986): 398–99. Goldin found that in Philadelphia in the early 1790s, for example, 93 percent of artisanal widows were artisans.

3. Mills and More: Women's Business and the First Industrial Revolution, 1830–1880

1. Information on Rebecca Pennock Lukens may be found in the Lukens Steel Company Papers (hereafter LSCP), Hagley Museum and Library, Wilmington, Delaware. See also Caroline Bird, *Enterprising Women* (New York: W. W. Norton, 1976), 53–56, for a brief popular treatment of Lukens's life.

2. See the entries for these terms in *The Oxford English Dictionary,* 2d ed., s.v. "business," "profession," and "occupation."

3. *Corporations* are legal entities that assume the same rights and responsibilities as individuals and bureaucratic forms that connect stockholders to trustees and employees. The mid-nineteenth century witnessed a growth in the use of corporate legal entities for business purposes. See Oscar Handlin and Mary Handlin, "Origins of the Amer-

ican Business Corporation," *Journal of Economic History* 5 (May 1945): 1–23.

4. *Primogeniture* is the practice of recognizing the oldest son's claim to all or the bulk of a family estate.

5. The state laws relating to married women's property in the nineteenth century were too complex and diverse to do justice to them here. In addition, the reasons states adopted different legal systems in former Mexican and French territories that shared a civil law tradition beg for further analysis, especially in relation to women's marital property and inheritance rights. See Norma Basch, *In the Eyes of the Law: Women, Marriage, and Property in Nineteenth-Century New York* (Ithaca, N.Y.: Cornell University Press, 1982), 15–29; Joan Hoff, *Law, Gender, and Injustice: A Legal History of U.S. Women* (New York: New York University Press, 1991), 117–36; and Joan Jensen, ed., *Promise to the Land: Essays on Rural Women* (Albuquerque: University of New Mexico Press, 1991), 1–24.

6. Carole Shammas, "Re-Assessing the Married Women's Property Acts," *Journal of Women's History* 6 (Spring 1994): 9–30.

7. Wendy Gamber, "A Precarious Independence: Milliners and Dressmakers in Boston, 1860–1890," *Journal of Women's History* 4 (Spring 1992): 60.

8. The Lukens Steel Company Papers contain evidence that Rebecca's mother tried to wrest control of the company from her in favor of her older brother. According to Rebecca's testimony, this seems to have been a case of internal family tensions between mother and daughter rather than a belief that Rebecca, as a woman, was unfit to lead the company. See Rebecca Lukens's testimony dated September 10, 1850, LSCP.

9. Suzanne Lebsock, *The Free Women of Petersburg: Status and Culture in a Southern Town, 1784–1860* (New York: W. W. Norton, 1985).

10. Ann Braude, *Radical Spirits: Spiritualism and Women's Rights in Nineteenth-Century America* (Boston: Beacon Press, 1989), 2.

11. Joyce W. Warren, ed., *Ruth Hall and Other Writings [by] Fanny Fern* (New Brunswick, N.J.: Rutgers University Press, 1986). The quotes appear on pp. 146–47 and 173 of the novel, emphasis in the original.

12. Joan M. Jensen, *Loosening the Bonds: Mid-Atlantic Farm Women, 1750–1850* (New Haven, Conn.: Yale University Press, 1986), chapter 6.

13. Household Account Book, 1838–42, Victorine du Pont Baudry, in E. I. du Pont de Nemours Papers, Group 6, Series A—Eleuthera (du

Pont) Smith, Box 14; Eleuthera D. Du Pont Smith to Mrs. James [Mary] Wilkinson, December 20, 1861, Du Pont Family Papers, E. I. du Pont de Nemours Papers, emphasis in original. Both in Hagley Museum and Library, Wilmington, Delaware.

14. Janet LeCompte, "The Independent Women of Hispanic New Mexico, 1821–1846," in *New Mexican Women: Intercultural Perspectives*, edited by Joan Jensen and Darlis Miller (Albuquerque: University of New Mexico Press, 1986), 75.

15. Quoted in J. F. Elliott, "The Great Western: Sarah Bowman, Mother and Mistress to the U.S. Army," *Journal of Arizona History* 30 (Spring 1989): 1–26.

4. Personal Work: Women's Business in a Corporate World, 1880–1930

1. Quoted in Margaret Duckworth, "Maggie L. Walker," in *Notable Black American Women*, edited by Jesse Carney Smith (Detroit, Mich.: Gale Research, 1992), 1189–90.

2. Duckworth, in "Maggie L. Walker," pp. 1188–93, notes that the bank was still in existence as of 1992 under the name Consolidated Bank and Trust Company.

3. Upton Sinclair, *The Jungle* (New York: Penguin Books, 1986). *The Jungle* was first published in 1906 and was instrumental in garnering public support for pure food and drug acts. For a fictional treatment of the impact of big business methods on agriculture, see *The Octopus* (Cambridge, Mass.: Riverside Press, 1958), by Sinclair's contemporary, Frank Norris, first published in 1901.

4. The word *feminism* achieved widespread use in the United States by 1914. It was borrowed from the French women's movement. See Nancy Cott, *The Grounding of Modern Feminism* (New Haven, Conn.: Yale University Press, 1987), 14–15.

5. Jim Crow laws set up arbitrary and insurmountable obstacles to voting, such as the necessity to recite the Declaration of Independence backward or to pass an examination on the intricacies of constitutional law. They were used to prevent African-Americans from exercising the right to vote.

6. Alice Kessler-Harris, *A Woman's Wage: Historical Meanings and Social Consequences* (Louisville: University Press of Kentucky, 1990), chapter 1. The quote appears on p. 13.

7. Irene W. Hart, *How to Make Money Although a Woman* (New York: J. S. Ogilvie, 1895).

8. [Gertrude G.] de Aguirre, *Women in the Business World or Hints and Helps to Prosperity* (Boston: Arena, 1894).

9. The notions of fetal rights and fetal viability were unknown in the nineteenth century. Physicians made their case on the basis of medical treatments for women.

10. Lockwood's case has a larger legal significance. In the late-nineteenth-century battle over the use and meaning of the term *persons* and the extent of the equal protection clause in the Fourteenth Amendment, the Supreme Court in *Lockwood* allowed states to define "persons" as "male." The principles expressed in *Lockwood* stood until the case was overturned in 1971. On the Lockwood case, see Joan Hoff, *Law, Gender, and Injustice: A Legal History of U.S. Women* (New York: New York University Press, 1991), 183–84.

11. Robyn Muncy, *Creating a Female Dominion in American Reform, 1890–1935* (New York: Oxford University Press, 1991).

12. The field survives today in a much-expanded form as human ecology.

13. The phrase is Mark H. Rose's in *Cities of Light and Heat: Domesticating Gas and Electricity in Urban America* (University Park: Pennsylvania State University Press, 1995), chapter 3.

14. "Association of Bank Women," *Pacific Banker* 2 (October 1932): 176.

15. Elizabeth Barry, "Where Women Bankers Excel," *Coast Banker* 36 (May 1926): 541.

16. Elizabeth F. Briscoe, Letter to E. E. Pratt, New York School of Philanthropy, February 12, 1910, Joseph Bancroft & Sons Company Records, Hagley Museum and Library, Wilmington, Delaware.

17. Fannie B. Rosser Papers, William R. Perkins Library, Duke University, Raleigh, North Carolina.

18. Joan Curl Elliott, "Madame C. J. Walker," in *Notable Black American Women*, edited by Jesse Carney Smith (Detroit, Mich.: Gale Research, 1992), 1184–88.

19. Wendy Holliday, "Hollywood's Modern Women: Screenwriting, Work Culture, and Feminism, 1910–1940" (Ph.D. diss., New York University, 1995).

20. Ally Acker, *Reel Women: Pioneers of the Cinema, 1896 to the Present* (New York: Continuum, 1991), 21–29.

21. Williams is best known for *The Flames of Wrath*, which she pro-

duced in 1923. George P. Johnson Collection, Special Collections, University of California, Los Angeles Libraries. I am grateful to Jerry Butters for information on Williams.

22. D. B. Jones Company Papers, 1884–1956, and Edith McConnell Records, 1937–1945, both in Hagley Museum and Library, Wilmington, Delaware.

5. Crisis Management: Women and Business at Midcentury, 1930–1963

1. Lauder's autobiography is as much an attempt to maintain an air of mystery as it is to record truth. It is, however, a superb demonstration of Lauder's lifelong self-identification with her products. Estée Lauder, *Estée: A Success Story* (New York: Random House, 1985); the quote appears on page 18. Her unauthorized biography is by Lee Israel, *Estée Lauder: Beyond the Magic* (New York: Macmillan, 1985). A useful overview is found in John N. Ingham and Lynne B. Feldman, "Estée Lauder," in *Contemporary American Business Leaders: A Biographical Dictionary* (Westport, Conn.: Greenwood Press, 1990), 330.

2. The quotation is from the film *Rosie the Riveter*, a documentary on women's work experiences during World War II.

3. In 1973 women could still be singled out for gender-based exemptions to jury service because of pregnancy, the existence of small children, or simply embarrassment at appearing in public. Joan Hoff, *Law, Gender, and Injustice: A Legal History of U.S. Women* (New York: New York University Press, 1991), 223–28. Chinese exclusion laws were repealed in 1943. Ronald Takaki, *A Different Mirror: A History of Multicultural America* (Boston: Little, Brown, 1993), 273, 387.

4. Quoted in Robert Sobel and David B. Sicilia, *The Entrepreneurs: An American Adventure* (Boston: Houghton Mifflin, 1986), 220.

5. D'Ann Campbell, *Women at War with America: Private Lives in a Patriotic Era* (Cambridge, Mass.: Harvard University Press, 1984), 105–11.

6. Robert Sobel, in *The Age of Giant Corporations: A Microeconomic History of American Business, 1914–1992*, 3d ed. (Westport, Conn.: Greenwood Press, 1993), 122–23, points out that "petroleum, automobiles, aircraft, [and] chemicals" did well and that "the leaders in practically every industry not only survived . . . but often emerged

stronger than they had been in 1929." Unfortunately, these were not areas that saw many female proprietors or workers.

7. Quoted in Alice Kessler-Harris, *A Woman's Wage: Historical Meanings and Social Consequences* (Louisville: University Press of Kentucky, 1990), 57.

8. This market involvement has continued, and Acoma pottery has an international reputation for artistic and technical excellence. Terry R. Reynolds, "Women, Pottery, and Economics at Acoma Pueblo," in *New Mexican Women: Intercultural Perspectives*, edited by Joan M. Jensen and Darlis Miller (Albuquerque: University of New Mexico Press, 1986), 279–300.

9. I am grateful to Lois Spatz for providing details of Fanny Stahl's life, "Biography of Fanny Stahl, Founder of Stahl's Knishes in Brighton Beach, New York," compiled by Dora Stahl Engelberg and edited by Lois Spatz, August 1996, copy in author's possession.

10. Rosser's and Randolph's stories are based on materials in the Fannie B. Rosser Papers, William R. Perkins Library, Duke University, Raleigh, North Carolina.

11. Babette Kass and Rose Feld, *The Economic Strength of Business and Professional Women* (New York: National Federation of Business and Professional Women's Clubs, 1954).

12. Quoted in Takaki, *A Different Mirror*, 269–70.

13. Stephanie Kwolek went on to invent Kevlar in 1965, the material from which bulletproof vests, and now such things as canoes, are made. And, yes, she is a distant relative. Anne L. Macdonald, *Women and Invention in America* (New York: Ballantine Books, 1992), 373–75.

14. Quoted in Elaine Tyler May, *Homeward Bound: American Families in the Cold War Era* (New York: Basic Books, 1988), 87.

15. U.S. Department of Health, Education, and Welfare and Department of Labor, *Day Care Services, Form and Substance: A Report of a Conference, November 17–18, 1960* (Washington, D.C.: U.S. Government Printing Office, 1960); U.S. Department of Labor, *Employed Mothers and Child Care*, Women's Bureau Bulletin No. 246 (Washington, D.C.: U.S. Government Printing Office, 1953).

16. Based on an interview with Helen Fritchie Kwolek (my mother), August 1996.

17. This discussion is based on Kass and Feld, *Economic Strength*. The quotations are from a memorandum from Erma Romanik, National Legislation Committee Chair, to all state presidents and legislative committee chairs of local Business and Professional Women's

Clubs, May 3, 1957, Elva M. Chandler Papers, Hagley Museum and Library, Wilmington, Delaware.

18. The discussion of the survey results in this text is flawed by the fact that the authors often treat the "respondents" as the "membership" when clearly the respondents are a self-selected sampling of the total members. However, a response rate of 11 percent is close to a random sample. In my discussion I have tried to note these distinctions.

19. U.S. Department of Labor, *Women in Higher-Level Positions*, Bulletin of the Women's Bureau No. 236 (Washington, D.C.: U.S. Government Printing Office, 1950), 82–83.

20. Elva M. Chandler Papers.

21. Hanna Papanek, quoted in Rosabeth Moss Kanter, *Men and Women of the Corporation* (New York: Basic Books, 1977), 108–26.

22. Guyencourt Nurseries, Inc. Papers and Homsey Architects, Inc. Papers, both in the Hagley Museum and Library, Wilmington, Delaware.

23. Nasatir produced such films as *One Flew over the Cuckoo's Nest, Annie Hall*, and *The Big Chill*, among others.

24. Quoted in Takaki, *A Different Mirror*, 275.

6. Difference at Work: The Renewal of the Businesswoman, 1963–2000

1. "Women in Business: A Global Report Card," *Wall Street Journal*, July 26, 1995, sec. B, pp. 1–12.

2. Stephanie Mansfield, "Dawn Undaunted," *Lear's* (October 1993): 66–69, 106. See also Dawn Steel, *They Can Kill You but They Can't Eat You: Lessons from the Front* (New York: Pocket Books, 1993).

3. Joan Hoff, *Law, Gender, and Injustice: A Legal History of U.S. Women* (New York: New York University Press, 1991), 229.

4. "Title 41—Public Contracts and Property Management," part 60–20, Sex Discrimination Guidelines, *Federal Register* 35, no. 111 (June 9, 1970): 8888–89.

5. The first wave was the movement that spanned the late nineteenth and early twentieth centuries and focused on suffrage.

6. Patricia Zavella, *Women's Work and Chicano Families: Cannery Workers of the Santa Clara Valley* (Ithaca, N.Y.: Cornell University Press, 1987).

7. Hoff, *Law, Gender, and Injustice,* 288.

8. The quote is from Lenore J. Weitzman, *The Divorce Revolution: The Unexpected Social and Economic Consequences for Women and Children in America* (New York: Free Press, 1985), xii, cited in Hoff, *Law, Gender, and Injustice,* 292.

9. Hoff, *Law, Gender, and Injustice,* 294–95.

10. Susan Chira, "Family Leave Is Law, Will Things Change?" *New York Times,* August 15, 1993, p. 3.

11. Catherine MacKinnon, *Sexual Harassment of Working Women* (New Haven, Conn.: Yale University Press, 1979), 1.

12. Quoted in Hoff, *Law, Gender, and Injustice,* 429.

13. Quoted in Gary N. Powell, *Women and Men in Management* (Newbury Park, Calif.: Sage, 1993), 133.

14. Oneil R. Soto, "Lending Women in Business a Hand; Project helps when banks won't," *Long Beach (California) Press Telegram,* 30 May, 1995, B-1.

15. Defined by annual sales and number of employees, female ownership or controlling interest, and owner involvement in daily management. Eric Schmuckler, "The Top 50 Women Business Owners," *Working Woman,* May 1996, 52.

16. Quoted in Mike Sheridan, "Mother's Nature," *Sky Magazine,* January 1995, 60, 64.

17. Paul Noglows, "Oprah: The Year of Living Dangerously," *Working Woman,* May 1994, 55.

18. Some of the argument in this section is based on original research. I collected and tabulated all of the popular magazine literature on female managers published between 1960 and 1990. Using a random-sampling technique, I read approximately 50 percent of this collection.

19. Survey Results, Boyle/Kirkman Associates, Inc., ca. 1975, The "X" Company Collection, p. 37, Hagley Museum and Library, Wilmington, Delaware (hereafter "X" Company). This company granted access to its archival materials on condition that it remain anonymous. Julia Kagan, "How Management Myths Hurt Women," *Working Women,* December 1980, 75.

20. Minutes, Executive Committee Meeting, January 21, 1976, Human Resources Department, "X" Company.

21. Quoted in Sterling G. Slappey, "Those Powerful Powder Puff Executives," *Nation's Business* 58 (November 1970): 81.

22. Vincent Bozzi, "Assertiveness Breeds Contempt," *Psychology Today* 21, no. 15 (September 1987): 15.

23. Patricia Sellers, "Women, Sex, and Power," *Fortune*, August 5, 1996, 44.

24. On these two examples, see Mary Cunningham, *Power Play: What Really Happened at Bendix* (New York: Simon & Schuster, 1984), and Ann Hopkins, *So Ordered: Making Partner the Hard Way* (Amherst: University of Massachusetts Press, 1996).

25. Alex Taylor III, "Why Women Managers Are Bailing Out," *Fortune*, August 18, 1986, 16–18.

26. Minutes, "Human Relations Task Force," February 6, 1975, "X" Company. Survey, Boyle/Kirkman, 36, "X" Company.

27. "The Managerial Mother," *Working Woman*, December 1987, 117–18, 121–22, 124–26.

28. Ann Hughey and Eric Gelman, "Managing the Woman's Way," *Newsweek*, March 17, 1986, 46–47; Survey, Boyle/Kirkman, 37, 34, "X" Company.

29. Hughey and Gelman, "Managing the Woman's Way," 46.

30. Sharon Nelton, "Making Men Comfortable," *Nation's Business*, May 1987, 4.

31. Michael J. Carter and Susan Boslego Carter, "Women's Recent Progress in the Professions or, Women Get a Ticket to Ride after the Gravy Train Has Left the Station," *Feminist Studies* 7, no. 3 (Fall 1981): 477–504.

Bibliographic Essay

It would be impossible to discuss thoroughly all of the works relevant to a synthetic treatment of women's business history such as this one. This book has drawn on sources from a variety of areas, including women's, economic, labor, and business history; anthropology; sociology; and information taken from government, corporate, public, and private archives, national business organizations, World Wide Web sites, contemporary journalism, and the popular press. As this is written, dissertations, books, and articles are under construction or in press that represent an explosion of interest in and scholarship about women's business history. The following bibliographic essay is meant to be a brief introduction to what will, I suspect, become an increasingly complex and diverse field of study. I have included those works most relevant or important to the conceptualization of this book. However, this discussion is not meant to be definitive.

ARCHIVAL COLLECTIONS

The Hagley Museum and Library, Wilmington, Delaware, houses numerous collections with information on women and business, including entrepreneurs, inventors, managers, and workers. See Lynn Catanese's comprehensive *Woman's History: A Guide to Sources at the Hagley Museum and Library* (Westport, Conn.: Greenwood Press, 1997). The collections listed here are only a small portion of those in this repository that deal with women.

Joseph Bancroft & Sons Company Records
Rose Campbell Papers
Nora C. Edwards Papers

Mary Hallock Greenewalt, 1918–1939. Papers of P. S. duPont
D. B. Jones Company Papers, 1884–1956
Lukens Steel Company Papers
Edith McConnell Records, 1937–1945
E. I. duPont de Nemours Papers
Wurtz Family Papers
The "X" Company Papers

Additional primary sources on women and business can be found in the Fannie B. Rosser Papers, William R. Perkins Library, Duke University, Raleigh, North Carolina, and the Wells Fargo Archives, San Francisco, California, and at World Wide Web sites such as Baker Library's "Unheard Voices: American Women in the Emerging Industrial and Business Age"
    (http://www.library.hbs.edu/hc/unheard=_voices/)

PUBLISHED PRIMARY SOURCES
Newspapers, Journals, and Magazines

Abbreviations
FOR   *Fortune*
LS   *Lear's*
NW   *Newsweek*
NYT   *New York Times*
TM   *Time*
WSJ   *Wall Street Journal*
WW   *Working Woman*

Bamford, Janet. "America's Top Women Business Owners." *WW*, May 1994, 39–51.
Billard, Mary. "Women on the Verge of Being CEO." *Business Month*, April 1990, 26–47.
Bozzi, Vincent. "Assertiveness Breeds Contempt." *Psychology Today*, September 1987, 15.
Brailsford, Karen V. "The Feminine Art of Management." *Black Enterprise*, February 1987, 102–4.
Chira, Susan. "Family Leave Is Law; Will Things Change?" *NYT*, August 15, 1993, p. 3.
Gabor, Andrea. "Crashing the 'Old Boy' Party." *NYT*, January 8, 1995, p. 1.

Gross, Jane. "Revenge of a Former Talking Head: Seen Less but Heard More [Christine Craft]." *NYT*, August 15, 1993, p. 7.

Hochman. David. "Movers and Shakers: On the Road with Salt-N-Pepa." *US*, August 1994, 54–58.

Hughey, Ann, and Eric Gelman. "Managing the Woman's Way." *NW*, March 17, 1986, 46–47.

Jacobs, Deborah L. "Back from the Mommy Track." *NYT*, October 9, 1994, pp. 1, 6.

Kagan. Julia. "How Management Myths Hurt Women." *WW*, December 1980, 75.

Kantrowitz, Barbara. "Advocating a 'Mommy Track.' " *NW*, March 13, 1989, 45.

Karlen, Neal. "Love among the Ruins [Courtney Love]." *US*, August 1994, 77–84, 90–91

Laws, Margaret. "The Superior Sex." *WW*, March 1984, 16.

"Madam Executive." *TM* February 18, 1974, 76.

"The Managerial Mother." *WW*, December 1987, 117–18, 121–22, 124–26.

Mansfield, Stephanie. "Dawn Undaunted." *LS*, October 1993, 66–69, 106.

Meyer, Pearl. "Women Executives Are Different." *Dun's Review*, January 1975, 46–48.

Nelton, Sharon. "Making Men Comfortable." *Nation's Business*, May 1987, 4.

Nemy, Enid. "Intuition? It's Not a Woman's Monopoly." *NYT*, July 5, 1971, p. 1.

Noglows, Paul. "Oprah: The Year of Living Dangerously." *WW*, May 1994, 52–55, 94.

Overton, Elizabeth. "What Makes an Executive Woman?" *WW*, January 1980, 35–37, 62–63.

Ryan, James. "And the Producer of the Movie Is. . . ." *NYT*, September 24, 1995, pp. 13, 22–23.

Saddler, Jeanne. "SBA Vows More Lending for Minorities and Women." *WSJ*, November 7, 1994, p. 1

Samuels, Patrice Duggan. "Enterprise." *LS*, January 1994, 18.

Schmuckler, Eric, and Janet Bamford. "The Top 50 Women Business Owners." *WW*, May 1996, 31–52.

Schoonover, Jean Way. "Why Corporate America Fears Women." *Vital Speeches*, April 15, 1974, 414–16.

Sellers, Patricia. "Women, Sex, and Power." *FOR*, August 1996, 42–57.

Sheridan, Mike. "Mother's Nature [Gertrude Boyle]." *Sky Magazine*, January 1995, 54–58, 60–61, 64.

Slappey, Sterling G. "Those Powerful Powder Puff Executives." *Nation's Business*, November 1970, 80–88.

Solomon, Jolie. "Operation Rescue." *WW*, May 1996, 54–59.

Taylor, Alex, III. "Why Women Managers Are Bailing Out." *FOR*, August 18, 1986, 16–23.

Thomas, Paulette. "Success at a Huge Personal Cost." *WSJ*, July 26, 1955, p. 1.
"Women in Business: A Global Report Card." *WSJ*, July 26, 1995, pp. 1–12.

Books

Adams, Elizabeth Kemper. *Women Professional Workers: A Study Made for the Women's Educational and Industrial Union*. New York: Women's Educational and Industrial Union, 1930.

Campbell, Dorcas. *Careers for Women in Banking and Finance*. New York: E. P. Dutton, 1944.

deAguirre, [Gertrude G.]. *Women in the Business World or Hints and Helps to Prosperity*. Boston: Arena, 1894.

Gildersleeve, Genevieve N. *Women in Banking: A History of the National Association of Bank Women*. Washington, D.C.: Public Affairs Press, 1929.

Gilman, Charlotte Perkins. *Women and Economics*. New York: G. P. Putnam's Sons, 1912 (first edition 1899).

Hart, Irene W. *How to Make Money Although a Woman*. New York: J. S. Ogilvie, 1895.

Kass, Babette, and Rose Feld. *The Economic Strength of Business and Professional Women*. New York: National Federation of Business and Professional Women's Clubs, 1954.

Schreiner, Olive. *Woman and Labor*. New York: Frederick A. Stokes, 1911.

Seward, Anne. *The Women's Department: Bank Department Series*. New York: Bankers Publishing, 1924.

Smedley, Dora, and Lura Robinson. *Careers in Business for Women*. New York: E.P. Dutton, 1945.

DEMOGRAPHIC INFORMATION
Government Documents and Census Reports

Anyone who has worked with census materials knows the frustrations of their constantly shifting or too-broad categories, and the changing topical interests of the census formulators. Before the 1970 federal census, it is difficult to discover how many women were sole proprietors. From the late nineteenth century, the category "proprietors, managers, and officials" lumped together entrepreneurs with salaried professionals. The most thorough and useful discussion of the federal census in relation to women's economic experience is found in Claudia Goldin, *Understanding the Gender Gap: An Economic History of American Women* (New York: Oxford University Press, 1990).

Bureau of the Census. *Statistics of Women at Work, Based on Published Information Derived from the Schedules of the 12th Census, 1900*. Washington, D.C.: U.S. Government Printing Office, 1907.

———. *Special Reports. Occupations at the Twelfth Census*. Washington, D.C.: U.S. Government Printing Office, 1904.

———. *13th Census of the United States Taken in the Year 1910*. Vol. 4, *Population 1910, Occupation Statistics*. Washington, D.C.: U.S. Government Printing Office, 1914.

———. *People of the United States in the Twentieth Century*. Edited by Irene Taeuber and Conrad Taeuber. Washington, D.C.: U.S. Government Printing Office, 1971.

———. *Historical Statistics of the United States*. Washington, D.C.: U.S. Government Printing Office, 1975.

———. *Women-Owned Businesses, 1972: Preliminary Report*. Washington, D.C.: U.S. Government Printing Office, 1976.

———. *Statistical Abstract of the U.S.: 2000*. Washington, D.C.: U.S. Government Printing Office, 2000.

———. *Woman-Owned Businesses, 1977* Washington, D.C.: U.S. Government Printing Office, 1980.

———. *Woman-Owned Businesses, 1987*. Washington, D.C.: U.S. Government Printing Office, 1990.

Erickson, Ethel. *The Employment of Women in Offices*. Bulletin of the Women's Bureau, No. 120. Washington, D.C.: U.S. Government Printing Office, 1934.

Ferriss, Abbott L. *Indicators of Trends in the Status of American Women*. New York: Russell Sage Foundation, 1971.

Hooks, Janet. *Women's Occupations through Seven Decades*. Bulletin of the Women's Bureau, No. 218. Washington, D.C.: U.S. Government Printing Office, 1947.

U.S. Department of Commerce. *Women-Owned Businesses, 1972*. Washington, D.C.: U.S. Government Printing Office, 1976.

U.S. Department of Commerce, Bureau of the Census. Economic Censuses (1987). *Survey of Minority-Owned Business Enterprises: Summary*. Washington, D.C.: U.S. Government Printing Office, 1991.

U.S. Department of Health, Education, and Welfare and Department of Labor. *Day Care Services, Form and Substance: A Report of a Conference, November 17–18, 1960*. Washington, D.C.: U.S. Government Printing Office, 1960.

U.S. Department of Labor. *Employed Mothers and Child Care*. Bulletin of the Women's Bureau, No. 246. Washington, D.C.: U.S. Government Printing Office, 1953.

———. *Women in Higher-Level Positions*. Bulletin of the Women's Bureau, No. 236. Washington, D.C.: U.S. Government Printing Office, 1950.

U.S. Small Business Administration, Office of Advocacy. *Small Business in the American Economy*. Washington, D.C.: U.S. Government Printing Office, 1988.

Compilations

The ongoing series of volumes compiled and published by the Women's Research and Education Institute provide extremely useful statistical information on women's status in a variety of areas including health, employment, and business. See Paula Ries and Anne J. Stone, eds., *The American Woman, 1992–93: A Status Report, Women and Politics* (New York: W. W. Norton, 1992); Sara E. Rix, ed., *The American Woman, 1987–88: A Report in Depth* (New York: W. W. Norton, 1987) and *The American Woman, 1988–89: A Status Report* (New York: W. W. Norton, 1988); and Cynthia Costello and Barbara K. Krimgold, eds., *The American Woman, 1996–97: Where We Stand, Women and Work* (New York: W. W. Norton, 1996); and Cynthia B. Costello and Anne J. Stone, eds., *The American Woman, 2001–2002: Getting to the Top* (New York: W. W. Norton Co., 2001).

The National Foundation for Women Business Owners, headquartered in Silver Spring, Maryland, maintains an Internet site and publishes useful materials that range in their degree of detail. *NFWBO News*, the organization's quarterly report, includes information on the status of women business owners. Other useful publications by this organization include *A Compendium of National Statistics on Women-Owned Businesses in the U.S.* (September 1994), *Going Global: Women-Owned Businesses in the International Marketplace* (1995), *Women-Owned Businesses: Breaking the Boundaries* (April 1995), and *1996 Facts on Women-Owned Businesses: Trends among Minority-Owned Firms* (1997). Organizations such as Catalyst (http://www.catalystwomen.org) and the International Center for Research on Women (http://www.icrw.org) compile information and support research on women in business. Women Incorporated (http://www.womeninc.com) is an important resource for information on women business owners, and provides numerous services for its membership.

GENERAL INFORMATION
Economy and Business

Few historical fields have been so thoroughly defined by the world-view of one historian. Alfred Chandler's *The Visible Hand: The Managerial Revolution in American Business* (Cambridge, Mass.: Harvard University Press, 1977) has structured a firm-centered approach to business history and remains a thought-provoking source of debate. See also his

Scale and Scope: The Dynamics of Industrial Capitalism (Cambridge, Mass.: Harvard University Press, 1990) and responses to the book in "*Scale and Scope*: A Review Colloquium," *Business History Review* 64 (Winter 1990): 690–735. For textbooks representative of the spectrum of issues in business history, see Keith L. Bryant Jr. and Henry C. Dethloff, *A History of American Business* (New Brunswick, N.J.: Prentice-Hall, 1983) and Mansel G. Blackford and K. Austin Kerr, *Business Enterprise in American History* (Boston: Houghton Mifflin, 1986).

Gender's relationship to business development is part of a larger exploration of cultural categories in business development. Among the earliest works to deal extensively with the social aspects of business is Thomas Cochran, *Business in American Life: A History* (New York: McGraw-Hill, 1972). More recent treatments include Wendy Gamber, "Gendered Concerns: Thoughts on the History of Business and the History of Women," *Business and Economic History* 23 (Fall 1994): 129–40; Alice Kessler-Harris, "Ideologies and Innovation: Gender Dimensions of Business History," *Business and Economic History* 2nd ser., 20 (1991): 45–51; Angel Kwolek-Folland, "The African American Financial Industries: Issues of Class, Race, and Gender in the Early 20th Century," *Business and Economic History* 23 (Winter 1994): 85–107; Kenneth Lipartito, "Culture and the Practice of Business History," *Business and Economic History* 24 (Winter 1995): 1–41; and Juliet Walker, "Racism, Slavery, and Free Enterprise: Black Entrepreneurship in the United States before the Civil War," *Business History Review* 60 (Autumn 1986): 343–82 and "Black Entrepreneurship: An Historical Inquiry," *Business and Economic History* 2nd ser., 12 (1983): 37–55. A collection of previously published essays on women and business can be found in Mary Yeager, ed., *Women in Business* (London: Elgar, 1999. Studies of specific industries include Angel Kwolek-Folland, *Engendering Business: Men and Women in the Corporate Office, 1870–1930* (Baltimore: Johns Hopkins University Press, 1994), on life insurance and banking; Ruth Milkman, *Gender at Work: The Dynamics of Job Segregation by Sex during World War II* (Urbana: University of Illinois Press, 1987), on the electrical and automotive industries; and Mark H. Rose, *Cities of Light and Heat: Domesticating Gas and Electricity in Urban America* (University Park: Pennsylvania State University Press, 1995). Juliet E. K. Walker's path breaking *The History of Black Business in America: Capitalism, Race, Entrepreneurship* (New York: Macmillan Library Reference, 1998) details the rich history of African American businesses, including information on women.

An excellent overview and synthesis of the literature on small business is found in Mansel G. Blackford, *A History of Small Business in America* (New York: Twayne, 1991). On family firms, see Philip Scranton, "Small Business, Family Firms, and Batch Production: Three Axes for Development in American Business History," *Business and Economic History* 2nd ser., 20 (1991): 99–106; and the essays in Geoffrey Jones and Mary B. Rose, eds., "Special Issue on Family Capitalism," *Business History* 35 (1993). Scranton's brief essay "Understanding the Strategies and Dynamics of Long-Lived Family Firms," *Business and Economic History* 2nd ser., 21 (1992): 219–27; and Heidi Hartmann, "The Family as the Locus of Gender, Class, and Political Struggle: The Example of Housework," *Signs* 6 (Spring 1988): 366–94, suggest the importance of understanding internal family dynamics. On nineteenth-century family business, see Clyde Griffen and Sally Griffen, "Family and Business in a Small City, Poughkeepsie, New York, 1850–1880," *Journal of Urban History* 2 (May 1975): 316–38. For an example of one African-American family involved in several types of business, see Dorothy Burnett Porter, "The Remonds of Salem, Massachusetts: A Nineteenth-Century Family Revisited," *Proceedings of the American Antiquarian Society* 95 (1985): 259–95. Naomi Lamoreaux discusses female family members involved in early banking in *Insider Lending: Banks, Personal Connections, and Economic Development in Industrial New England* (Cambridge, Mass.: Harvard University Press, 1994). Nicole Woolsey Biggart includes the recent use of marital partnerships as business structures in her *Charismatic Capitalism: Direct Selling Organizations in America* (Chicago: University of Chicago Press, 1989).

Several synthetic treatments of women's history are particularly useful to issues surrounding business development. See, for example, Teresa Amott and Julie Matthaei, *Race, Gender, and Work: A Multi-Cultural Economic History of Women in the United States* (Boston: South End Press, 1996); Karen Anderson, *Changing Woman: A History of Racial Ethnic Women in Modern America* (New York: Oxford University Press, 1996): Patricia Hill Collins, *Black Feminist Thought: Knowledge, Consciousness, and the Politics of Empowerment* (Boston: Unwin Hyman, 1990); Sara Evans, *Born for Liberty: A History of Women in America* (New York: Free Press, 1989); Claudia Goldin, *Understanding the Gender Gap*, cited above; Jacqueline Jones, *Labor of Love, Labor of Sorrow: Black Women, Work, and the Family from Reconstruction to the Present* (New York: Random House, 1985); Alice Kessler-Harris, *A Woman's*

Wage: Historical Meanings and Social Consequences (Louisville: University of Kentucky Press, 1990) and *Out to Work: A History of Wage-Earning Women in the United States* (New York: Oxford University Press, 1982); and Julie Matthaei, *An Economic History of Women in America: Women's Work, the Sexual Division of Labor, and the Development of Capitalism* (New York: Schocken Books, 1982).

Sociologists interested in organizational theory have profitably used gender to understand the "nonrational" nature of business organization. See, for example, Joan Acker, "Hierarchies, Jobs, Bodies: A Theory of Gendered Organizations," *Gender and Society* 4 (June 1990): 139–58; Gibson Burrell, "Sex and Organizational Analysis," *Organization Studies* 5 (1984): 97–118, and "No Accounting for Sexuality," *Accounting Organization and Society* 12 (1987): 98–110; David Collinson and David Knights, eds., *Gender and the Labour Process* (Hampshire, England: Gower, 1986); Robin Leidner, "Serving Hamburgers and Selling Insurance: Gender, Work, and Identity in Interactive Service Jobs," *Gender and Society* 5 (June 1991): 154–77; and Kathryn M. Moore. "Towards a Synthesis of Organizational Theory and Historical Analysis: The Case of Academic Women," *Review of Higher Education* 5 (Summer 1982): 233–43.

Comparing how businesses organize various social categories could suggest similarities with other types of organizations. Kathryn N. Tuttle's 1996 dissertation ("What Became of the Dean of Women? Changing Roles for Women Administrators in American Higher Education, 1940–1980," University of Kansas), for example, draws extensive comparisons between the development of managerial roles in business and in higher education (a timely topic given the fetish among university administrators for business models) by focusing on twentieth-century debates over race and gender in university administrative positions.

Women's Status

The history of the law in relation to women in the United States is complicated by several factors. There were two European sources—common and civil law—for our legal system, each tempered in the Revolution and the state-making and constitutional processes that followed. In addition, there is no single law but rather layers of law: municipal, county, state, and federal statutes governing everything

from the property rights of married women to citizenship status; the
law as made by legislatures and as interpreted by courts; and the
social consensus on which legal procedures rest. In terms of women's
history, at any given time any or all of these could be in conflict. Widows, for example, have historically been a particularly revealing category for legal study. See, for example, Ida Blom, "The History of
Widowhood: A Bibliographic Overview," *Journal of Family History* 16
(1991): 191–210.

Information on inheritance laws, which reveal a great deal about
women's status, can be found in Carole Shammas, Marylynn Salmon,
and Michel Dahlin, *Inheritance in America from Colonial Times to the
Present* (New Brunswick, N.J.: Rutgers University Press, 1987). For an
excellent overview of national debates and federal constitutionalism in
relation to women, see Joan Hoff, *Law, Gender, and Injustice: A Legal
History of U.S. Women* (New York: New York University Press, 1991).
A useful survey of women's legal status within the family is found in
Elizabeth Pleck, *Domestic Tyranny: The Making of American Social
Policy against Family Violence from Colonial Times to the Present* (New
York: Oxford University Press, 1987).

On women's economic, social, and legal status before the nine-
teenth century, see Joy Day Buel and Richard Buel Jr., *The Way of
Duty: A Woman and Her Family in Revolutionary America* (New York:
W. W. Norton, 1984), about Mary Fish Silliman; Lois Green Carr,
Philip D. Morgan, and Jean Russo, *Colonial Chesapeake Society*
(Chapel Hill: University of North Carolina Press, 1988); Helen S.
Carter, "Legal Aspects of Widowhood and Aging," in *On Their Own:
Widows and Widowhood in the American Southwest, 1848–1939*, edited
by Arlene Scadron (Urbana: University of Illinois Press, 1988);
Jonathan Chu, "Debt and Taxes: Public Finance and Private Economic
Behavior in Postrevolutionary Massachusetts," in *Entrepreneurs: The
Boston Business Community, 1700–1850*, edited by Conrad E. Wright
and Katheryn P. Viens (Boston: Northeastern University Press, 1997),
on Abigail Adams; Claudia Hughes Dayton, *Women before the Bar:
Gender, Law, and Society in Connecticut, 1639–1789* (Chapel Hill: Uni-
versity of North Carolina Press, 1995); Toby L. Ditz, *Property and Kin-
ship: Inheritance in Early Connecticut, 1750–1820* (Princeton, N.J.:
Princeton University Press, 1986); Claudia Goldin, "The Economic
Status of Women in the Early Republic: Quantitative Evidence,"*Journal
of Interdisciplinary History* 16 (Winter 1986): 375–404; the essays in
Ronald Hoffman and Peter J. Albert, eds., *Women in the Age of the*

American Revolution (Charlottesville: University Press of Virginia, 1989); Stephen Innes, ed., *Work and Labor in Early America* (Chapel Hill: University of North Carolina Press, 1988); Larry Koger, *Black Slaveowners: Free Black Slave Masters in South Carolina, 1790–1860* (Jefferson, N.C.: McFarland, 1985); David T. Konig, "A Summary View of the Law of British America," *William and Mary Quarterly* 50 (January 1993): 42–50; Gary B. Mills, "Coincoin: An Eighteenth Century 'Liberated Woman,'" *Journal of Southern History* 42 (1976): 205–22; Mary Beth Norton, *Liberty's Daughters: The Revolutionary Experience of American Women* (Ithaca, N.Y.: Cornell University Press, 1980); Marylynn Salmon, *Women and the Law of Property in Early America* (Chapel Hill: University of North Carolina Press, 1986); and Lisa Wilson, *Life after Death: Widows in Pennsylvania, 1750–1850* (Philadelphia: Temple University Press, 1992).

On the development of nineteenth-century gender ideals for white women, see Nancy Cott, *The Bonds of Womanhood: Women's Sphere in New England, 1780–1835* (New Haven, Conn.: Yale University Press, 1977); and Linda Kerber, *Women of the Republic: Intellect and Ideology in Revolutionary America* (Chapel Hill: University of North Carolina Press, 1980). On the connections among ideas about sexuality, demographic decline, and race in the nineteenth century, see Nancy Cott, "Passionlessness: An Interpretation of Victorian Sexual Ideology, 1790–1850," in *A Heritage of Her Own*, edited by Nancy F. Cott and Elizabeth H. Pleck (New York: Simon & Schuster, 1979), and Daniel Scott Smith, "Family Limitation, Sexual Control, and Domestic Feminism in Victorian America," in *Clio's Consciousness Raised*, edited by Mary S. Hartman and Lois Banner (New York: Harper & Row, 1974). On the history of masculinity, see E. Anthony Rotundo, *American Manhood: Transformations in Masculinity from the Revolution to the Modern Era* (New York: Basic Books, 1993). A useful summary of these issues can be found in John D'Emilio and Estelle B. Freedman, *Intimate Matters: A History of Sexuality in America* (New York: Harper & Row, 1988).

A good summary of the issues involved in the changing legal status of women in the nineteenth century can be found in Carole Shammas, "Re-Assessing the Married Women's Property Acts," *Journal of Women's History* 6 (Spring 1994): 9–30. Other insightful studies of women, property, and the law in the nineteenth century include Norma Basch, *In the Eyes of the Law: Women, Marriage, and Property in Nineteenth-Century New York* (Ithaca, N.Y.: Cornell University

Press, 1982); Richard H. Chused, "Married Women's Property Law: 1800–1850," *Georgetown Law Journal* 71 (1983): 1359–1425; the introduction in Joan M. Jensen, ed., *Promise to the Land: Essays on Rural Women* (Albuquerque: University of New Mexico Press, 1991); Marylynn Salmon, "Republican Sentiment, Economic Change, and the Property Rights of Women in American Law," in *Women in the Age of the American Revolution*, edited by Hoffman and Albert, cited above; and Riva B. Siegel, "Home as Work: The First Woman's Rights Claims Concerning Wives' Household Labor, 1850–1880," *Yale Law Journal* 103 (March 1994): 1073–1217. For similar developments elsewhere, see Lee Holcombe, *Wives and Property: Reform of the Married Women's Property Law in Nineteenth-Century England* (Toronto; University of Toronto Press, 1983); and Constance Backhouse, "Married Women's Property Law in Nineteenth-Century Canada," *Law and History Review* 6 (1988): 211–57.

The best treatment of the suffrage and women's movements in the twentieth century is Nancy Cott's *The Grounding of Modern Feminism* (New Haven, Conn.: Yale University Press, 1987). On divorce, see Glenda Riley, *Divorce: An American Tradition* (New York: Oxford University Press, 1991); and Lenore J. Weitzman, *The Divorce Revolution: The Unexpected Social and Economic Consequences for Women and Children in America* (New York: Free Press, 1985). On the issues facing African-American women, see Gail Bederman, *Manliness and Civilization: A Cultural History of Gender and Race in the United States, 1880–1917* (Chicago: University of Chicago Press, 1995), especially the chapter on Ida Wells Barnett. For women's status generally in the twentieth century, see William Chafe, *The Paradox of Change: American Women in the Twentieth Century* (New York: Oxford University Press, 1991); Elaine Tyler May, *Homeward Bound: American Families in the Cold War Era* (New York: Basic Books, 1988); and Rosalind Rosenberg, *Divided Lives: American Women in the Twentieth Century* (New York: Hill & Wang, 1992). On the relation of the depression and World War II to women's experience, see Allan Bérubé, *Coming Out under Fire: The History of Gay Men and Women in World War II* (New York: Penguin, 1990); D'Ann Campbell, *Women at War with America: Private Lives in a Patriotic Era* (Cambridge, Mass.: Harvard University Press, 1984); Susan M. Hartmann, *American Women in the 1940's: The Home Front and Beyond* (Boston: Twayne, 1982); Annelise Orleck, " 'We Are the Mythical Thing Called the Public': Militant Housewives during the Great Depression," *Feminist Studies* 19 (Spring 1993):

147–72; and Susan Ware, *Holding Their Own: American Women in the 1930s* (Boston: Twayne, 1982). Useful studies of women and business in the cold war period include Debra Michals, "Beyond 'Pin Money': The Rise of Women's Small Business Ownership, 1945–1980," (Ph.D. diss., New York University, forthcoming). On women and the civil rights movements of the mid-twentieth century, see Sara Evans, *Personal Politics: The Roots of Women's Liberation in the Civil Rights Movement and the New Left* (New York: Random House, 1979); Alice Echols, *Daring to Be Bad: Radical Feminism in America, 1967–1975* (Minneapolis: University of Minnesota Press, 1989); Winifred Wandersee, *On the Move: American Women in the 1970s* (Boston: Twayne, 1988); Peter Mattheissen, *In the Spirit of Crazy Horse* (New York: Viking Press, 1983); and Olga Rodriguez, ed., *The Politics of Chicano Liberation* (New York: Pathfinder Press, 1977).

Economy, Business, and Historical Periodization

Historians of the colonial and early national period interested in economic change continue to debate to what degree North America before 1830 was a capitalist economy: whether it was a traditional society on the verge of capitalism, a precapitalist economy, or a society already infused with capitalist principles. For excellent summaries of this debate, see Allan Kulikoff, *The Agrarian Origins of American Capitalism* (Charlottesville: University Press of Virginia, 1992), chapter 1; and Winifred Barr Rothenberg, "The Market and Massachusetts Farmers, 1750–1855," *Journal of Economic History* 41 (June 1981): 283–314. Capitalism, consumption, and the nature of the colonial economy are explored in James Axtell, *Beyond 1492: Encounters in Colonial North America* (New York: Oxford University Press, 1992); Richard L. Bushman, *The Refinement of America* (New York: Knopf, 1992); Christopher Clark, *The Roots of Rural Capitalism: Western Massachusetts, 1780–1860* (Ithaca, N.Y.: Cornell University Press, 1990); Bruce Mann, *Neighbors and Strangers: Law and Community in Early Connecticut* (Chapel Hill: University of North Carolina Press, 1987); John J. McCusker and Russell R. Menard, *The Economy of British North America, 1607–1789* (Chapel Hill: University of North Carolina Press, 1985); Nancy Grey Osterud, "Gender and the Transition to Capitalism in Rural America," *Agricultural History* 67 (Spring 1993): 14–29; Edwin J. Perkins, *The Economy of Colonial America* (New York:

Columbia University Press, 1988) (which also has a succinct chapter entitled "Women in the Colonial Economy"); Winifred Barr Rothenberg, *From Market-Places to a Market Economy: The Transformation of Rural Massachusetts, 1750–1850* (Chicago: University of Chicago Press, 1992); Carole Shammas, *The Pre-Industrial Consumer in England and America* (New York: Oxford University Press, 1990); Janet Thomas, "Women and Capitalism: Oppression or Emancipation? A Review Article," *Comparative Studies in Society and History* 30 (1988): 534–49; and Wright and Viens, eds., *Entrepreneurs*, cited above. On the connections among consumption and the industrial revolution, see Jane Humphries, " 'Lurking in the Wings . . . ': Women in the Historiography of the Industrial Revolution," *Business and Economic History* 2nd ser., 20 (1991): 32–44, and Jan de Vries, "The Industrial Revolution and the Industrious Revolution," *Journal of Economic History* 54 (June 1994):249–70.

General works on economic change in the nineteenth century include Sidney Ratner, James H. Soltow, and Richard Sylla, *The Evolution of the American Economy: Growth, Welfare, and Decision Making* (New York: Basic Books, 1979); Charles Sellers, *The Market Revolution: Jacksonian America, 1815–1846* (New York: Oxford University Press, 1991); and Alan Trachtenberg, *The Incorporation of America: Culture and Society in the Gilded Age* (New York: Hill & Wang, 1982). On the impact of the cash-based economy on the social and economic value of women's domestic work, see Jeanne Boydston, *Home and Work: Housework, Wages, and the Ideology of Labor in the Early Republic* (New York: Oxford University Press, 1990). On business in the twentieth century, see Robert Sobel, *The Age of Giant Corporations: A Microeconomic History of American Business* (Westport, Conn.: Greenwood Press, 1993).

The relationship between the industrial and market revolutions and women's paid labor has received attention from labor and social historians. See Mary Blewett, *Men, Women, and Work: Class, Gender, and Protest in the New England Shoe Industry, 1780–1910* (Urbana: University of Illinois Press, 1988); and Thomas Dublin, *Women at Work: The Transformation of Work and Community in Lowell, Massachusetts, 1826–1860* (New York: Columbia University Press, 1979) and *Transforming Women's Work: New England Lives in the Industrial Revolution* (Ithaca, N.Y.: Cornell University Press, 1994).

Consumption and the market are two crucial and developing areas of research. Useful monographs include Thomas S. Dicke, *Franchis-*

ing in America: The Development of a Business Method (Chapel Hill: University of North Carolina Press, 1992); Jackson Lears, *Fables of Abundance: A Cultural History of Advertising in America* (New York: Basic Books, 1995); Roland Marchand, *Advertising the American Dream* (Berkeley and Los Angeles: University of California Press, 1985); David Monod, *Store Wars: Shopkeepers and the Culture of Mass Marketing* (Toronto: University of Toronto Press, 1996); Jennifer Scanlon, *Inarticulate Longings: The Ladies' Home Journal, Gender, and the Promises of Consumer Culture* (New York: Routledge, 1995); and Susan Strasser, *Satisfaction Guaranteed: The Making of the American Mass Market* (New York: Pantheon Books, 1989) on retailers and markets. On women and the modern consumer economy, see especially Kathy Peiss, *Hope in a Jar: The Making of American Beauty Culture* (New York, 1998) and Katina L. Manko, "Ding Dong! Avon Calling!: Gender, Business, and Door-to-Door Selling, 1890–1962" (Ph.D. diss., University of Delaware, 2001) on the cosmetics industry; and Virginia Scharff, *Taking the Wheel: Women and the Coming of the Motor Age* (New York: Free Press, 1991).

The literature on nineteenth-century business organization favors industrial and engineering models of managerial development. For treatments of the advent of industrial management, see Jeremy Attack, "Firm Size and Industrial Structure in the United States during the Nineteenth Century," *Journal of Economic History* 46 (June 1986): 463–75; and Walter Licht, *Working for the Railroad: The Organization of Work in the Nineteenth Century* (Princeton, N.J.: Princeton University Press, 1983), especially chapter 1. For the British example, see Sidney Pollard, "The Genesis of the Managerial Profession: The Experience of the Industrial Revolution in Great Britain," *Studies in Romanticism* 4 (Winter 1965): 47–80. On the various types of nineteenth-century management theory, see Kwolek-Folland, *Engendering Business*, cited above. Peter Dobkin Hall, in *The Organization of American Culture 1700–1900: Private Institutions, Elites, and the Origins of American Nationality* (New York: New York University Press, 1982), argues that nonprofit corporations were among those that gradually took over many functions of the family during the nineteenth century and thus assumed managerial roles. Lori Ginzberg cogently argues for the connections among domestic management, reform organizations, and the development of a nonprofit managerial model in *Women and the Work of Benevolence: Morality, Politics, and Class in the 19th-Century United States* (New Haven, Conn.: Yale University Press, 1990), especially chapter 2.

In addition to the work of Alfred Chandler already discussed, on the growth and implications of corporate forms and bureaucratic management, see Kwolek-Folland, *Engendering Business*, cited above; Daniel Nelson, ed., *A Mental Revolution: Scientific Management since Taylor* (Columbus: Ohio State University Press, 1992); David E. Nye, *Image Worlds: Corporate Identities at General Electric, 1890–1930* (Cambridge, Mass.: Harvard University Press, 1985); Philip Scranton, *Proprietary Capitalism: Textile Manufacture at Philadelphia, 1800–1885* (New York: Cambridge University Press, 1983); Sharon Hartman Strom, *Beyond the Typewriter: Gender, Class, and the Origins of Modern American Office Work, 1900–1930* (Urbana: University of Illinois Press, 1992); Andrea Tone, *The Business of Benevolence: Welfare Work in America* (Ithaca, N.Y.: Cornell University Press, 1997); JoAnne Yates, *Control through Communication: The Rise of System in American Management* (Baltimore: Johns Hopkins University Press, 1989); and Oliver Zunz, *Making America Corporate, 1870–1920* (Chicago: University of Chicago Press, 1990). On professionalism and Progressive reform, see Burton J. Bledstein, *The Culture of Professionalism: The Middle Class and the Development of Higher Education in America* (New York: W. W. Norton, 1976); and Robert H. Wiebe, *The Search for Order, 1877–1920* (New York: Hill & Wang, 1967).

Good sources on the history of the middle class are Mary P. Ryan, *Cradle of the Middle Class: The Family in Oneida County, New York, 1790–1865* (New York: Cambridge University Press, 1981); and Stuart M. Blumin,*The Emergence of the Middle Class: Social Experience in the American City, 1760–1900* (New York: Cambridge University Press, 1989). For the English case, see Leonore Davidoff and Catherine Hall, *Family Fortunes: Men and Women of the English Middle Class, 1750–1850* (Chicago: University of Chicago Press, 1987). On the antebellum African-American middle class, see James Oliver Horton, "Freedom's Yoke: Gender Conventions among Antebellum Free Blacks," *Feminist Studies* 12 (Spring 1986): 51–75. There is no firm agreement on what constitutes a definition of the middle class. For a discussion of some of the issues involved, see Kathleen Canning, "Gender and the Politics of Class Formation: Rethinking German Labor History," *American Historical Review* 97 (June 1992): 736–68.

Autobiographies, Biographies, and Encyclopedias

Several encyclopedias and biographical dictionaries include some entries on women, among them William Davis, *The Innovators: The Essential Guide to Business Thinkers, Achievers, and Entrepreneurs* (New York: AMACOM, 1987); Glenn Porter, ed., *Encyclopedia of American Business History* (New York: Scribner, 1980); and Robert Sobel and David Sicilia's *The Entrepreneurs* (Boston: Houghton Mifflin, 1986). For useful (although celebratory) short biographies of several contemporary businesswomen, see Joseph J. Fucini and Suzy Fucini, *Entrepreneurs: The Men and Women behind Famous Brand Names and How They Made It* (Boston: G. K. Hall, 1985). A more thorough treatment of modern female public-sector managers is Judith A. Leavitt's *American Women Managers and Administrators: A Selective Biographical Dictionary of Twentieth-Century Leaders in Business, Education, and Government* (Westport, Conn.: Greenwood Press, 1985). For a comprehensive bibliography on African-American women, see Darlene Clark Hine, ed., *Black Women in United States History* (Brooklyn: Carlson, 1990).

For individual biographies of African-American businesswomen, see John Ingham and Lynne Feldman, eds., *African American Business Leaders: A Biographical Dictionary* (Westport, Conn.: Greenwood Press, 1994); and Jesse Carney Smith, ed., *Notable Black American Women* (Detroit, Mich., 1992). In addition to entries on Maggie Lena Walker in these sources, see Elsa Barkley Brown, "Womanist Consciousness: Maggie Lena Walker and the Independent Order of St. Luke," *Signs* 14 (Spring 1989): 610–35. Useful profiles of female writers, playwrights, and screenwriters can be found in Randall Clark, ed., *Dictionary of Literary Biography* (Detroit, Mich.: Gale Research, 1986).

There are some popular treatments of businesswomen. Although now somewhat dated, probably the most thorough and accurate of the popular synthetic treatments of women's business history is Caroline Bird's collection of biographies, *Enterprising Women* (New York: W. W. Norton, 1976). On Lydia Pinkham, see Sarah Stage, *Female Complaints: Lydia Pinkham and the Business of Women's Medicine* (New York: W. W. Norton, 1979). Cecee McCarty is discussed in Juliet E. K. Walker, "Racism, Slavery, and Free Enterprise: Black Entrepreneurship in the United States before the Civil War,"*Business History Review* 60 (Autumn 1986): 343–82. On the Demorests, see Ishbel Ross,

Crusades and Crinolines: The Life and Times of Ellen Curtis Demorest and William Jennings Demorest (New York: Harper & Row, 1963). Margaret Walsh discusses the relationship between the Demorests' product and management and that of their main competitor, E. Butterick & Co., in "The Democratization of Fashion: The Emergence of the Women's Dress Pattern Industry," *Journal of American History* 66 (September 1979): 299–313. On the Everleigh sisters, who ran brothels in Chicago, see Caroline Bird, *Enterprising Women*, cited above. Lynn Hudson reconstructs Mary Ellen Pleasant's life in "Mary Ellen Pleasant" (Ph.D. diss., University of Indiana, 1996). On Ruth Barnett, see Ricky Solinger, *The Abortionist: A Woman against the Law* (New York: Free Press, 1994). Helen Schultz is discussed in Margaret Walsh, "Iowa's Bus Queen: Helen M. Schultz and the Red Ball Transportation Company," *Annals of Iowa* 53 (1994): 329–55; and "Not Rosie the Riveter: Women's Diverse Roles in the Making of the American Long-Distance Bus Industry," *Journal of Transport History* 3d ser., 17 (1996): 43–45. Emily W. Leider's recent biography of Mae West, *Becoming Mae West* (New York: Farrar, Straus & Giroux, 1997), places her firmly within the development of the entertainment industry in the early twentieth century. Estée Lauder's unofficial biography is by Lee Israel, *Estée Lauder: Beyond the Magic* (New York: Macmillan 1985). On Kim Polese, see Robert H. Reid, *Architects of the Web* (New York: John Wiley & Sons, 1996), chapter 3. Roland Westwood's recent biography of Georgia White Clark, *Woman of the River* (Logan: Utah State University Press, 1997), emphasizes her role in the development of tourism.

Autobiographies of specific individuals include Mary Kay Ash, *You Can Have It All* (Rocklin, Calif: Prima Publishing 1995); Mae West's entertaining *Goodness Had Nothing to Do with It* (New York: Belvedere, 1959); Sydney Barrows and William Novak, *Mayflower Madam: The Secret Life of Sydney Biddle Barrows* (New York: Arbor House, 1986); Mary Cunningham, *Power Play: What Really Happened at Bendix* (New York: Simon & Schuster, 1984); Ann Hopkins, *So Ordered: Making Partner the Hard Way* (Amherst: University of Massachusetts Press, 1996); and Dawn Steel, *They Can Kill You but They Can't Eat You: Lessons from the Front* (New York: Simon & Schuster, 1993).

ETHNICITY, RACE, AND GENDER

The literature on gender and race as social categories, language, and the role of difference in historical reconstruction is voluminous.

Among the most useful works in the field are the following: Margaret L. Anderson and Patricia Hill Collins, eds., *Race, Class, and Gender: An Anthology* (Belmont, Calif.: Wadsworth 1992); Judith Butler, *Gender Trouble: Feminism and the Subversion of Identity* (New York: Routledge, 1990); Jane Flax, "Postmodernism and Gender Relations in Feminist Theory," *Signs* 12 (Summer 1987): 621–43; Evelyn Brooks Higginbotham, "African American Women's History and the Metalanguage of Race," *Signs* 17 (Winter 1992): 251–74; Gerda Lerner, *The Creation of Patriarchy* (New York: Oxford University Press, 1986); George E. Marcus and Michael M. Fischer, *Anthropology as Cultural Critique: An Experimental Moment in the Human Sciences* (Chicago: University of Chicago Press, 1986); Naomi Quinn and Dorothy Holland, eds., *Cultural Models in Language and Thought* (New York: Cambridge University Press, 1987); and Joan W. Scott, *Gender and the Politics of History* (New York: Columbia University Press, 1988).

On language, gender, landscape, and colonization, see Ramón Gutiérrez, *When Jesus Came, the Corn Mothers Went Away: Marriage, Sexuality, and Power in New Mexico, 1500–1846* (Stanford, Calif.: Stanford University Press, 1991); Annette Kolodny, *The Land before Her: Fantasy and Experience of the American Frontiers, 1630–1860* (Chapel Hill: University of North Carolina Press, 1984), and *The Lay of the Land: Metaphor as Experience and History in American Life and Letters* (Chapel Hill: University of North Carolina Press, 1975); Carolyn Merchant, *Ecological Revolutions: Nature, Gender, and Science in New England* (Chapel Hill: University of North Carolina Press, 1989); and Louis Montrose, "The Work of Gender in the Discourse of Discovery," in *New World Encounters*, edited by Stephen Greenblatt (Berkeley and Los Angeles: University of California Press, 1993). On the roots of these metaphors in Western European culture, see Henry Nash Smith, *Virgin Land: The American West as Symbol and Myth* (Cambridge, Mass.: Harvard University Press, 1950); and John R. Stilgoe, *Common Landscapes of America*, 1580–1845 (New Haven, Conn.: Yale University Press, 1982).

For background on Native Americans and colonization, see Gutiérrez, cited above; Daniel Usner, *Indians, Settlers, and Slaves in a Frontier Exchange Economy: The Lower Mississippi Valley before 1783* (Chapel Hill: University of North Carolina Press, 1992); and Richard White, *The Middle Ground: Indians, Empires, and Republics in the Great Lakes Region, 1650–1815* (New York: Cambridge University Press, 1991). Literature on the economic activities and status of Native

American women is uneven, and much of it is located within the context of other issues. Some particularly useful works for the colonial period include Priscilla Buffalohead, "Farmers, Warriors, Traders: A Fresh Look at Ojibway Women," *Minnesota History* 48 (Summer 1983): 236–44; Carol Devens, *Countering Colonization: Native American Women and Great Lakes Missions, 1630–1900* (Berkeley and Los Angeles: University of California Press, 1992); Ellice B. Gonzalez, *Changing Economic Roles for Micmac Men and Women: An Ethnohistorical Analysis* (Ottawa: National Museums of Canada, 1981); Robert S. Grumet, "Sunksquaws, Shamans, and Tradeswomen: Middle Atlantic Coastal Algonkian Women during the 17th and 18th Centuries," in *Women and Colonization: Anthropological Perspectives*, edited by Mona Etienne and Eleanor Leacock (New York: Praeger, 1982); Joan Jensen, "Native American Women and Agriculture: A Seneca Case Study," *Sex Roles* 3 (1977): 423–42; and Sylvia Van Kirk, *Many Tender Ties: Women in Fur-Trade Society, 1670–1870* (Norman: University of Oklahoma Press, 1980).

A new translation is now available of the amazing autobiography of Catalina de Erauso, *Lieutenant Nun: Memoir of a Basque Transvestite in the New World*, translated by Michele Stepto and Gabriel Stepto (Boston: Beacon Press, 1996). Useful studies that include information on Hispanic, Spanish, and Dutch women in colonial America include Silvia M. Arrom, *The Women of Mexico City, 1790–1857* (Stanford, Calif.: Stanford University Press, 1985); Edith Couturier, "Women and the Family in Eighteenth-Century Mexico: Law and Practice," *Journal of Family History* 10 (Fall 1985): 204–304; Jay Kinsbruner, "Petty Capitalism in Spanish America: The Pulperos of Puebla, Mexico City, Caracas, and Buenos Aires," *Dellplain Latin American Studies*, no. 21 (1987), especially pp. 13–18; Elizabeth Kuznesof, "A History of Domestic Service in Spanish America, 1492–1980," in *Muchachas No More: Household Workers in Latin American and the Caribbean*, edited by Elsa M. Chaney and Mary Garcia Castro (Philadelphia: Temple University Press, 1989); essays in Joan Jensen and Darlis Miller, eds., *New Mexican Women: Intercultural Perspectives* (Albuquerque: University of New Mexico Press, 1986); Elizabeth Kuznesof and Robert Oppenheimer, "The Family and Society in Nineteenth-Century Latin America: An Historiographical Introduction," *Journal of Family History* 10 (Fall 1985): 215–34; the essays in Asunción Lavrin, ed., *Latin American Women* (Westport, Conn.: Greenwood Press, 1978); and Colin M. MacLachlan and Jaime E. Rodriguez O., *Forging of the Cos-*

mic Race: A Reinterpretation of Colonial Mexico (Berkeley and Los Angeles: University of California Press, 1980). For information on Dutch women, see Linda Briggs Biemer, *Women and Property in Colonial New York* (Ann Arbor, Mich.: UMI Research Press, 1983); and Donna Merwick, *Possessing Albany, 1630–1710: The Dutch and English Experience* (New York: Cambridge University Press, 1990).

For African-Americans' business activities in the mid-nineteenth century, see W. B. Hartgrove, "The Story of Maria Louise Moore and Fannie M. Richards," *Journal of Negro History* 1 (January 1916): 23–33; Whittington B. Johnson, "Free Blacks in Antebellum Savannah: An Economic Profile," *Georgia Historical Quarterly* 64 (Winter 1980): 418–31; Suzanne Lebsock, *The Free Women of Petersburg: Status and Culture in a Southern Town, 1784–1860* (New York: W. W. Norton, 1985); Philip D. Morgan, "The Ownership of Property by Slaves in the Mid-Nineteenth-Century Low Country," *Journal of Southern History* 49 (August 1983): 399–420; Jane Rhodes, "Race, Money, Politics, and the Antebellum Black Press," *Journalism History* 20 (1994): 95–106, which includes information on newspaper owner Mary Ann Shadd Cary; and Loren Schweninger, "Black-Owned Businesses in the South, 1790–1880," *Business History Review* 63 (Spring 1989): 22–60, and "Property Owning Free African-American Women in the South, 1800–1870," *Journal of Women's History* 1 (Winter 1990): 13–44. On African-American entrepreneurs in New York City, see Martha S. Putney, "New York City Directory Listing of Occupations of Blacks in the 1840s and 1850s and Black-Owned Businesses in the 1840s: An Analysis," *Journal of the Afro-American Historical and Geneological Society* 9 (1988): 58–63.

On African-American business in the twentieth century in addition to Juliet Walker's work, cited above, see J. H. Harmon Jr., Arnett G. Lindsay, and Carter G. Woodson, *The Negro as Businessman* (College Park, Md.: McGrath, 1929); Abram L. Harris, *The Negro as Capitalist: A Study of Banking and Business among American Negroes* (New York: Negro Universities Press, 1936); Alexa B. Henderson, *Atlanta Life Insurance Company: Guardian of Black Economic Dignity* (Tuscaloosa: University of Alabama Press, 1990); Debra Michals, "The Meaning of Ownership: Black Women Beauticians in the Civil Rights Era," unpublished seminar paper (1993, in my possession); Walter B. Weare, *Black Business in the New South: A Social History of the North Carolina Mutual Life Insurance Company* (Urbana: University of Illinois Press, 1977); and Robert E. Weems Jr., "The History of the Chicago Mutual

Assurance Company: An Examination of Business as a Black Community Institution" (Ph.D. diss., University of Wisconsin-Madison, 1987).

Ivan H. Light's *Ethnic Enterprise in America: Business and Welfare among Chinese, Japanese and Blacks* (Berkeley and Los Angeles: University of California Press, 1972) is useful on the issue of ethnic entrepreneurship, although he does not cover women's businesses. See also Scott Cummings, *Self-Help in Urban America: Patterns of Minority Enterprise* (Port Washington, N.Y.: Kennikat Press, 1980). On Hispanic women, see Sarah Deutsch, *No Separate Refuge: Culture, Class, and Gender on an Anglo-Hispanic Frontier in the American Southwest, 1880–1940* (New York: Oxford University Press, 1987); Donna J. Guy, "The Economics of Widowhood in Arizona, 1880–1940," in *On Their Own*, edited by Scadron, cited above; Vicki Ruiz, *Cannery Women, Cannery Lives: Mexican Women, Unionization, and the California Food Processing Industry, 1930–1950* (Albuquerque: University of New Mexico Press, 1987); and Patricia Zavella, *Women's Work and Chicano Families: Cannery Workers of the Santa Clara Valley* (Ithaca, N.Y.: Cornell University Press, 1987). On Jewish women in the West, see Andrea Katzman, "Developing Identities in the Heartland: Jewish Women in Kansas City during World War II" (master's thesis, University of Kansas, 1996).

GENDER AND TECHNOLOGY
The relation between gender and technology is a growing area of scholarly interest. In addition to Mark Rose's work cited above, see the essays in a special issue of *Technology and Culture*, "Gender Analysis and the History of Technology," 38 (January 1997); Ruth Schwartz Cowan, *More Work for Mother: The Ironies of Household Technology from the Open Hearth to the Microwave* (New York: Basic Books, 1983); Lisa A. Marovich. "Fueling the Fires of Genius: Women's Inventive Activities in American War Eras" (Ph.D. diss., University of California-Los Angeles, 1998); David Sicilia, "Selling Power: Marketing and Monopoly at Boston Edison, 1886–1929" (Ph.D. diss., Brandeis University, 1991); and Susan Strasser, *Never Done: A History of American Housework* (New York: Pantheon, 1982).

Anne L. Macdonald does justice to women inventors in *Feminine Ingenuity: Women and Invention in America* (New York: Ballantine, 1992). The papers of two twentieth-century women inventors in the Hagley Museum and Library Collection are particularly rich: Nora C. Edwards, who invented a skirt elevator and whose papers document her attempts to patent her invention and start a business, and Mary Hallock Greenewalt, who invented a sound and light machine.

WOMEN AND BUSINESS
Agriculture

On changes in women's nineteenth-century agricultural role, see Joan E. Cashin, *A Family Venture: Men and Women on the Southern Frontier* (Baltimore: Johns Hopkins University Press, 1991); John Mack Faragher, *Sugar Creek: Life on the Illinois Prairie* (New Haven, Conn.: Yale University Press, 1986); Joan Jensen, *Loosening the Bonds: Mid-Atlantic Farm Women, 1750–1850* (New Haven, Conn.: Yale University Press, 1986); Sally McMurry, *Transforming Rural Life: Dairying Families and Agricultural Change, 1820–1885* (Baltimore: Johns Hopkins University Press, 1995); and Nancy Grey Osterud, *Bonds of Community: The Lives of Farm Women in Nineteenth-Century New York* (Ithaca, N.Y.: Cornell University Press, 1991). For the twentieth century, see Deborah Fink, *Agrarian Women: Wives and Mothers in Rural Nebraska, 1880–1920* (Chapel Hill: University of North Carolina Press, 1992), and *Open Country, Iowa: Rural Women, Tradition, and Change* (Albany: State University of New York Press, 1986); Katherine Jellison, *Entitled to Power: Farm Women and Technology, 1913–1963* (Chapel Hill: University of North Carolina Press, 1993); Laurie Mercier, "Montanans at Work: Businesswomen in Agricultural Communities," *Montana* 40 (1990): 77–83; and Mary Neth, *Preserving the Family Farm: Women, Community, and the Foundations of Agribusiness in the Midwest, 1900–1940* (Chapel Hill: University of North Carolina Press, 1995).

Prostitution

On prostitution and the nineteenth-century sex trade, see Timothy J. Gilfoyle, *City of Eros: New York City, Prostitution, and the Commercialization of Sex, 1790–1920* (New York; W. W. Norton, 1992); Barbara Meil Hobson, *Uneasy Virtue: The Politics of Prostitution and the American Reform Tradition* (Chicago: University of Chicago Press, 1990); and Donna J. Seifert, "Within Site of the White House: The Archaeology of Working Women," *Historical Archaeology* 25 (1991): 82–108. On prostitution in the American West, see Anne M. Butler, *Daughters of*

Joy, Sisters of Misery: Prostitutes in the American West, 1865–1890 (Urbana: University of Illinois Press, 1985); Lucie Cheng Hirata, "Free, Enslaved, and Indentured Workers in Nineteenth-Century America: The Case of Chinese Prostitution," *Signs* 5 (Autumn 1979): 3–29; Darlis Miller, "Foragers, Army Women, and Prostitutes," in *New Mexican Women*, edited by Jensen and Miller, cited above; Eugene Moehring, *Resort City in the Sunbelt: Las Vegas, 1930–1970* (Las Vegas: University of Nevada Press, 1995); and Paula Petrik, "Capitalists with Rooms: Prostitution in Helena, Montana, 1865–1900," *Montana* 31–32 (1981–82): 28–40. On prostitution and Progressive Era reform, see Ruth Rosen, *The Lost Sisterhood: Prostitution in America, 1900–1918* (Baltimore: Johns Hopkins University Press, 1982). Studies of prostitution in the twentieth century include Beth Bailey and David Farber, *The First Strange Place: Race and Sex in World War II Hawaii* (Baltimore: Johns Hopkins University Press, 1992); Ivan Light, "From Vice District to Tourist Attraction: The Moral Career of American Chinatowns, 1880–1940," in *Crime and Justice in American History*, vol. 8, edited by Eric Monkkonen (New York: K. G. Saur, 1992); and Jody Miller, "Gender and Power on the Streets: Street Prostitution in the Era of Crack Cocaine," *Journal of Contemporary Ethnography* 23 (1995): 427–52. Recent interpretations emphasize the business and labor aspects of the sex trade. See, for example, Barbara Sherman Heyl, *The Madam as Entrepreneur: Career Management in House Prostitution* (New Brunswick, N.J.: Transaction Books, 1979), and Valerie Jenness, *Making It Work: The Prostitutes' Rights Movement in Perspective* (New York: Aldine de Gruyter, 1993).

Women in the West

Overviews of women in the West include Julie Roy Jeffrey, *Frontier Women: The Transmississippi West, 1840–1880* (New York: Hill & Wang, 1979); and Glenda Riley, *The Female Frontier: A Comparative View of Women on the Prairie and Plains* (Lawrence: University Press of Kansas, 1988). For women in specific cultural and geographic areas, see Georgellen Burnett, *We Just Toughed It Out: Women in the Llano Estacado* (El Paso: Texas Western Press, 1990); J. F. Elliot, "The Great Western: Sarah Bowman, Mother and Mistress to the U.S. Army," *Journal of Arizona History* 30 (Spring 1989): 1–26; Deena J. González, "The Widowed Women of Santa Fe: Assessments on the Lives of an

Unmarried Population, 1850–80," in *On Their Own*, edited by Scadron, cited above; Katherine Harris, *Long Vistas: Women and Families on Colorado Homesteads* (Niwot: University Press of Colorado, 1993); Janet LeCompte, "The Independent Women of Hispanic New Mexico, 1821–1846," in *New Mexican Women*, edited by Jensen and Miller, cited above; JoAnn Levy, "Forgotten Forty-Niners," *American History Illustrated* 26 (1992): 38–49; and Mary C. Wright, "Economic Development and Native American Women in the Early Nineteenth Century," *American Quarterly* 33 (Winter 1981): 525–36. Patricia Y. Stallard's *Glittering Misery: Dependents of the Indian Fighting Army* (Norman: University of Oklahoma Press, 1992) discusses the role of women in the western army. An excellent approach to issues of multiculturalism in the West is Peggy Pascoe's *Relations of Rescue: The Search for Female Moral Authority in the American West, 1874–1939* (New York: Oxford University Press, 1990).

Professions, Occupations, and Entrepreneurship

Research on colonial Anglo-American women, and particularly their economic and business dealings, is fairly extensive and has generated some recent interest. Useful works on women and business include three early monographs—Elisabeth Dexter's two books, *Colonial Women of Affairs: A Study of Women in Business and the Professions in America before 1776* (New York: Houghton Mifflin, 1931), and *Career Women of America, 1776–1840* (Francestown, N.H.: Marshall Jones, 1950); and Julia Cherry Spruill, *Women's Life and Work in the Southern Colonies* (New York: Russell & Russell, 1969). The most extensive explorations of the connections among Anglo-American women's social and economic lives can be found in numerous publications by Laurel Thatcher Ulrich, among them *A Midwive's Tale: The Life of Martha Ballard, Based on Her Diary, 1785–1812* (New York: Vintage Books, 1991); *Good Wives: Image and Reality in the Lives of Women in Northern New England, 1650–1750* (New York: Oxford University Press, 1982); and "Housewife and Gadder: Themes of Self-Sufficiency and Community in Eighteenth-Century New England," in *"To Toil the Livelong Day": America's Women at Work, 1780–1980*, edited by Carol Groneman and Mary Beth Norton (Ithaca, N.Y.: Cornell University Press, 1987). On businesswomen, see Patricia Cleary, " 'She Merchants' of Colonial America: Women and Commerce on the Eve of the

Revolution" (Ph.D. diss., Northwestern University, 1989) and " 'She Will Be in the Shop': Women's Sphere of Trade in Eighteenth-Century Philadelphia and New York," *Pennsylvania Magazine* 119 (July 1995): 181–202; Frances May Manges, "Women Shopkeepers, Tavernkeepers, and Artisans in Colonial Philadelphia" (Ph.D. diss., University of Pennsylvania, 1958); and Mary Beth Norton, "A Cherished Spirit of Independence: The Life of an Eighteenth-Century Boston Businesswoman," in *Women of America: A History*, edited by Carol Berkin and Mary Beth Norton (Boston: Houghton Mifflin, 1979). David W. Conroy includes some information on women tavern keepers in his *The Public Houses: Drink and the Revolution of Authority in Colonial Massachusetts* (Chapel Hill: University of North Carolina Press, 1995).

For useful overviews of nineteenth-century female entrepreneurship keyed to particular geographic areas, see Susan Ingalls Lewis, "Female Entrepreneurs in Albany, 1840–1885," *Business and Economic History* 2nd ser., 21 (1992): 65–73; and Lucy Eldersveld Murphy, "Businesswomen and Separate Spheres in the Midwest, 1850–1880," *Illinois Historical Journal* 80 (Autumn, 1987): 155–76.

Most studies of female entrepreneurs tend to focus on types of business. One recent collection of essays useful for the 1980s is Oliver Hagan, Carol Rivchun, and Donald Sexton, eds., *Women-Owned Businesses* (New York: Praeger, 1989). On women in literature, see Susan Albertine, "Breaking the Silent Partnership: Businesswomen in Popular Fiction," *American Literature* 62 (1990): 238–61; Sherilyn Cox Bennion, *Equal to the Occasion: Women Editors of the Nineteenth Century West* (Reno: University of Nevada Press, 1990); Susan Coultrap-Mc-Quin, *Doing Literary Business: American Women Writers in the Nineteenth-Century* (Chapel Hill: University of North Carolina Press, 1990); Autumn Stanley, "Scribbling Women as Entrepreneurs: Kate Field (1838–96) and Charlotte Smith (1840–1917)" *Business and Economic History* 2nd ser., 21 (1992): 74–83; and Joyce W. Warren, ed., *Ruth Hall and Other Writings [by] Fanny Fern* (New Brunswick, N.J.: Rutgers University Press, 1986). On women ministers and religion, see William L. Andrews, ed., *Sisters of the Spirit: Three Black Women's Autobiographies of the Nineteenth Century* (Bloomington: Indiana University Press, 1986); Louis Billington, "Female Laborers in the Church: Women Preachers in the Northeastern United States, 1790–1840," *Journal of American Studies* 19 (1985): 369–94; and Ann Braude, *Radical Spirits: Spiritualism and Women's Rights in Nineteenth-Century America* (Boston: Beacon Press, 1986). Two excellent sources on women and theater are Jane K. Curry, *Nineteenth-Century American Women Theater Managers* (Westport, Conn.: Greenwood Press, 1994); and Faye E. Dudden, *Women in the American Theatre: Actresses and Audiences, 1790–1879* (New Haven, Conn.: Yale University Press, 1994). On women's role in education, see Barbara Solomon, *In the Company of Educated Women: A History of Women and Higher Education in America* (New Haven, Conn.: Yale University Press, 1985); and Mary Hurlbut Cordier, *Schoolwomen of the Prairies and Plains: Personal Narratives from Iowa, Kansas, and Nebraska, 1860s–1920s* (Albuquerque: University of New Mexico Press, 1992).

On women scientists, see Margaret Rossiter's two excellent volumes, *Women Scientists in America: Struggles and Strategies to 1940* (Baltimore: Johns Hopkins University Press, 1982) and *Women Scientists in America: Before Affirmative Action, 1940–1972* (Baltimore: Johns Hopkins University Press, 1995). On the employment of female scientists in industry, see Regina Blaszczyk, "Where Mrs. Homemaker Is Never Forgotten: Lucy M. Maltby and the Home Economics Department at Corning Glass Works, 1929–1965," in *Rethinking Women and Home Economics in the Twentieth Century*, edited by Sarah Stage and Virginia Vicenti (Ithaca, N.Y.: Cornell University Press, 1995).

The literature on nineteenth-century milliners and dressmakers is becoming increasingly rich. By far the most thorough study is Wendy Gamber's *The Female Economy: The Millinery and Dressmaking Trades, 1860–1930* (Urbana: University of Illinois Press, 1997). Sources that cover more specific areas include Elizabeth Keckley, *Behind the Scenes, or Thirty Years a Slave and Four Years in the White House* (New York, 1868; reprint ed., New York: Oxford University Press, 1988); Lucy Eldersveld Murphy, "Business Ladies: Midwestern Women and Enterprise, 1850–1880," *Journal of Women's History* 3 (Spring 1991): 65–89; and Amy Simon, " 'She Is So Neat and Fits So Well': Garment Construction and the Millinery Business of Eliza Oliver Dodds, 1821–1833" (master's thesis, University of Delaware, 1993).

The literature on women office workers is extensive. See Cindy Sondik Aron, *Ladies and Gentlemen of the Civil Service: Middle-Class Workers in Victorian America* (New York: Oxford University Press, 1987); Margery Davies, *Women's Place Is at the Typewriter, 1870–1930* (Philadelphia: Temple University Press, 1982); Ileen DeVault, *Sons and Daughters of Labor: Class and Clerical Work in Turn-of-the-Century*

Pittsburgh (Ithaca, N.Y.: Cornell University Press, 1990); Lisa Fine, *The Souls of the Skyscraper: Female Clerical Workers in Chicago, 1870–1930* (Philadelphia: Temple University Press, 1981); Kwolek-Folland, *Engendering Business*, cited above: Elyce Rotella, *From Home to Office: U.S. Women at Work, 1870–1930* (Ann Arbor, Mich.: UMI Research Press, 1981); Carole Srole, " 'A Position That God Has Not Particularly Assigned to Men': The Feminization of Clerical Work, Boston, 1860–1915" (Ph.D. diss., University of California—Loss Angeles, 1984); and Sharon Strom, *Beyond the Typewriter*, cited above.

The relation between gender and work, particularly professional occupations, has been explored in several specific contexts. For an excellent overview of the issues, see Ava Baron's "Gender and Labor History: Learning from the Past, Looking to the Future," in her collection *Work Engendered: Toward a New History of American Labor* (Ithaca, N.Y.: Cornell University Press, 1991). On the relation between feminization and the professions, see Michael J. Carter and Susan Boslego Carter, "Women's Recent Progress in the Professions or, Women Get a Ticket to Ride after the Gravy Train Has Left the Station," *Feminist Studies* 7 (Fall 1981): 477–504. For the status of African-American women, see Delores P. Aldridge, "African-American Women in the Economic Marketplace: A Continuing Struggle," *Journal of Black Studies* 20 (December 1989): 129–54. On women in retail sales, see Susan Porter Benson, *Counter Cultures: Saleswomen, Managers, and Customers in American Department Stores, 1890–1940* (Urbana: University of Illinois Press, 1988). On department stores and the changes in the dressmaking and millinery trades, see Wendy Gamber, *The Female Economy*, cited above, chapter 2; and William Leach, *Land of Desire: Merchants, Power, and the Rise of a New American Culture* (New York: Pantheon Books, 1993). On education and professional development, see Barbara Solomon, *In the Company*, cited above. On the gendering of social welfare and librarianship, respectively, see Daniel J. Walkowitz, "The Making of a Feminine Professional Identity: Social Workers in the 1920s," *American Historical Review* 95 (1990): 1051–75; and Abigail Van Slyck, *Free to All: Carnegie Libraries and American Culture, 1890–1920* (Chicago: University of Chicago Press, 1995). On women and banking, see Sara Alpern, "Women in Banking: Early Years," *The Encyclopedia of American Business History and Biography* (New York: Facts on File, 1990), 468–71. On women in management, see Sara Alpern, "In the Beginning: A History of Women in Management," in *Women in Management: Trends, Issues, and Chal-*

lenges in Managerial Diversity, edited by Ellen A. Fagenson (Newbury Park, Calif.: Sage, 1993); Kwolek-Folland, *Engendering Business*, cited above; Gary N. Powell, *Women and Men in Management* (Newbury Park, Calif.: Sage, 1993); and Sharon Strom, *Beyond the Typewriter*, cited above. For the twentieth-century history of women attorneys and judges, see Cynthia Fuchs Epstein, *Women in Law*, 2d ed. (Urbana: University of Illinois Press, 1993). On Native American women as managers and bureaucrats for the Bureau of Indian Affairs, see Lisa E. Emmerich, " 'Right in the Midst of My Own People': Native American Women in the Field Matron Program," *American Indian Quarterly* 15 (1991): 201–16.

On women and medicine, see Barbara Melosh, *"The Physician's Hand": Work Culture and Conflict in American Nursing* (Philadelphia: Temple University Press, 1982); James Mohr, *Abortion in America: The Origins and Evolution of National Policy, 1800–1900* (New York: Oxford University Press, 1978); and Regina Morantz-Sanchez, *Sympathy and Science: Women Physicians in American Medicine* (New York: Oxford University Press, 1985).

Women ministers are discussed in Cynthia Grant Tucker's *Prophetic Sisterhood: Liberal Women Ministers of the Frontier, 1880–1930* (Boston: Beacon Press, 1990). Women's role in reform has been extensive and extensively researched. An excellent source is Robyn Muncy, *Creating a Female Dominion in American Reform, 1890–1935* (New York: Oxford University Press, 1991). Susan M. Yohn's work in progress, tentatively titled *"Let Christian Women Set the Example in Their Own Gifts": The Business of Protestant Women's Organizations*, promises to link the female reformist tradition with modern business culture.

The literature on women in entertainment is quite extensive, although much of it tends toward the celebratory or sensationalistic. My discussion of women in the film industry is based on the solid scholarship of Ally Acker, *Reel Women: Pioneers of the Cinema, 1986 to the Present* (New York: Continuum, 1991); Wendy Holliday, "Hollywood's Modern Women: Screenwriting, Work Culture, and Feminism, 1910–1940" (Ph.D. diss., New York University, 1995); Karen Ward Mahar, "Gendering the Studio: Women and Work in the American Film Industry, 1916–1928" (Ph.D. diss., University of Southern California, 1996); Judith Mayne, *Directed by Dorothy Arzner* (Bloomington: Indiana University Press, 1994); Larry May, *Screening out the Past: The Birth of Mass Culture and the Motion Picture Industry* (Chicago:

University of Chicago Press, 1980); and Robert Sklar, *Movie-Made America: A Cultural History of American Movies* (New York: Vintage Books, 1975). On celebrities as cultural icons, see Susan Ware, *Still Missing: Amelia Earhart and the Search for Modern Feminism* (New York: W. W. Norton, 1993). On women and regional music, see Kristine McCusker, " 'It Wasn't God Who Made Honky Tonk Angels': Women, Work, and Industry in the New South, 1920–1952" (Ph.D. diss., Indiana University, forthcoming); and Chris Strachwitz and James Nicolopulos, ed., *Lydia Mendoza: A Family Autobiography* (Houston, Tex.: Arte Público, 1993). A good overall history of rodeo is found in Kristine Fredriksson's *American Rodeo: From Buffalo Bill to Big Business* (College Station: Texas A&M University Press, 1985). On women in rodeo, see MaryLou LeCompte, *Cowgirls of the Rodeo: Pioneer Professional Athletes* (Urbana: University of Illinois Press, 1993). Women in professional sports are covered in Susan K. Cahn's *Coming on Strong: Gender and Sexuality in Twentieth-Century Women's Sports* (Cambridge, Mass.: Harvard University Press, 1994). For the history of women's involvement in the national park system, including their work as managers, educators, scientists, and rangers, see Polly Welts Kaufman, *National Parks and the Woman's Voice: A History* (Albuquerque: University of New Mexico Press, 1996).

Index

abolitionism: and republican motherhood, 54; and spiritualism, 69

abolitionist movement, 67

abortion: as a business, 101, 164–165; in law, 101; and the medical profession, 100–101

accountants. *See* professions

Acoma. *See* Native Americans

Adams, Abigail, 36

Adams, Hannah, 43

Addams, Jane, 103

advertising, 69, 160; and African-Americans, 193; and beauty products, 130; and female consumers, 130; and female executives, 141, 201; and gender stereotypes, 70, 196; and prostitution, 65; and television, 140–141

advice literature, 98–99

affirmative action, 173–179, 198–200, 205, 210; and management, 214; and small business, 190

African-American Cosmopolitan Chamber of Commerce (Chicago), 193

African-Americans: and advertising, 193; and artisans, 39; and banking, 116; and beauty products, 126; and civil rights movement, 174; and class status, 53–54; and community activism, 146; as consumers, 117; and divorce rate, 95; and earnings, 175; and economic activism, 193; and education, 53; as entrepreneurs, 10; and ethnic business, 115–118; and family support, 60; and farming, 124; as *femes sole*, 59; and gains in occupations, 97; and insurance, 8; and laundry, 85, 146; and midwifery, 31; as ministers, 68; and motion picture industry, 122; and mutual aid societies, 85; and New Deal, 147; and office work, 97; and philanthropy, 198; and professional sports, 162-163; in professions, 175; and property, 52, 60; and racial betterment, 54, 193; and sharecropping, 165; and sole proprietorships, 196; and television industry, 197–198; as traders, 44; and voting, 147; as writers, 43

Africans, 16–17; women as traders, 44–45

agents, women as, 77, 200–201

"agents of necessity," 25

agribusiness, 5; and family farming, 161–162

Agricultural Adjustment Act, 144

agriculture, 13–14, 18; in Depression, 144; and extension services, 124; and family farms, 61; and Native Americans, 20; and New Deal policies, 140; and new technologies, 123–124; on slave plantations, 14; and women's household economy, 78

The Author

Angel Kwolek-Folland is a Professor of History and Director of the Center for Women's Studies and Gender Research at the University of Florida. She is the author of *Engendering Business: Men and Women in the Corporate Office, 1870–1930* (Baltimore: Johns Hopkins University Press, 1994) and numerous articles and essays.

The Editor

Dr. Kenneth J. Lipartito is professor of history at Florida International University of Miami, Florida. He holds a Ph.D. in history from the Johns Hopkins University and has published extensively in the field of economic and business history. He is the author of *The Bell System and Regional Business: The Telephone in the South* and *Baker and Botts in the Development of Modern Houston*. His work has appeared in leading journals, including the *American Historical Review*, the *Journal of Economic History*, the *Business History Review*, and *Industrial and Corporate Change*. Dr. Lipartito was appointed Newcomen Fellow at the Harvard Business School for the years 1989 to 1990. In 1995 he was awarded the IEEE Life Members Award for the best article in the history of electrical technology, as well as the Newcomen Society Award for Excellence in Business History Research and Writing by the Business History Conference.